A MEMOIR
ROHIT JAGESSAR

KISS & Breathe
ONLY THE BROKEN ONES WILL RISE

Copyright © Rohit Jagessar

Published by Rohit Jagessar

This book may be purchased in bulk for educational or business use. Please contact: kissandbreathe@gmail.com

Copyright 2022

All rights reserved under International and Pan-American Copyright Conventions. No part of this book may be reproduced in any form or by any electronic or mechanical means, including information storage and retrieval systems, without permission in writing from the publisher, except by a reviewer, who may quote brief passages in a review.

ISBN 9798985688801

Cover photography: Reproduced with permission by iStock and Canva
Design and typesetting: Richard Carreau Design

Printed in The United States

https://www.facebook.com/organicenergybooks

https://www.instagram.com/rohitjagessar

A memoir is an account of something noteworthy that happened in life. The best ones leave a lasting impression and perhaps the author's life lessons for us to ponder. My book is dedicated to you, my readers, and it is my sincere hope you will find some of your story in mine.

CHAPTER 1

Deep within the raging ocean, there is calm and peace, and if we are to find ours, we too, must go deep within.

It was three in the morning when I arrived in Mumbai from Beijing, leaving behind the Great Wall, and checked into the Taj Hotel overlooking the Gateway of India.

Around six, crystal clear water fell from the nozzle of the shower. The steady flow brought to mind a larger expanse.

One of water, and one of story.

My grandmother used to tell me stories about the endless stretch of water she and her parents, along with many others, crossed by ship arriving at an unknown place.

One million people were taken from India to colonies far and wide to labor on sugar plantations. Over time their stories were translated into lyrics and music. It was these lyrics that brought me to this land on this day.

I stepped out of the shower to the sound of coffee cups gently tinkling outside of the front door.

Room service placed three cups of coffee onto the desk. The young woman bringing the coffee glanced around. She seemed a bit puzzled that no one else was in the room. I thanked her, and she left.

I looked over to the bed and saw my production bag lying on it. My notes were scattered next to it. My Sony Walkman was lying on the pillows where I had rested my head for a few short hours.

I collected my notes and brought them to the desk, letting the palms of my hands rest on top. I quietly stilled my mind.

"Let it breathe, Rohit," my grandmother would tell me.

On my journey to this day, I was mindful of her wisdom.

I was thinking of the day ahead. I had rehearsed for it. As I reflected, I reached for the phone sitting on the far edge of the desk and phoned Trinidad and Tobago to speak to my long-time friend and collaborator, Moean Mohammed, a man who never minced words.

"Rohit, the situation is such that you will have to be careful this time around. This is not the early 80s when we were a team of hitmakers with Kanchan and Babla."

Five years earlier, in the summer of 1986, Kanchan and Babla had gone their own way. During this time, they had made four albums with other producers. None of the albums went anywhere; it was one flop after the other.

"Let me tell you like it is. Like it or not, Kanchan and Babla are finished. They have returned to their days of obscurity. They are back to square one. Their audience has dwindled to a few people again, just as it was before you managed and produced them. I want you to know lightning doesn't strike twice at the same place. I want you to think about that."

Moean went on to tell me that piracy had finished his once flourishing record business in Trinidad.

"Now, I have to re-think. And I am telling you, like a father to a son, to do the same."

He then became somber and said, "I don't know what magic you infused into the early 80s that made us kings. What a time that was Rohit. What a time that was."

I quietly placed the phone down on the receiver and sat back, reflecting on his fatherly advice.

During the separation he spoke of, while Kanchan and Babla were making four albums with other producers, I had focused my energy and purpose on bringing the music of my people who came by ship to a broader audience.

It was the advent of the digital age, and I introduced to the mainstream American and European music store shelves, a modest catalog on compact disc of Afro-and Indo-Caribbean music and select Bollywood and Indian classical titles.

These world beat music titles introduced our heritage to mainstream audiences.

Should I manage to resuscitate Kanchan and Babla and make another successful album of Indo-Caribbean music, it would also resurrect the music of the people who came by ship. If I accomplished this, the broken would rise.

As I walked toward the recording studio, I did not notice the noise and bustle in the busy streets. I was focused on how I would make Kanchan and Babla successful again, which would mean the music of the people who came by ship would continue to be celebrated.

I entered the familiar building and took a short elevator ride to a hallway leading to a familiar door. The sign on the door read: Western Outdoor Recording Studios.

I paused at the door, took a deep breath and steadied my mind. I was ready, and I gently pushed the door open. Familiar faces revealed themselves. It was as if time had stood still.

Babla was the first to step forward and embrace me. Once a struggling musician selling grains in a local market, he had put together a band, and promoters booked shows for them at small venues. In time a singer joined his band. Her name was Kanchan. In the 1980s, I had worked with Kanchan and Babla, and we produced several records that reached the Top 10 charts and brought the music of the Indo-Caribbean people to a broader audience. But five years ago, we had gone our separate ways to pursue our own projects. Babla and I were reunited this day, and Kanchan would join us in three days.

Along with the musicians, we broke the coconut in reverence of the Goddess Saraswati, the goddess of music, knowledge, and wisdom. Soon thereafter, I took my seat behind the recording board next to the recording engineer, and the tape started rolling.

CHAPTER 2

Some songs are a lyrical quest for liberation!

On this day, twelve musicians laid down the rhythm tracks. In three days, Kanchan would arrive and record the lyrics, guided by the nuances and emotions of the music we recorded that day.

The minute we started recording, it dawned on me why those four albums went off track. I stopped the musicians.

There was complete silence throughout the studio. I placed both of my elbows onto the edge of the recording board then brought my face into the palms of my hands and held it there. My fingers sat upon my brows. After some time, I calmly got up and walked from the control room into the next room, where the rhythm players sat in a far corner.

On the other side of the room was a microphone. In three days, Kanchan would be standing behind it to weave the lyrics of the people who came by ship into song.

A trail of earthy-fragranced smoke traveling from a small bundle of incense sitting on the floor flowed toward me.

I could feel the presence of my grandmother's stories of how the burning of the sugar plants would take place before the cutting, and how ships took laborers from India to colonies far and wide in countries such as Guyana, Trinidad, Suriname, Fiji, Mauritius, Belize and Jamaica. They wrote the lyrics of the songs that depicted life in these colonies, laboring on the sugar plantations. I have picked ten of these songs and have come here to record them for this album.

I walked past the rhythm musicians to the last room of the studio, where the violinist sat. He was an older man in his 80s.

While sitting behind the recording console, I observed him playing the tune without any poetic and lyrical feel or expression. He followed the score given to him by the arranger who had no understanding of the experiences of plantation life, and no knowledge of what had happened to these people to have caused them to write and sing these songs in the sugar belts where they toiled.

If I am to bring the imprint of these people's emotions as they toiled in the fields into this recording, I must first get the violinist to interpret those emotions. Kanchan would, in turn, interpret his violin with her voice. If she was again to be the heartbeat of the people who came by ship, I must first help the violinist understand the emotions.

I sat beside this older gentleman. He seemed relieved by my presence, and I took him on the journey of the indentured woman toiling in the sugar fields. The early morning dew causes the dirt to paste under her bare feet as she walks miles away from her home. She carries her lunch pot, wrapped in an old rag, on her head. She balances it with the sway of her cutlass, held in her hand. The teeth of the file she would use to sharpen her cutlass are gripped and fastened between a piece of cloth tightly banded around her waist.

She walks the path to where the sugar plants are standing, stalks bending on both sides of her. In her movements, a lyrical rhythm is developing. Should it rise sufficiently, these songs of liberation will be heard.

She reaches her hand to her head and places all that is on it down on the ground. In front of her is the large expanse of fields.

She bends her back, and her eyes move down the sugar plant, stopping at its root. She cuts close to it, leaving a stump from which a new plant will someday breathe to life again. She raises her bent back to reset her posture, then bends again — with each bent motion, she brings up a harvest.

"With each bend of your violin, I want you to tell her story so that we too can bring up a harvest on this day."

The older gentleman fell into the well of his imagination. He stilled his eyes. It became apparent to me that he too saw footprints.

Soon, he immersed himself in the poetry of the life of an indentured woman toiling so the colonial masters could fill their coffers.

"I want you to bring and hold the soul of that toiling woman within the strains of your violin, so when Kanchan sings to the nuances of your violin, she too will see and feel the women who toiled in the sugar fields. These songs are the poetry of liberation for the people who once toiled these lands. Therefore, each bend of your violin must reflect this poetry, their emotions, and their lyrical quest for liberation."

Three days later, Kanchan stood behind the microphone. It had been standing and waiting for five long years for her. We were recording her vocals for the song *Leggo Me Na Raja*.

Until then, she hadn't heard the violin's emotions that awaited her. I had been careful for this to be an element of surprise when she heard it for the first time. I wanted her to understand it was a new beginning, one that held the promise of a different result, an even greater result than we had realized when we collaborated years before.

Kanchan took her place behind the microphone and heard a recording that held the true emotions of the indentured woman. It unspooled note by note into her earphone.

As she neared the first verse, she looked at me, and I sensed she needed my help. I motioned for her to bring her hand to her waist and "grip her file," then bring up her wrist and turn it into dance. Once she reached the interlude, the space placed between sections of lyrics, the momentum from this movement brought her to lean forward, and she became one with this song.

We were not new to each other. Purpose had brought us together many moons before this day. It happened when I was a teenager and was still living in Black Bush Polder, some ten thousand miles away from where we stood in this recording studio.

CHAPTER 3

In the darkest of night
There is light somewhere in the world
There is always light somewhere within you.

Only the sound of our footsteps could be heard in the still air of this day. The dark, pitch road we walked upon blurred in mirage under the intense heat of the Guyana sun. But as my family and I walked some ten miles from Friendship Village to Black Bush Polder, our bare feet did not burn. They were light, and our hearts were glad. This day held a promise.

My father, Ramnarain — who everyone referred to as Manny — wore a smile as we made the long trek, and when he smiled, we all smiled. Though we were leaving our home behind, an air of beginning could be felt among us. I can still feel it, today. It is thought in my family the birth of a child will bring good luck. In 1963, that is exactly what happened. My sister Betty was born, and my family received its first real chance at life.

During the 1960s, Guyana became the main rice and vegetable producer in the Caribbean. Dense swamplands, we locals called savannas, were cleared and drained. Roads were stretched through, and the government developed housing tracts to keep up with demand. When Black Bush Polder, a new settlement in the county of Berbice, was opened, families came from far and wide to the new opportunities its promise held. We settled here at Lot 172, Mibicuri North, Black Bush Polder.

With my three eldest sisters, Ivereen, Leela, and Shanti, married and settled into their husbands' homes in this same county and my newly born sister, Betty, being carried in the arms of my other sister, Datsy, my brother and I and my parents joined the more than fifteen hundred other Afro-Guyanese and Indo-Guyanese families from across the country and started our new life in Black Bush Polder.

Life on those seventeen-and-a-half titled acres was toilsome yet perfect. By the time I was six, my morning started the same way each day. At four thirty, the rooster would begin its daily call, and my head would pop up from my bed made of jute, spread on our wooden floor. I would throw on one of my two pairs of clothes and head out to gently coax our cow, Buri, from her night's rest. After a long stare and a few strong words exacted at the rooster for waking us up so early again — for this was our friendly tradition — I nudged Buri out of the homestead yard and onto the fringes of the rice fields.

Here, many times I would simply sit and watch Buri and the other cows of the village grazing on fresh, dew-covered grass.

My mother, Rattie, known to all as Nellie, had told me of the importance of cows and that they too were mothers to us all. If a child's mother cannot provide milk, the child would be nourished by the cow's milk. She also taught the art of ancient remedy of Ayurveda stretching back to the motherland, India, telling me that when people are unwell, it's cow's milk and ghee, a highly clarified butter made from milk, that nourishes them back to health. She taught me that when cows give birth, colostrum — the first milk — gives the new calf strength; when people drink the first milk, our immune systems become strong, and we become healthy.

I remember feeling such great happiness as I would watch my cow graze, as if the more she ate, the more I was somehow accomplishing for our family. My mother's words had given me a stronger connection to Buri, though at the time, I didn't understand just how strong it was.

Then, one day around noon, when no one else was at home, I noticed Buri pacing nervously around her large barn. What could be the matter, I thought. I was very in tune with her moods and movements but had never seen her in such a state.

I walked over to her, and it was then that I felt it — a sensation as if a part of my consciousness had awoken. Immediately, I knew what Buri was telling me and that something big was about to happen. That an event was about to take place, and for this event to be successful, she needed to be alone.

My mind raced. I had to tell someone. The world had to know an event was about to happen. But no one was there. I ran to my neighbor's yard, and unable to contain my excitement, I blurted out the big announcement as soon as the first person came into my view.

"Our cow is going to give birth!"

I covered my mouth and held my breath as soon as the final word escaped.

It hit me in that moment of excitement: no one knew Buri was pregnant. I had always let her graze for as long as she wanted, and her normal shape was well-rounded.

"How do you know?" one of my neighbors asked, peeking over the low picket fence that separated our yard.

By that time, Buri was back resting calmly, and all seemed normal "to eyes that only see."

I had no answer. It was the feeling within that led me to know that it was going to happen. I concentrated on the sensation as my prophecy was being dismissed by my neighbors with laughter and a little teasing. But their response was not my business. I knew she was going to give birth.

"Don't stare at her," I said, and the laughter stopped. "She needs to be alone."

I moved to a place where I could watch her, in case she needed my help. I didn't have to answer those who questioned. The feeling was there, and once it was there, I knew it would be true and it would happen.

Bam! Suddenly, she stood up, and a large orange bladder-like bag came out from behind her. In a moment, she had given birth to the most beautiful calf that I had ever seen. Within minutes, her newborn went from limping on its elbows to standing firmly on its tiny hooves as its mother welcomed it into the world with a thorough bath.

A chorus of inquiries rang out around me, "How did you know? How did you know?"

They were drowned out by my thoughts. Now we will have milk! A mother's milk! Colostrum! First milk! We will get a stronger immune system. And I would get to milk her every morning.

Later that day, my grandmother would tell me, in the manner she explained things, that the sensation I felt was the awakening of the intuitive side of my being.

My grandmother held great wisdom. Each night, when darkness would cast its shadows across the settlement, the only light that could be seen was a faint glow from a makeshift bottle lamp, lit with a little kerosene, sitting on the floor, in the center of the main room. Each home could afford only one, and that was enough.

We would gather around the lamp while my grandmother told us stories from times completely unknown to my siblings and me. We learned much about the roots of our history through those stories: how my grandparents and great-grandparents were brought over from India to Guyana on ships to work under the labor system called indentureship; how they lived in tenement ranges, called logies, made of trunks and branches, barely any protection against the severe Guyana climate; how this system ended in 1917. That year my father was born.

"You see," my grandmother would say, "his birth was a lucky one."

So vivid were my grandmother's stories, that I could see the ships crossing unknown and dangerous oceans, see the people, and feel their strength. Her stories went to the well of my imagination, and I saw another world beyond Black Bush Polder. My imagination wandered through the village where my ancestors had lived in India. It crossed the ocean with them, saw my life in the logies alongside them. My connection to these people was strong.

And with every story told, the dots connected more clearly in my young and developing mind. These people were bound by indentureship; however, their bodies and minds were free. They knew that both the body and the mind held power, and like clay, they could use these to alter and change the course of their life over time — mold and fashion it to their liking. And if my ancestors could, then so could I.

Each night, when the stories were over, I would step away from our lamp and into the absolute darkness of the night. I would tread carefully to the back of the house to urinate outside. It was an easy task navigating through the darkness of the night. However, I was mindful to listen intently through every breath for any sound, any disturbance whatsoever in the nearby bushes that might signal wild and dangerous animals had made their way from the savannas and into the fringes of the clearing and the housing areas. Not only did this nightly ritual begin to develop my senses of sound, smell, and touch, but intuition as well.

At six o'clock each morning, I would help my parents take care of our two-and-a-half-acre homestead. This was part of the seventeen and a half acres we had rented from the government. The remaining fifteen acres were for the cultivation of rice.

At our homestead, we planted every vegetable that would grow in Guyana's hot, moist conditions. My grandmother would tend the garden, and I recall her being very focused among plants, her movements caring, and her touch gentle.

She would sometimes tell me, "Be careful how you walk among the plants, Rohit. They have feelings too, you know."

One day, she took me by the hand and led me to the far side of the house. She showed me herbs and roots that she had planted and cultivated apart from the rest in our garden. Here, she was serious and soft in her mannerisms, as though what she was revealing was a great treasure and could only be regarded with the utmost respect. She described each of the plants to me by holding her hands out and showing me the shape of their leaves. Once I could remember how each shape was different, she would send me out to a place within the savanna undisturbed by man.

"There, you will find the same herbs and roots growing wild," she told me.

This became a ritual. Every day, I went out and gathered the plants for her, and every day, by late afternoon, the villagers would begin to arrive at our home.

I would sit on the floor, and both my grandmother and my mother would greet the arriving villagers, who would take turns describing their ailments. I would grind up the leaves, stems, barks, and roots for their well-being as my grandmother had taught me. Turmeric was always the final ingredient to these natural, homegrown organic medicines.

The only thing resembling government healthcare in Black Bush Polder was a makeshift room where a "dispenser" would dole out medicines from a bottle sitting on an old wooden table. Villagers would say whatever their ailment was, and this "doctor" would push a long needle deep into that bottle, draw some of the liquid out, and inject it into their arms. It didn't take long before the villagers began avoiding the government's version of medicine.

One day, I woke up feeling feverish. My skin was hot against the cool air, but everything inside felt cold. I was surprised when my grandmother told my brother to accompany me to the village "doctor" instead of taking care of me with our homemade goodies.

As we walked down the path from our house, my brother reminded me of the tales about that long needle and how it pierces the skin to lodge into the bone. I couldn't — I wouldn't go to that horrible place. I had only one choice: get rid of this fever.

At first, I started to think it. I am not sick! I am not sick! I am not sick!

The thoughts became so strong that the more I said them, the more they became true.

I yelled out loud, "I am not sick."

My brother looked at me with wide eyes. "You're delirious," he said. He grabbed my hand and began pulling me toward that horrid injection.

Before fear could appear, I knew that I had to run away from what I did not want. I tore away from him and ran fast. The chase was on. I was steps ahead of him, running toward our home, imagining I was the jaguar, our country's national animal.

And all the while, I kept on shouting, "I am not sick! I am not sick! I am not sick!"

By the time I reached our home, I fell to my knees on the street and through the sweat stinging my eyes, I saw my grandmother's approaching feet. Her kind laughter sent a familiar wave through me, and I felt immediately connected again with her. I also realized the lesson she was teaching me.

"What keeps you alive?" she asked in her calm voice.

"Food," I said.

She laughed a bit more. "Keep breathing, Rohit," she assuringly said, then walked away from my brother and me.

As I saw her feet disappear, my focus returned to my own presence. I took her parting words as a command and began concentrating on my breath. I drew in deep inhales and let longer exhales out, filling the atmosphere.

With each breath in, I felt strength and all that was good for me returning. With each exhale, I felt the chills leave through my pores.

My grandmother returned with a warm rag and a cup of simmering hot tea. Gently wiping away the sweat from my forehead, she handed me the cup and said, "Here. Drink this. It will balance your body's temperature, which in turn will balance your energy."

The natural smell awakened my senses. Once I had taken a few more sips, she motioned for me to follow her.

"Come," she said. "There is work to be done."

I licked my lips as I followed her into the house. The taste of ginger, turmeric, and fever grass lingered.

It still lingers to this day. This is what medicine should truly taste like. It is all the medicine we will ever need if we only remember to remind ourselves to KISS and breathe; keep it simple and breathe.

During that young, pure period in my life, I already knew, and still believe now, that I have never experienced a more perfect time. I did not know then how much my life was about to change. I would soon embark on a strange journey. It was called school.

CHAPTER 4

When you seek guidance from others, some will show you who they are rather than pointing you to your true potential.

On the morning of my first day of school, everything I had learned and regarded as normal was changing.

I told you that I only had two pairs of clothes. The truth is, there were three. This third set of trousers and shirt had laid neatly folded in a small chest of drawers in our modest home.

I remember on many occasions asking my mother when I would be able to wear them, to which she would always reply, "When you are older."

On that morning, I remember her pulling those clothes out of their drawer, and I immediately knew something was happening. It was like the air changed around me. I remember her gently unfolding them in front of me while I jumped up and down, unable to contain myself. I was older! No matter where I am in the world, the smell of mothballs still pulls me back to that moment.

After dressing, she handed me a small aluminum container and told me it was my lunchbox and not to eat it before lunchtime. What a strange morning this was. And it was made stranger still when she placed a coin into my pocket and told me to buy something during my break at school.

Lunchbox! School! Buy something! This was all new to me. I didn't even know what school meant. I knew my older siblings had gone there, and that it kept them away from home for many hours during the day, but never until this moment had I thought to ask them what it was.

And what could someone buy there? I had never bought anything in my young life. I had never needed to buy anything. Everything I needed was right here, in our home and on our land. And what would I learn at school? Here at home and on this land, I learn to cultivate and grow things, to bring wellness to others, and well-being to myself.

I asked my mother these questions, and she told me that school was a place where I would go to learn. Learn? The thought made no sense. I had been learning my entire life right here. I had been learning the most important things: the farm, Buri and the other animals, Ayurveda, organic energy, herbs, breathing, and balance. What else could there be which was so important to take me away from what I had come to know as perfect?

My head was still reeling with unanswered questions as my mother guided me out of the house. As I emerged into the outside air that morning, another set of experiences awaited me. There was my dad, with our old rusted bicycle, gesturing me toward him. His face was calm, but even at the age of six, I could see that there was an anticipation in his eyes, a quiet excitement.

I mounted the bike's crossbar, and as we rolled down the bare dirt street, neighbors began greeting us. However, something was unusual. They were calling out more to me than to my dad.

I couldn't understand the cause of this excitement. The attention was overwhelming. I was important. I was a star that morning. I smiled uncontrollably, with new-found fame, forgetting all of the graciousness I had learned up until then.

This continued as we turned from our dirt street onto the main pitch road and passed people on foot. I continued to bathe in their seeming admiration.

I saw an old man dressed in a ragged shirt and short pants. Both his knees were swollen, and he was struggling toward his destination. His condition was similar to those who would come to our home for Ayurveda and organic energy wellness, but I was too distracted by my new importance to focus on his plight. Riding on a throne of metal, I was invincible, and as the wind blew through my hair and cooled my head under the hot sun, the day seemed mine to command.

As the road continued, we came to a wooden bridge. It stretched across a large expanse of flowing water. Suddenly, this new throne upon which I sat became a place of fear. I had never been here before, never seen so much water moving so fast. Sensing my apprehension, my dad stopped at the foot of the bridge.

"It's okay, my son. This water flows from the main waterway into the tributaries that help our plants grow in our garden at home. It leads to our home."

In his calm manner, my father explained this waterway as serving the greater good, and this is why he did not fear it. When we see and understand the purpose of things, fear has no place in them.

"You see, Rohit, I want you to pay close attention to this moment because I will not always be there with you all of the time, and you will have to cross bridges all by yourself."

As we left the bridge behind, a new landscape stretched out before me. The houses here were larger than any I had seen. However, they stood so close together. Maybe it was these houses that my older sister Datsy and my brother Prakash were telling me about; the place where rich people lived.

However, now seeing where rich people lived, I realized that there was barely any richness here, no space for a garden, and certainly not enough for a cow. How could anyone live in these conditions, I wondered?

Soon, we turned onto a tree-lined street, and through the branches, glimpses of a never-ending wooden structure peeked out at me. My eyes, my focus, my mind, my imagination were now pulled toward this building. What could lay inside it?

My dad must have noticed both my amazement and my puzzlement.

He calmly said, "School," and then turned into the entrance.

I saw the other children. There were so many, more than I had ever seen in any one place. They were approaching from every direction. Some arrived on foot, while others by bicycle. They looked like me. But then I noticed others stepping out of cars and running through the open front gate of the school.

I beheld what others would later call "wealth." Having encountered some of the deadliest sins that morning, I too found my wealth along my journey that day. Shedding my ego I saw purpose and found my wealth in its realization.

It is believed that whatever a child learns by the time they turn six, will be foundational to how they live their life. They will either use those experiences to propel themselves forward through their pursuits or be held back by them.

In some ways, I was also starting to learn from my father, in the way he knew how to explain it, Albert Einstein's theory of relativity of how one thing works with the other.

This morning, in less than an hour, I had also seen and experienced vanity, pride, fear, and apathy. And I had been introduced to my ego.

The teacher wasted no time showing us who was in charge at school. He was tall and held a cane in his hand at all times. When he asked a question, any wrong answer resulted in a strike from his cane. I was terrified. Even when he asked a question I thought I might know the answer to, I remained silent, my words stilled by fear. The curiosity with which I had lived, up until this moment, was extinguishing.

My father's words about fear, spoken to me only minutes before I had to face fear by myself, were already proving true. I tried to see purpose, but this fear had none. This teacher's actions were meaningless.

It started as a slight tightness within, barely noticeable, but grew until my breathing had changed. How could this be a place for me? How could anyone learn anything here?

It was barely an hour into school when I got up. I could take no more. I clenched my fists, harnessing my inner jaguar and ran out of the room, out of the building and onto the street. Reaching the outside, I looked around but didn't know which direction home was. The fear of the experience was still clouding my intuition. And once I became aware of this, I closed my eyes, and stilled my mind. My breath returned to me, and with it my calm and my focus. I was now safe.

Opening my eyes, I saw the trees lining the street in front of me. That's it! I knew where I was standing. All I had to do now was run past those trees, and I would find my way home.

I ran and ran, and the farther I ran, the better I felt. Then saw the bridge in the distance.

There, I remembered my dad's words and my grandmother's lessons. "Rohit, you must always remember to find your center, your balance."

I pictured myself crossing the bridge and then standing safely on the other side — strong and brave. This was my life, and I was in control of it, not that teacher.

I arrived at our home. No one was there, so I sat on the stair of our front porch and, in a state of courage, in the protection of all that was normal, ate the contents of my lunchbox, living life on my terms again.

In a single morning, one man in one environment had attempted to crush the love of learning and curiosity I had acquired in the first six years of my life. Instead, I took actions that helped me to stay away from him and his environment.

As I sat there on the porch, thinking of how to move forward, how to deal with school, my dad came riding up. He nearly fell over his bike when he saw me home much earlier than I was supposed to be, then asked why I was not at school.

After I told him the story of what had happened, he looked at me and said, "Rohit, that man can only teach you from where he, himself, stands. And you can only learn from where you sit. He may have much knowledge to share with you, however, only you can be your true teacher. If you believe you will learn, make it your purpose, and you will learn."

CHAPTER 5

The magic is within.

Some seven years later, at the age of thirteen, my mother and I made the two-mile trek from our home to the trench that ran along the border of our rice field. It was certainly not my first visit. I had been helping my parents with the rice harvest since I was six. However, that year would forever stay in my memory.

It was the end of the rice-growing season, and soon, rice-cutting combines would start arriving in Black Bush Polder to cut the dried rice plants, extract the grains, and funnel them into jute bags.

We swam across a tributary, a fifteen-foot-wide trench. I stood by my mother's side as she began to survey the state of the field. It had been draining into the trench for several days, and just by looking out over the expanse of our paddy field, she could estimate how many bags of grains it was likely to yield. Any number less than 100 bags would mean a loss, and a loss would mean a difficult year ahead for us, farming more vegetables and catching and selling more fish to make ends meet and pay the government its rent.

A quick pronouncement from her usually meant a favorable one. However, this moment stretched out, and my mother remained silent as she looked. The silence and her body language spoke more to me than any words could. The yield would not be sufficient.

Months before, during the preparation and sowing of the field, the tractor had gotten stuck in the wet soil, creating a deep impression in one corner of the field. Soon, the rains came, turning this impression into a deep pond.

Even so, the pond was not very large and at most meant the loss of a few bags. However, there was a bigger problem, which we did not know the extent of until now. Unusually hard rains had bent the rice stalks toward the ground, damaging much of the crop. With the field drained, the damage was plain for my mother to see.

My mother stepped forward, and I followed her immediately looking around to find a solution. She inspected the damage, and though the prospects seemed bleak to her, my mother was strong, and in situations like this one, she would look to the future with great determination. The rain might have bent the rice plants but not her determination and strength.

I heard her take in her characteristic deep breath then bravely exhale, "We will have to work hard to pay the government its rent, son."

The words were said in a tone of optimism and full of belief and purpose that everything would be alright. This has always been my memory of my mother: optimism and strength in the face of hardship and adversity.

We turned back and walked toward the trench to return home. She began to explain what we would have to do to earn enough money over the next many months. As she spoke, I kept looking around. Soon, a sound carried my thoughts away from her words. There was a slight ripple coming from the pond, and at once, I knew it to be the sound of fish.

I turned, facing this watery oasis as we walked back, and all I could think about was how this gaping hole in our rice production might end up being the solution to its shortfall.

During the draining of the fields, fish that had spent the entire season feeding around the rich roots of the rice plants in the flooded fields would intuitively escape the soon-to-be-dried field and become abundant in the trenches. And, as was usual during this period, my father, my brother, and I, along with all the villagers, would go out each day with nets to seine these trenches.

This was an important part of our income. The first few days were always met with good catches; however, with the increase of fish in the market, the price would become low. As the fields finished their natural course of draining, the catch slowed, and with the reduction of fish in the market, the price would increase again. This was a seasonal exercise, and one by that time in my life, I fully understood.

This year, I had a secret. I kept thinking about the pond. I visualized it daily as the fields drained and the fish yield slowed more and more in the trenches. Still, I remained silent about my plan regarding the bounties held in our field.

Many days after the draining was complete, my father and I went to the field to determine whether it was dry enough for harvest. Our dogs accompanied us. On this day, we hardly caught any fish from the trench to feed our dogs and our family, much less to sell at the market.

As the day stretched on, our dogs kept running back and forth from the pond to me, as though their instincts knew what my plan was. It was as if they were telling me: Why are you still fishing here in the trenches when you know there is an abundance to be had over there, in the pond?

After some time, it became apparent we were straining water rather than fishing. It was time!

I told my father of my plan, and we went to the pond. The first cast of my net brought more fish than we had caught in the entire previous week. The catch was good. So good that this pond by itself brought enough money at the market to make up for the crop's entire shortfall. We even made a little profit, and my mother bought an item of new clothing for each family member and balloons for the children on our street. It was a festive day.

It is a lesson I would never forget: opportunity is always there for the one who looks for it, for those who have a purpose to find it. The more I looked for opportunities in my life, and the more I believed I would find them, the more I would discover them.

With the harvest finally behind us, it was time to prepare the field for the next season. First, we would have to set fire to the dried stalks of the already harvested rice plants. This may sound dangerous, but in truth, it was usually a simple and relatively safe task, one I had been helping with since I could remember. However, this year was a bit unusual.

There is a small window of time between the harvesting and burning of the rice fields, and that year, our neighbor, owner of the field next to ours, was running late. He had not secured a combine, and his field was not yet harvested. However, if we were to catch the next crop, we had to burn our field that day.

This was so because heavy rains were forecast for later that day, signaling the rainy season had arrived earlier than usual.

The rain was predicted to be so heavy that it could flood the fields, and the burning of our field would have to be postponed to another day, another time.

The rice stalks were crisp and dried. A single mishap that day, a single ember floating across the narrow three-foot dam separating our field from our neighbors, could spell disaster for their entire crop, perhaps burning it to the ground. Delaying any longer could spell disaster for our next crop. We could not wait another day.

My father and I arrived at our field that morning with our purpose and two boxes of matches in hand. We waited until the sun had finished drying the morning's dew off the stalks.

A sudden shade cast itself across the field. I observed as my father, with the box of matches in his hand, looked up into the darkening clouds. With outstretched hands, he was determining both the wind speed and its direction. I mindfully continued to observe his reading of both weather and wind.

The field was divided into two halves. We walked to the middle, and my father struck the first match. The technique was simple: start the burn in the middle of the field and against the wind so it will burn slowly and evenly toward our neighbor's field. This slow burn would give us sufficient time to contain the fire, should it spread too quickly and try to jump the narrow dam onto our neighbor's field. The dam had a green growth of wild weeds, and the fire, burning against the wind, would be too weak to cross over it into our neighbor's field.

The moment my father struck the first match, so too did the day's storm show its first strike. A bright bolt of lightning flashed low in the distance to announce that the rains were only a short time away. As sound followed light, a deafening thunder rolled across the fields, carrying with it strong winds.

The winds blew hard against the fire, holding it at an even slower pace than we had hoped for. At that rate, the burn would take too long, and the rains would surely beat us to the finish line and perhaps to our next crop.

However, the lesson learned was fresh in my mind: purpose is in the hands of those who hold it, and opportunity is in the hands of those who act upon it.

I strode forward in confidence, ahead of the slow-burning fire, and as I had observed my father earlier, I too held my hand out against the wind, gauging its speed. Scanning the field's width and averaging the wind's speed and power, I walked to a point about thirty feet ahead of the slow-moving burn and struck the match, going against the norm, burning with the wind and its full strength and speed.

Working with the wind, this fire would burn at full speed, perhaps more than four times the rate of the oncoming slow-moving burn. I felt no concern. My father was also a carpenter and had learned this trade from his father. And he had always advised me that in everything I do, I must be mindful to measure twice and cut once.

I had measured this wind speed twice, perhaps even three times before striking the match. And by applying all I had learned, I could see in my mind's eye the course to be true, and so it would be.

My father looked up and saw what I had done. I saw his eyes race toward our neighbor's field, measuring the distance between it and the oncoming rage spreading toward it while also moving toward the slow burn.

He was overcome with a moment's fear and sat down by the now charred remains behind his slow-moving burn and closed his eyes. I saw his expression change as he realized it was his teachings I had articulated. When he opened his eyes again, there was no fear remaining in them. It was clear that my father had realized my actions would lead us to another crop.

As this raging fire grew closer to the original one, both my father and I kept looking at this reality. Soon, it had burned to the perfect width and collided with the existing slow-moving fire, and they both seamlessly canceled each other out in a satisfying conclusion.

With the realization that this new strategy would help us accomplish our purpose, we finished the burn safely and without incident before the heavy rains started.

After our task was complete, we swam back across the trench, with bolts of lightning followed by loud cracks of thunder across the darkening sky. The rains brought one of the greatest floods we had ever witnessed in Black Bush Polder. Our task was completed with perfect timing, and our pond was refilling and replenishing. Knowing full well that the floods would destroy our neighbor's chances of harvest, I imagined the pond could be of rescue to them too.

That evening, I overheard my father narrating the entire story to my mother and my siblings. His account ended with the words, "Our son, and your brother, is now a man." There are no more endearing words for a son to hear from his father, and I have carried them as a badge of strength to this day.

It is said that a good beginning makes for a good ending. That year, the rice crop would prove the saying true. From that first day burning the dried stalks to the eventual harvest, a more perfect season could not have been asked for. In the end, we reaped more than three hundred bags, more than twice the amount of any crop before. When my father brought home the money — and the goodies it had afforded — we invited our neighbors to our home for a modest celebration and spent the evening recounting the story of the season, from burn to harvest.

And the gaping hole in our field, our pond, again proved to be as bountiful as had the crop before. In addition to helping our neighbor, it also provided an extra piece of clothing for each family member.

That harvest felt like a turning point for my family. There seemed to be less of an air of survival surrounding our daily activities and more one of living and the formation of two banks — one of money and one of karma.

CHAPTER 6

The color of light is black. It is a canvas waiting for the light to shine on it. Light your purpose there, and you will see it shine the brightest.

We had a yearly tradition for as long as my memory stretches back of taking two special trips from Black Bush Polder into Rose Hall, the town where my high school was located. These trips were to the movies.

My brother Prakash, our friends, and I would make the trip together twice each year. The trips allowed me to develop a sense of handling the coins my mother gave me — twelve coins totaling $3.00. Two coins were for my bus fare, eight for my lunch, snacks, and refreshments, and the remaining two for my admission into the cinema.

The excitement was so overwhelming, and the decision of which cinema to attend required serious deliberation. There were two locations, Apollo in Rose Hall Town itself and

Roopmahal in the neighboring settlement of Port Mourant. Each cinema showed a different Bollywood movie.

As large as that decision weighed on our young minds, picking the wrong movie would have changed the rest of my life.

After a long conference among us, debating the pros and cons between our choices, we settled on Roopmahal in Port Mourant to see the movie *Dharmatma*, a Bollywood film with a plot loosely based on the Hollywood film *The Godfather*. And, as with almost all Bollywood movies, it featured songs.

Soon, there was darkness in the cinema, and I could make out the curtain opening and moving to both sides, slowly revealing the screen in the center. The anticipation was building. After the trailers, the screen went dark again.

A crackling sound was heard, similar to a phonograph needle, as it is placed on a record's very first scrapings. A few scratches appeared on the screen. The sound abruptly stopped, and the screen went dark once again. A few seconds later, a few broken lines reappeared across the screen once more.

We sat quietly anticipating the movie to begin, when in the still of this moment, I felt a slight tingling sensation in the palms of my hands.

I closed my eyes and calmed my mind, allowing it, this sign, to develop further. I stretched my fingers out to their limit, rolled them back into a tight fist, and held them tightly shut, protecting and holding within that which would be soon revealed to me.

The movie finally started, and after some time, I heard her voice.

It was not the voice of India's Nightingale, Lata Mangeshkar. Neither was it any of the other Indian superstar singers of the day.

The voice pierced into my consciousness and found a home. As the song ended, I slowly allowed myself to relax back into my seat. I opened my now warm hands and gently placed them, one on top of the other, over my brows.

I knew with full awareness something had happened. I knew that a higher purpose had brought me here to this very cinema and this moment.

I did not know her name, nor where she was or how to find her, but that did not matter. How I would find her did not concern me. The mission of the higher purpose that caused our meeting on this day would be revealed. I believed this. I held it within, took a deep breath, exhaled and enjoyed the rest of the movie. That was the last movie I would see in Guyana.

The money my father brought home from the harvest came at just the right moment. My eldest sister, Ivereen, and her family had already moved to the United States, and she had sponsored us to live there also. We had been focusing on getting the money to pay for such a significant move, and the harvest had brought that to us.

On the 30th day of May in 1976, I along with my parents and my brother Prakash and my sister Betty, boarded a Pan American flight out of Georgetown, Guyana. Some six hours later, we arrived at JFK Airport in New York City.

CHAPTER 7

Spring awakens kindness, compassion, love, and emotions. The rise of vibration.

I was now fifteen.

We joined my sister Ivereen, her husband, Harry, and their daughter, Diane, on a short bus ride followed by a longer train ride to where they lived at 500 West 135th Street in Spanish Harlem, a section of Manhattan.

In my young man's memory, both the train and the bus were plastered with posters and banners of God Bless America. It immediately dawned upon me that this was the land of great patriots.

Realizing my curiosity, Ivereen pointed out that this was the year of the country's Bicentennial celebration. Still, the thought of people who were thankful for their bounties remained within me. What a land, I thought.

My first sight of the city and lasting first image of this new country was like walking into a perfect painting. And with each step that day, more and more of the beauty around me revealed itself.

I observed the Manhattan skyline standing out in brilliantly hued colors against an overcast backdrop on that spring day. Cool winds and spring flowers breathed life into a city that held the promise for an eventful summer.

As I threaded together my first moments in this new land, coming from a village, this environment could have been overwhelming; however, the lessons I had learned from my grandmother back in Black Bush Polder stayed with me and kept me present in the moment. This is how I was mindfully able to observe each facet of the new and beautiful frame. One by one, one step after the other, then collectively in all of their beauty, I realized the entire portrait. My grandmother had taught me to see the good in all things.

She would say, "Rohit, to see the beauty, one must first look within."

And although she did not make the trip with us, I decided this is how I would see this new home of ours. Like with my country, here I would look for and find the goodness in all the things I saw and felt. And for the next four decades, to this very day, that is still the America I see: a constitution blessed with an abundance of goodness, kindness, and the true spirit of freedom.

A few months later, we moved with my sister and her family, settling in Richmond Hill in Queens. It was from here that I would travel by train to Manhattan to continue my high school education.

One day, as we were waiting for our teacher to arrive in class, I sat, as usual, reading about the great country's history. I was quietly absorbing the way English was spoken.

In Black Bush Polder, I was accustomed to speaking in Creolese, a disjointed English. Reading not only quenched my thirst for knowledge about the land I now lived in but also improved my English. As I read, I would often mouth the words to myself to have a feel for the sound.

"Learn English, man!" came the harsh tone of someone to the far side of me.

I looked toward him as a matter of courtesy. He was tall and wore a sneer across his face, which appeared to be right at home there.

"No one can understand a word you say," he continued.

"Yeah!" another one joined in. "Go back to your country, foreigner!"

This new one was not so tall yet wore a similar sneer. They must practice together, I thought.

Both stood a moment later, and their sneers deepened into scowls of hatred as they moved toward my desk. Two more joined them, all puffing themselves up like roosters squaring for a fight; the clock within I understood so well.

I was not afraid.

"The more pressure there is in any situation, the calmer you must become, Rohit," my grandmother used to tell me.

She had taught me to breathe and hold to my purpose, to have the reality I saw in my mind's eye. I had seen this throughout my life, and so I had no fear this situation would be any different. And besides, I was used to setting whole fields on fire. What do I have to fear from four young men? Yes, some of them were tall. I had once faced a tall, large bridge. They might have been boastfully strong. My strength was in the wisdom I observed and learned.

I assumed that the teacher would be arriving in about five minutes. This is the time I needed to buy.

The ticking of the clock on the wall became my guidepost. I could now hear it clearly. It merged with the rhythm of my breathing.

So much so, that their words, "Let's beat him up!" and "Let's kill him!" slowly faded into the background. I began thinking about my next movements as they crowded and imposed themselves further. I became even more prepared, thinking of a ram goat back in my village in Black Bush Polder.

It was a large ram with a habit of reversing some steps, then dashing its head forward into the smaller animals on our farm. Having seen this, I strode out to face him. Our eyes locked.

He took some measured shuffling steps backward and then decisively stopped.

I opened my tightly closed fists, outstretched my fingers as far as they would go then held them out in front of me. We were both ready.

He started his charge — charging forward with all of his might.

His horns absorbed the blow in the bend of my elbows and knees. I pushed him away, and he came at me again and got the same result. We continued this way for several minutes, and finally, the ram stepped away. He would have no more of it.

It saw me not as an animal to be beaten, but a friend with whom to spar.

Before my assailants could follow through with their inclinations, the teacher walked in. Sensing what had happened, he asked us to shake hands and make up.

As we shook, they sensed peaceful intent through my continued calmness. They remained there standing.

My classmates and I became friends that day. They asked me how I remained so calm. I told them about life back in Black Bush Polder — harvesting herbs from the dangerous savannas, helping my grandmother heal others, lighting rice fields on fire, and running like a jaguar — all adventures they too lived, but only in books.

The more I told them, the more inquisitive they grew, and the more they wanted to know. Soon, other students were drawing their chairs closer. Before long, the teacher himself had decided to allot time to these stories, justifying their inclusion in the curriculum as "social studies." I could not have been happier to oblige.

In the stories I first told them about the three-foot alligator I had pulled out of the trench, the alligator soon grew to four feet, then five, six, seven feet and more. I think at one point it might have been around twenty feet. They never called me out on this casual discrepancy; we were friends. The America I knew and know values courage.

CHAPTER 8

In the state of observation, burdens are shed, and there are no consequences to bear.

In the spring of 1978, my family moved into our own apartment in Richmond Hill. My brother Prakash, who used to talk about serving his great country, had joined the U.S. Army. My sister Betty was in seventh grade, and I was in my junior year of high school.

About a month before the end of my junior year of high school, I noticed an advertisement on a large display: Get Your High School Equivalency Diploma. There was a line of fine print stating that current students were ineligible. This fine print did not concern me. Soon I'd be off for the summer. Surely then, I will not be considered a current student.

I took the test as soon as school closed for summer vacation. My high school equivalency diploma came in the mail a week before school reopened for the fall semester. So, when the semester began, I went to school only for the first day. I said goodbye to my teachers and friends and started the next chapter of my life. But I never stopped being a student.

I had not considered the unique situation completing school early created for me. I was too young to be out of school and too young to be employed.

I saw it as an opportunity. This city I lived in was teeming with activity. With a little effort, a young enterprising mind could always find a way to earn some money and, perhaps, some wisdom along the way.

After asking around to every person I knew, I soon found myself gainfully employed with a 4:30 a.m. paper route. This new beginning for work in a new land was very familiar to me. In Black Bush Polder, it was the rooster's clock that rang at the stroke of 4:30 a.m. that started my workday.

Here in New York, I started by delivering the papers on foot with my mother's shopping cart. I soon saved up to afford my first bike.

I fastened a couple of old milk crates to the handlebar, and a route that, at first, would take me several hours to complete, now took much less time. After that, I would comb the streets of New York looking for work until returning home for dinner around 5 p.m. In the evening, I would walk across the street, volunteering to pack groceries at the Key Food supermarket. A few shoppers would occasionally give me coins.

One evening, I helped an elderly lady with her bags of groceries to her car. She searched her purse for coins. Realizing there were none, she handed me a dollar bill. I told her to wait for a minute and hurried off to my home for a dollar's worth of coins. But upon offering it to her, she smiled and told me to keep it, then reopened her purse and handed me yet another dollar. It was my biggest tip, and I deposited it in both of my banks — my helping her went straight to my Bank of Karma, and her tip went straight to my Bank of Money.

All told, my weekly earnings at that time averaged around $30 per week.

The America I know rewards you for your efforts.

It was around nine o'clock one night when our phone rang. It was a call from Guyana. My grandmother had experienced the occasion of "birth." She had shed her frail frame, broken with the passage of time. Everything she had observed in this and previous lives, all of her wisdom and all of her actions would be realized again in a brand-new frame. The broken one will rise.

All of the care that she had gifted to my family and me would now be gifted back to her by her new family, so the wheel of her life would turn one notch closer to her journey of achieving Moksha — a higher form of being.

I knew that she now belonged to others, and it was time for me to let her go and set her free. She taught me that the purpose of life is to live, and the fundamental principle of this event of life is to leave this body naturally when the time comes. She taught me should I ever force it, I will return to where I had left off, learn the lesson from which I ran, and only then would I be able to continue onwards.

Therefore, we should only welcome death whenever it comes to us naturally.

It had been nearing spring then, and I was reminded of the parallel between the seasons of nature and the seasons of life and birth. My grandmother had gone through the autumn of her life with us, weathered the winter of transition, and would now be entering the spring of a new life.

And one day, she would experience a birth when she enters into the state of the perfect vibration, where every burden dissolves, and the being exists in its highest and lightest form — Moksha — where there are no burdens to bear and each being exists in perfect unity with their universe.

The universe that exists all around us survives on air, minerals, and more. And so, too, do we as individuals. Each of us is a complete universe unto the self. We do not know when we will enter Moksha. However, if we are mindful while we build our vibrations and rise toward it, we can experience its shades right here and right now.

One of its shades can be experienced in the presence of mind where no burden exists. This can be attained by letting go of the judgment of experience itself, when you can see and hear all surrounding you and recognize it is neither good nor bad. It only is. Then you will shed all burdens toward it. That is a shade of Moksha.

This was a freeing thought. To see everyone around you and be mindful they are moving through their journey with their own challenges, living and growing at different stages on the same path. Over time, we will all emerge into the complete bliss and harmony of Moksha.

I thought much about this principle. I committed myself to engaging with people through the lens of this belief. It was my purpose.

And in this way, I welcomed the "birth" of my grandmother. I recommitted myself to the practice of her teachings. I spent many hours in quiet mindfulness, being aware of the promise I had given to her that I would work hard and build the legacy for our family that she had prophesied those many years before.

One day, I ventured out into Richmond Hill and found the streets were nearly empty. Almost everyone was either at school or at work, and the tree-lined streets felt light.

In this calmness, I felt completely free. Absolute clarity of thought and action was mine to command. It was as if I was the only person walking this great land, and whatever I wanted to do, I was free to do. I took that feeling and transformed it into my purpose. I believed I would experience something impactful that day, and because I could feel it within, I knew it would happen. I remained in this awareness and went where it took me.

I took the train and randomly got off in Astoria, another part of Queens. There will be work for me here, I thought, or something important.

A few steps from the subway exit was a small oriental grocery store. It was in this store I discovered my purpose — one that would grow and shape my life and the lives of many over the next four decades.

As I walked through the doors of this grocery store, I noticed a few records lying half covered in an old cardboard box. Records in a grocery store?

I looked closer and it was then that I saw them. These were no ordinary records, these were records belonging to my heritage — Indo-Caribbean records. As I scanned through the records, I looked toward the cashier and noticed there didn't appear to be any cultural link between her and these records.

"Wow! Do you listen to this music?" I probed.

"No," she replied through a hearty laugh. "I don't know anything about it. There are a few people from, I don't know, Trinidad maybe, living in the neighborhood, and one of them left the box. Why? Are you from there too?"

"Well, I am from Guyana. We are neighbors with Trinidad. And Suriname too." I extended my hand toward her.

After a moment's hesitation, she reached out, and we shook hands.

"I am from Korea. Wow! Your hands are so warm!"

She was right. While these records may have no cultural connection with her, I immediately felt connected with them. And having realized this connection, I began to feel a familiar tingle in the palms of my hands.

I nodded, and turned back to the records. This time, I crouched down to look more closely. The sensation in my palms was a signal — a vibration telling me this is what was meant for me today.

They were all singles — 45 RPM vinyls. I examined them closely, one at a time.

I counted all of them. There were eighteen in total. All had the name Windsor Records printed across them and marked: Made in Trinidad and Tobago.

It dawned upon me, with great clarity, that this record label must represent all of the popular Indo-Caribbean singers. Although I knew that she was a Bollywood singer from India, I still wondered, might she be among these records?

As I momentarily drifted, I remembered.

When life leaves a gaping hole, it is only giving you a head start. Dig deeper, and there you will find life's treasures. Precious metal and stone lie hidden, deep below the surface.

And having reflected upon this, I was leaving no stone unturned.

I scanned the records yet again for the names of any female singers. There were none. What I did see were male singers such as the hitmaker Sundar Popo. I didn't know her name anyway.

I had to have one of these records. I began searching my pockets for coins and managed to scrape together about $4.00. I also noticed I had a few subway tokens.

I asked the cashier how much it was for one.

She said, "It's $3.00."

I deliberated which one of these records I would take, for I only had enough money for one. Returning to the box, I pulled them out again, one by one, and chose the one which gave me the strongest feeling of connection.

I had taken the train to Astoria that day intending to find work, and in the awareness I would discover something important. I left with an idea represented by a record I now held close to me. I was consumed by the idea of that record.

I stepped back on the train, again not knowing where my next stop would be. As I searched for direction, I moved from carriage to carriage looking for someone, anyone, of Indian ancestry from the Caribbean or from places such as Fiji or Mauritius. I found an older gentleman.

Perfect, I thought. This man may be able to give me direction.

What he told me was invaluable. There were no Indo-Caribbean record stores in all of New York, but there are three Indo-Caribbean grocery stores that had a few of these records for sale. He was clear that since they were so scarce, they were very expensive at $3.00 each.

As he spoke, my young mind started drifting with his words causing him to wonder out loud, "Are you falling asleep?"

I replied, "I am awake."

I rewarded this man by showing him the record I had just bought and telling him where I had found it. His eyes grew wide. He was amazed I had seen it there. He had never seen such a place sell this kind of music. And to this day, I myself have never seen another oriental grocery store selling Indo-Caribbean records. I had been guided to the right place at the perfect time of my life.

I sat back as the train continued on. By the end of the day, I had completed my tour of the three stores the man on the train had told me about.

Like the oriental grocery store, the stores' selection of Indo-Caribbean records was thin — a grand total of eighty-seven 45 RPM records. I concluded this must be the full length and breadth of the Indo-Caribbean record business in New York, the greatest city in the world. This meant my people were denied their music.

This was a problem, and armed with a purpose, I felt within that I could solve it.

That evening, I headed back to Richmond Hill on the train with others returning home from work. It was time to start doing research for my immediate purpose. I arrived at my stop and stood at the steps of the subway to count the number of people of Indo-Caribbean background as they walked by. I stayed and counted until the last train that evening.

A friend of mine happened by, and as we walked home, he mentioned he was looking for work. Without any pause or doubt, I told him that I would hire him if he was still looking for work at the end of one year's time. He looked at me and laughed off my remark as though I was joking. I was serious.

I had left home that morning looking for work, and by the end of that very day, I was hiring.

A few more friends joined us as we walked, and all were given the same offer. They too, laughed and reacted much as the first had. But I held on to my purpose.

The America I know is a place where purpose thrives. It is bountiful and filled with opportunities.

All told, I spent $3.00 at the oriental grocery store that day. That was my investment in the record business. However, the real capital on this journey was purpose, the music of my heritage, and the people who came on ships.

CHAPTER 9

When life leaves a gaping hole, it is giving you a head start. Dig deeper, and there you will find life's treasures.

I vividly remember the night when I had returned home with my first record. It was 1978, before my eighteenth birthday, and as I lay in bed, my mind was consumed by the image of those other records lying in a few broken boxes across this great city.

Windsor Records! They were the largest Indo-Caribbean recording company in Trinidad and Tobago, a country some five hundred miles from Guyana and two thousand miles from where I then lay. I would need to contact them. What would I say? My young and developing mind began searching for answers. Data. I would need data.

This was before the advent of the internet. One could not pull up demographic data on the computer. In truth, I had no idea where to find the information I needed. So I did the next best thing.

I reflected back on the day we went to the U.S. Embassy in Guyana. I recalled there must have been around a dozen other Indo-Guyanese families with us in line that day, also waiting to get their visas. Assuming they would have been coming to America since the mid-60s, as individuals and later as families, I calculated a rough number of about fifteen thousand families coming from Guyana to the United States. To be conservative, I settled on ten thousand households. I added another five thousand from neighboring countries Trinidad and Tobago and Suriname, and landed on fifteen thousand Indo-Caribbean families as my final count. This was my market.

Although this market was extremely small, that there would only be eighty-seven Indo-Caribbean records in the whole of New York was baffling to me. Why was that the case? And why were these records collecting dust? This didn't make any sense in my young mind.

And then there were the concerts. These were even less prevalent than the records, occurring only in the smallest local venues — school auditoriums and places of worship — and only during holidays such as Diwali, the festival of lights. Admission to these events was normally fifty cents but certainly not more than one dollar per ticket.

Once a year or so, well-known Indo-Caribbean artists would travel to New York to perform. However, the audience was never more than two hundred and fifty people. Even this commanded only a five dollar admission price.

That very night, as I worked the numbers, I concluded that a population of around fifteen thousand families were spending a total of about $7,000 per year on Indo-Caribbean entertainment — an average of forty-six cents per family.

These families, like mine, would be what most Americans considered hyper-frugal. The new arrivals focused on building new lives for themselves and their children in this new land. They worked hard, but most did not bring in much more than the minimum wage of $2.90 per hour. Some worked for even less.

Back in Black Bush Polder, when the fish got scarce, the price was the highest.

So too it is with heritage. When the music of a people becomes scarce, they would someday pay a high price.

Could it be that this was the legacy my grandmother had prophesied for me and was hoping for on the day I left the shores of Guyana?

I could not bring myself to believe this low income was the cause of the void in Indo-Caribbean entertainment. During my research, I learned from one of the store owners that others had tried to build an Indo-Caribbean record business in New York City. They were two wealthy individuals who suffered the same fate as these dusty records. Having found few takers, they soon lost hope and gave up.

My grandmother and my mother had both ingrained in me never to leave anything unresolved. I strongly believed those previous individuals had lost hope and given up too soon. I would find the path forward that had eluded them. There was a reason why I had found the Indo-Caribbean records in an oriental grocery store.

In Black Bush Polder, it was uncommon to retire later than 9 p.m. The belief in the importance of a good night's rest was a part of our upbringing. Yet that night, for the first time, I lay awake until around 3 a.m. It was the first time I had broken one of my grandmother's golden rules.

As I lay there in the darkness of that night, I saw the path forward. Knowing fully the only way forward was to be found within, I searched deep, and there it was. For Indo-Caribbean records to emerge and become an industry, I must create a record with a voice so compelling that it would be an event in and of itself. The last thought I remember on that night was that I knew there was such a voice out there. Her voice.

CHAPTER 10

We find our purpose through observation.
The more mindful we become in observation,
the larger the canvas we paint in our lives.
They who master observation rise in vibration.

The next morning my first movement was to grab the record off the nightstand beside me. Windsor Records. How would I approach this mighty giant? What would I say on the call? Could I afford the call? How do I even call a foreign country?

I dialed zero, and the AT&T operator informed me a call to Trinidad would cost around $4.00 per minute. I would have to book the call with her in advance, and within forty-eight hours, she would call and connect me. Should I not pick up when the call was connected, I would still be charged for the first minute. What if the call went on for an hour? I told the operator I would call her back.

I would need to find full-time work if I was going to make this call. Fortunately, soon thereafter, on April 3rd, 1979, I turned eighteen and companies could now hire me.

I ventured out to Long Island City where I had heard a few jobs were available and found an opening for a shipping clerk. If I got this job, I would be able to make the call. And I was prepared. I had rehearsed my talking points many times.

Most important of all was my purpose. I wanted Indo-Caribbean music, the music of my heritage, to survive and thrive in this new land. I needed to make the call, and I needed the job.

During the interview, they asked if I had packaging and shipping experience.

"Yes, of course," I told them. "I worked several months for *The New York Times* in packaging and shipping." The fact that I was packing newspapers into milk crates and shipping them via my bicycle was none of their business.

I got the job. I would make $90 per week assisting the packaging and shipping clerk. The ball was rolling, and even better, I saw there were a few Indo-Caribbean workers. Great, I thought. I could pick their brains about what music they listen to for entertainment.

I started the next day and soon learned my fellow Indo-Caribbeans would not be the resource I had initially hoped for. They were from neighboring Trinidad and Suriname. Their actions demonstrated the same barriers as existed between the countries themselves.

I was from Guyana, and any attempts at conversation were ignored. And not only was there the country barrier, but also that of status. Their body language told me that my entry-level status did not permit me to speak to them in any capacity whatsoever. Any thought I had of gaining insight into what Indo Caribbeans living in America thought about their homegrown music was put on hold.

My early encounters with these coworkers did, however, teach me a great lesson. I was not prepared. If I was not able to capture the attention of those working alongside me, how would I be able to command the attention of a record company in Trinidad?

The answer became clear to me. I had to create a reason for them to listen to me. I needed to be able to show experience in the production and distribution of Indo-Caribbean music. I would need to produce at least one record. Only then would I be ready to make the phone call to Trinidad.

I was not deterred by the fact that I had never produced a record before. I had a belief in my purpose. I would continue to work and save up money to fulfill my responsibility to the music of my people. And I was confident the next step to achieving this purpose would become clear to me.

Soon, the next step was revealed.

CHAPTER 11

Purpose is in the hands of those who hold it, and opportunity is in the hands of those who act upon it.

Vision of Asia was the only Indian television program on the air in the greater New York market. It was a ninety-minute variety show airing on Sunday morning, produced by a family of Indian expats who had come to New York directly from the motherland.

Everyone of Indian ancestry, both Indian and Indo-Caribbean expats, looked forward to the program every week, and when it aired, all eyes were glued to the television.

As I watched that Sunday, a group of singers and musicians was featured, and as fate would have it, I recognized one of them. Sarojini was her name. She and her husband, Latchman Budhai, were from Guyana and had been in the very same line with my family as we had stood at the U.S. Embassy waiting for our visas.

I knew they lived only a few short blocks from our home in Richmond Hill. I went to visit them the very same day.

Their excitement at seeing me soon faded into confusion when I told them of the reason for my visit. I explained I wanted to make a record, but I also wanted to explore the idea of making a television show. From their expressions, it seemed they believed I had gotten my goals mixed up. Adding to their confusion was the fact that I was only eighteen years old and had zero experience in either the television or record business.

It was well known that those who came to the United States from India looked down upon all Indo Caribbeans as people of a lower social strata. The Trinidadians and Surinamese expats, in turn, looked down on the Guyanese. The Indian owners of Vision of Asia were an exception, and they featured Indo-Caribbean singers on their show.

The Budhais informed me the variety show was shot at the Vision of Asia studios. The studio retained creative control and sole ownership of all the content. They suggested that I try to make a similar deal. In this way, I would not have to pay for the production cost.

That was not what I had in mind. I wanted to film the program, pay all production costs, retain creative control, but have Vision of Asia air it for me.

Of course, the Budhais couldn't understand how I would manage this on my own.

"Look, Rohit," Latchman Budhai tried explaining, "you have no experience in records or television, and you are approaching both at the same time."

They had concerns, but in the end, they promised to approach the other singers with me the following Sunday.

As I rode the train to work the following morning, my thoughts were on how I would balance work, produce a one-hour television program, and then a record. The answer came to me as I walked through the door.

The supervisor spotted me and motioned me into her office. In very few words, she told me I was the new head of packaging and shipping and the man who currently held the position, the very person who had hired me, would now be working under me. She told me that my pay would increase to $290 per week and handed me an envelope, telling me it was a bonus.

After asking her why I was taking someone's bread away from them, she told me that my output in the short time I worked there was more than twice his.

As part of my learning, I had observed this man's body language to better my own skills at this task.

I motioned my supervisor to follow me to where the man, whose job I was being offered, stood. He looked up at me, and I used my gaze to signal that I intended to help him.

"Please, wrap that bundle," I said to him with the supervisor standing next to me.

He pulled a length of paper from the cutter and wrapped the bundle, completing the task slightly above his normal speed, but not fast at all.

My supervisor looked at me with a look of victory. "See? I told you. He is slow."

I asked the man to come around to the other side of the table. "Stand here," I gestured. "Now wrap the next parcel, please."

He did. Only this time, his speed was greatly improved.

My supervisor's eyes widened into saucers. "How is that possible?"

"His strength and pace are in his other hand," I explained.

In truth, what he also lacked was confidence and belief in his abilities and in a few simple gestures, I had given that to him. It was exactly what he was deprived of by our supervisor. She had never treated any of us as anything other than transactions. She never managed the talents of those she supervised.

I pulled my supervisor aside, thanked her for offering me the raise, and then informed her that I would leave the company.

Her eyes, still wide from the previous few minutes, reached an even greater circumference. "But why? You will still have your raise."

"Because here, you fire and demote people instead of teaching and cultivating their talents," I responded.

I stepped out of my first full-time job and headed straight for the studios of WNJU, Channel 47, in Newark, New Jersey. It was time for me to learn how much a sixty-minute variety show would cost to shoot.

CHAPTER 12

The shortest distance between our goals and opportunity is purpose.

I arrived at the WNJU, Channel 47, television studios at one o'clock in the afternoon the same day I had walked out of a promotion and pay raise at my first full-time job. I do not look back on my choice as right or wrong. I felt confident as I walked through the doors and shook the hand of the general manager at WNJU.

I managed to learn quite quickly that it would cost exactly $900 for a sixty-minute shoot and edits. I already knew from the Budhais that the singers and musicians would charge around $300 for their services. Therefore, the total for the production would be $1,200.

This did not come as a particularly big surprise, and as fate provided, this was the exact amount I had saved up as the result of all of my work.

Finished early with my reconnaissance mission, I decided to stop in Manhattan where a friend of mine worked in a fabric factory. Walking through the door, I met the owner, who informed me he had an immediate opening sweeping the floor and preparing the workspace from half past three in the afternoon until closing time.

"The pay is $40 per week." He made this offer with an air in his voice that made it perfectly clear that he believed it was unimportant, menial labor. "Take it or leave it."

I had a very different view of this man and the job. Like the owner of Vision of Asia, he too had come directly from India. I thought observing and interacting with him would help me prepare for my eventual meeting with the owner of Vision of Asia. The pay was much less, but the part-time work would allow me to devote my time producing a TV show and record. It was exactly what I needed.

"Where is the broom?" I calmly asked, and I made sure my face spoke of my appreciation for the work that would allow me to someday chart my way to bring the music of my heritage to the people.

He smirked, pointed to a closet in the far corner of the room, then walked off.

As I swept the concrete floors that afternoon, I wondered to myself how this guy's eyes would pop out of his head when he saw me on television, and I had a hearty laugh as I pressed the broom to the concrete.

With my immediate purpose and my new salary of $40 per week secured, I had enough money for everything I needed, mostly small amounts of food and subway tokens.

Each day, I traveled to Manhattan for work and, by evening time, to the Bronx for rehearsals for my TV show.

At other times, I continued to walk this great city, thinking about the Indo Caribbeans, the descendants of the people who came by ships, who I was on a journey to provide music for.

Why, I wondered, had they allowed their music to gather dust?

One day, I went to Sam Goody, one of the largest record stores at the time in Manhattan, hoping to catch a glimpse of how mainstream America was selling records. More than this, I wanted to begin preparing myself for the record industry, and being among records was part of this preparation.

Walking in, I was struck by the vastness of the space. Record bins, shelves, and displays of every conceivable kind full of records seemed to stretch on endlessly.

People were searching, thumbing through stacks of records, focused on reading labels, all happy to be there — all speaking the shared language of music. I felt a surge of energy run through me at the experience, and then, a thought came into my mind.

Since I had not seen Indo Caribbeans buying records in grocery stores, I wondered if I would see them here?

I spotted two people. I approached them, and both politely told me they had stopped by this store on their lunch break looking for their favorite disco records.

Disco was still popular at the time. And like them, I too loved disco music. In fact, my favorite film at the time was *Saturday Night Fever*. But disco was a cultural phenomenon that one day would fade. It will pass — one day it's bell bottoms, another day it's tight jeans. However, it's not the same with heritage. Heritage is deeply rooted within.

And seeing these two people reminded me of my heritage and prompted me to ask them whether they liked Indo-Caribbean music. And as I asked these music buyers, I waited with bated breath to exhale. I had waited to exhale since that day I first saw those eighty-seven records.

One of them said, "I don't listen to it. I only listen to disco music, but he does," pointing to the other.

Her friend then reminded me that the only places you could find Indo-Caribbean records were in local Indo-Caribbean grocery stores and they were almost always scratched up.

"Plus, $3.00 is far too much to pay for a 45 RPM record, scratched or not. Disco 45s cost less than half that amount."

Nothing they said was new information. On the one hand, some new arrivals, wanting to seem Americanized, had flat out denied any attachment to their own music. While on the other hand, those that held a strong attachment to the music could not find it, and if they did, at a price they wanted to pay for it.

To hear it, to have it confirmed from the very people I aimed to soon market this music to, was as valuable as any precious gem.

It reinforced my belief that should this music be allowed to continue to lay dormant, it would suffer the same fate as a group of Indian immigrants who arrived on the west coast of this great country more than a century before. Many had not paid attention to their heritage and lost their identity. If Indo-Caribbeans continued to be more and more separated from their own music, it would soon be pushed into oblivion and lost. I could feel my purpose deepening as I stood in the aisles of that record store.

Having finished carefully observing the Sam Goody record store that afternoon, I moved on to my job and put the broom to the concrete. By six thirty that evening, I was finished, and by eight I had arrived in the Bronx as the Indo-Caribbean singers and musicians were setting up to begin rehearsal for my television show.

At nine thirty we took a break for dinner. The flavors of all the home-cooked Caribbean food steaming out of their containers was a beautiful experience, bringing my mind into full nostalgia for the people and place I came from and that helped shape me. This was the perfect backdrop for me to sit and visualize the future.

I let my thoughts drift to the image in my mind of Windsor Records: vast and mighty, perhaps as spectacular as Sam Goody, or even more. And I brought my thoughts to more pressing questions. What will I say during my musical variety television show? And what will I wear as its host? I conjured up a vision of John Travolta in the movie *Saturday Night Fever*, and the suit he wore as he walked down the pavement in the opening sequence. That would do nicely, I thought, as I remembered the love of disco the two people in the Sam Goody record store had expressed.

And in that moment, as I sat there, I saw and felt exactly what my future would hold, confirming my purpose to bring Indo-Caribbean music to America.

That clarity of purpose and destination burned away any burdens that might have remained of the unknown. I exhaled. I breathed out a full, refreshing, and satisfying breath.

I saw a brand-new day for the present generation of my people, whose ancestors had once traveled the high and dangerous seas from India to the various colonies. And more than that, I saw one for other people.

They had come to the Caribbean from another continent — Africa. And my vision expanded to all the different people who had been brought to the Caribbean. I saw a new day for all of us. And this shared day was united with the language of music.

Music would work in the way that only it can, through sound. It is a magic that works even without words and is silent in that way, and yet, powerfully loud. I knew I had to work in silence to be heard the loudest.

For the next three weeks, I did exactly that. During every rehearsal, I quietly shaped the show and my part, confidently watched it unfold.

A month later, I walked into the studios of WNJU and this time stood on my mark at the center of the stage. The spotlight was hot. Purpose didn't allow my eyes to burn. I was focused. I allowed myself to become one with the microphone and used every second of time I had available to deliver my words.

Three hours later, my first project, a sixty-minute musical variety television show, was in the can. I had spent all the money I had in the world.

At the end of the show, seeing that I really did it, that I had spent all the money I had, the singers and musicians stood there wondering at the risk I had taken, especially at a time when immigrants in America were playing it safe, saving their money and building their new lives. I felt no risk at all. I remained calm and confident in the awareness that I had a purpose.

A week later, I put my vision to its first test. It was time to be a salesperson again, only this time, I intended to succeed.

When I was eight, I had collected a large bag of guava fruits. I stood by our school trying to sell them, hoping to make a few coins to help my family. That didn't turn out very well. It was a crash course for me in economics. I quickly learned that there was a reason no one else was trying to sell guavas. Everyone already had guavas. Most had their own tree, as we did in our yard. I learned that trying to sell something to people who already had it wasn't such a good idea. That experience taught me a lesson as a young child, and because I learned it when I was young, it was branded into my memory.

That would not be my experience this time. I had a product that no one else had and a marketing idea I was sure no one else had thought of.

The meeting with the owner of Vision of Asia, Dr. Banad N. Viswanath, was the following Monday, and I was joined by Latchman Budhai, who had agreed to accompany me and provide some friendly guidance.

Although two Indo-Caribbean expats were meeting with an Indian expat, the meeting began promisingly.

Dr. Viswanath sat with us and quietly watched the entire show, then went into complete silence, betraying no emotions.

After the long silence, he asked in a low voice, his words measured and carefully chosen, "How did you go about finding all the technical pieces to put together for this show?"

Before I could answer, more questions followed. Could this be the dawn of a new day for relationships of people sharing the same heritage, set apart only by their countries of birth? How did you find WNJU? How did you fund this program?

I remained silent and let my silence stretch out. The good doctor had just seen my work, and in my silence, he heard me the loudest.

Latchman, after shifting restlessly in his seat, started answering the questions. I observed them both.

The more Latchman explained, the more Dr. Viswanath seemed to drift off into wonderment, perhaps trying to equate my young teenage years with the process: the boldness of the idea of doing this on my own, the cost of the production, and the quality of its execution.

I remained silent, both my hands tightly closed. Our eyes were on the flashing timer on the video cassette machine, where the tape holding my production still rested.

Minutes passed, and the silence stretched on. Had they waited for me to speak first, we would likely still be sitting there to this day. I knew from Dr. Viswanath's body language that he saw a production of unusually high quality. He also saw that in a land where he was king, having the only Indian television show, there was now a challenger — a threat to his throne.

He knew I had a working relationship with WNJU television, the same television station from which he leased airtime to broadcast his program, Vision of Asia. He knew it would be possible for me to lease airtime from WNJU television and have my own television show.

This is why Latchman spoke with such excitement about the show I had produced, and why Dr. Viswanath was now visibly thinking. Realizing the facts, he stood up, walked across the room, opened a checkbook sitting on a small desk, and stood there with his back to us.

Then Dr. Viswanath broke his silence. "Mr. Rohit, how much have you spent producing the show?"

Latchman, eager for me to recover my investment and for me to make a profit, elbowed me, indicating that I should go high. But I knew this situation could go in several directions, and I only cared about one, the sustenance of the music of my people.

I got up and walked over to Dr. Viswanath and gently placed my hand on top of his and closed the checkbook. He was in both shock and puzzlement, perhaps even disappointment. He wanted me to accept a check, and he knew I knew why.

Then I spoke my first words. "Doctor, let's do a deal. In exchange for the rights to my show, I will accept a package of free airtime to show advertisements for an upcoming record I will be producing. Do not worry, I will not lease television airtime from WNJU and compete with you. I am not in the television business. I am in the record business."

An audible sigh of relief escaped the doctor, and every bit of tension that I might have been a competitor melted from his face.

With a broad smile, he said, "Rohit, you and I are like brothers. The only thing that separates us is I was born in India, and you in Guyana. From today onward, whenever you need airtime to market your records, just call me, and it's yours."

Realizing I had just bartered my $1,200 investment for thousands of dollars of free advertising, Latchman now understood and saw that a deal can be made after a checkbook is closed. He exhaled in relief.

Many years later, both of these gentlemen would tell me that they couldn't have imagined then how historic a day it was for Indo-Caribbean and Indian music and for its people, and for our collective heritage. I could. And I did — even then.

The following Sunday, my variety television show aired on Vision of Asia. It was viewed by the entire population of Indian expats from India and the Caribbean who lived in New York and surrounding communities. They saw me on stage in my *Saturday Night Fever* suit.

The next afternoon, I returned to work, picked up my broom, and began sweeping the concrete floors. This day, my boss looked on, and I could sense his puzzlement. He struggled to equate what he had seen on television the day before with what he was now witnessing.

This job was more important to me now than ever. It provided me with the money I needed to get around the city exploring the American record stores, recording studios, and Indo-Caribbean entertainment habits in the greatest city in the world.

It was time for me to make my first record and keep charting my way to finding her.

CHAPTER 13

Temperament is the rhythm in which we communicate the approach to our goals and how we navigate to a successful conclusion.

Ever since the day I left my home and found those records in that grocery store gathering dust, I had wanted to make that phone call to Windsor Records in Trinidad.

I had completed the first major step in my plan. Now came the next. I needed to make a record to get to the next step — making a phone call to Windsor Records.

And much like my television show, here too, I had no experience. I also had no money.

My travels around the city, searching out American record stores had shown me its length and breadth. I had a complete picture of this environment in my mind, like an illustrated map. There was the financial district, the fashion district, the diamond district, and Times Square — the epicenter of the entertainment industry, with many recording studios.

One morning, like so many before, I stepped out of my door and walked to the train, knowing where I wanted to go but without a specific address. I had full confidence my purpose would take me where I needed to be.

Stepping off at Times Square, I soon noticed a few signs for recording studios and followed my intuition to the door of one. I knocked and pushed open the door slightly to reveal a dark cave-like space inside. I knew I had come to the right place.

"Hello," I said, stepping inside and holding the door open behind me. "Is anyone here?"

A light turned on at the back of the space, and I noticed an older gentleman walking toward me. He switched on another light and upon reaching me, shook my hand.

My first thought was that this recording studio was small — much smaller than the one at WNJU TV.

"How did you find me here?" asked the man.

"I noticed there are many studios in this area. I'm visiting some of them."

"Yes," he said. "Several studios have popped up recently since the success of the *Saturday Night Fever* album. My business has taken a dive with all this new competition around."

"I would definitely give you a good deal if you book with me," he continued, as he showed me through the space. "Look here," he said, pointing to a framed picture on the wall. "This is where Liza Minnelli recorded her first single." He nodded toward an open studio. "She recorded her very first song right in that room."

"Perfect," I said. "I am also here to produce my first single."

Then I asked him a question I knew he would not be prepared for. As expected, it put him in a state of complete confusion. But I had to ask. "What is Liza Minnelli's date of birth? If you give it to me, I will consider booking your studio."

When I was a young boy, my grandmother told me of the importance of the sun, the moon, the stars, shapes, symbols, and numbers. That they carried great power to affect the purpose of those who understand them, and that I should be careful to look out for them.

My grandmother never stepped foot in any institution of learning that you would call a school, and so, she would interpret them in the best way she knew how. I took this information from early in my life and spent a great deal of time thinking and meditating on it.

In that studio, I had only to hear that Liza Minnelli was born on the twelfth for me to confirm I was in the right spot. I was born on the third, and the numerals of the number twelve, one, and two, added up to three. I understood then that as Liza Minnelli's producer had found her and recorded her, I too would find *her* and record her.

The man told me the cost for the recording would be $300, and upon my request, he wrote up the contract and handed it to me. I told him I would look it over and get back to him. Then I thanked him and walked out of the studio.

And although one of my two banks didn't have the $300 to pay for the recording session, the other one, my Bank of Karma, certainly did. It had a finely tuned purpose for the preservation of my heritage.

While working on my television show, I would occasionally continue my visits to the Indo-Caribbean grocery stores: two in Manhattan, one in the Bronx, and a newly opened one a few blocks from our home in Richmond Hill.

I had not been in the one near my home since my variety show had aired. As I neared the store, I focused my mind on the idea that some of the money I needed to make my record could possibly be in this store.

I thought to myself, maybe I could sell some of my records to this guy even before I produce it and then use the money to actually produce it. How do I sell a record even before I make that record?

My intuition prevailed. Before I had finished clearing the threshold of his store, I was met by the owner, this time with open arms. He had uncharacteristically rushed out from behind the counter on this day. He embraced me and told me how he had watched my television show. From that moment forward, he told all his family and acquaintances we were best friends. His enthusiasm was so great that he immediately introduced me to any customers in the store, praising my work. Everyone had seen the show, and everyone agreed and joined him in praise.

This was the moment I had been waiting for. My TV show had started a conversation in this dormant market. It confirmed these people had been denied quality entertainment at a price they could afford.

For the first time, I saw how Indo Caribbeans would respond to quality entertainment of their heritage and my vision. I had put in the work and had researched the demographic data as much as possible. I had visualized this moment and felt it within. The people's reaction in that grocery store was the confirmation I needed that all that is broken will rise.

"So, what is next?" the store owner asked with eager eyes. "When will be your next show?"

With a gesture, I indicated that we should move out of the range of general hearing, which only heightened his anticipation. I led him to a quiet corner of his store. His excitement was palpable, as though he was about to hear a great secret meant only for him. I saw in his eyes the same feeling I had felt when my grandmother shared the secrets of the Ayurvedic plants she had cultivated at the side of our home in Black Bush Polder.

And when we were out of range of anyone's hearing, I told him, "I am going to do something bigger, much bigger and I want you to be a part of it."

"I am with you all the way, Rohit," he said without hesitation, without even knowing what it was I planned to do.

I described how I was planning to produce a record and advertise it on television, and that I would put his store's name and its location on the advertisements as a place where the record was sold.

"What!" he was elated. "I am going to be on TV, too?"

"Of course," I said. "Your investment will be only $300."

I took out the contract I had received from the recording studio owner, and the store owner carefully took it from me with trembling hands, as though it were something sacred.

After looking it over for a brief moment, he looked up at me with wide eyes. "Done!" he said. "Let's do it. I am in."

I would repeat this process at the other three stores and by the end I had $1,200, the same amount I had invested in my television show. This time, I would only need to pay $600 to record my 45 RPM single, $300 for the studio, and $300 for the musicians. My first bank, my Bank of Karma, had always been profitable and now, for the first time, my second bank, the Bank of Money, had made a profit.

I was also several steps closer to contacting Windsor Records and closer to finding and recording *her*.

In 1980, by the time I turned nineteen years old, I had my first record available for sale at four locations across New York. As part of the deal I had made with them, each store owner bought two hundred copies. I advertised for them on television on Vision of Asia, referring to them not as grocery stores but as grocery and record stores.

On their part, Indo Caribbeans witnessed an Indo Caribbean record being marketed on television for the very first time and immediately responded to it. The seed of hope for Indo-Caribbean records in America was sown on that day.

After allowing some time for the popularity of this new record to grow, I traveled to the city with the second-highest population of Indo-Caribbean people in the international market, Toronto, Canada.

CHAPTER 14

*One must go to a place and
stand there to understand it.*

I departed in the evening, and by the next morning, the CN Tower had come into full view, adorning the Toronto skyline.

Although I had taken some records with me, hoping to find a few grocery stores there, my primary goal for this first visit was simple: observation.

I needed to gain a feel for the pace and rhythms of this city, its sights and sounds, and its people. I knew I could successfully sell records in a place once I took the time to know it. So I spent a good portion of my time simply moving through the city streets.

It was then a memorable event unfolded. This one event could well have brought the remainder of my journey to Windsor Records, and subsequently, to her, to a complete end. My path, which had begun in a grocery store in New York, faced its first major hurdle in another grocery store some five hundred miles from it.

I noticed an Indian grocery store and approached the gentleman standing behind the counter. I introduced myself and extended my hand.

As we shook hands, he said, "Hi, I am Mohan Singh. I am from India. Which part of the Caribbean are you from? Guyana or Trinidad or Suriname?"

My attention was drawn to the display of food products on the shelves behind the man, many of which I recognized since they were Indo-Caribbean food brands.

Realizing my curiosity, he laughed and said, "You must be wondering how come a guy from India is selling Indo-Caribbean groceries?"

"Although I am not from the Caribbean," he continued. "I do visit there regularly. I import vegetables from Trinidad and occasionally bring some Indo-Caribbean singers from there to do shows here in Toronto."

This last bit of information seemed odd for him to add. Then I realized why. He noticed that I had a record and an invoice book in my hand.

He was right; I was wondering. The first time I had met a grocery store owner back in New York, she had no direct link to entertainment except for a few dusty records. Here, a gentleman from India was telling me of his direct involvement with Indo-Caribbean entertainment.

He then gestured to the record in my hand and asked, "Are you in the record business, too?"

"I am. Why? Are you?" I responded. I wanted to be sure I hadn't misjudged the situation. He didn't tell me he was in the record business. He just said he brought in shows.

What he told me next would provide information that extended from where I stood all the way to Windsor Records in Trinidad.

"As a matter of fact," he said. "I just made an album with a group I brought here not so long ago. I'm sure you must have heard of them — The BWIA Indian National Orchestra of Trinidad and Tobago."

Immediately I sensed something amiss. Every Windsor Records I had seen had this orchestra. This is the first time I heard that another label had it.

Although I didn't personally know anyone at Windsor, nor had I ever spoken to anyone there, I felt this compelling sense of proprietorship toward it. Now I was even more interested in learning everything about this man and his album.

The man reached to the far side of the counter and retrieved the album. As he struggled to remove the shrink wrap from its cover, I saw that BWIA was printed on it in large bold type. He held out the record in front of me to see. Windsor Records was not printed on it.

Who was this man? Why was he recording Windsor artists? Was he their competitor?

I knew I would need answers before I could move forward, but to get them, I would have to remain patient.

My grandmother had told me, "the good fortune written in a person's hand cannot be taken away, and no one can erase it." She also said, "That which stands in the way of purpose, is merely a door, and all you have to do to realize your fullest potential is to open that door. It is as simple as that."

As I stood in a grocery store in Toronto, I was keenly aware of the door within, and as he placed the record on the turntable, I reached my fingers over my palms and clenched my hands closed. In this state of awareness, I heard the first scrapings of the needle on the vinyl record, and within seconds, it was playing. The man standing next to the turntable was brimming with pride.

Windsor had done all the heavy lifting. It had introduced this band, marketed and promoted it, and made it a household name throughout the Caribbean. But Windsor had not paid attention to the international market. This was why those records sat overpriced and dormant in those grocery stores back in New York and here in Toronto.

Others were now looking to reap what Windsor had sown.

The sound was beautiful. He turned up the volume, and soon, his entire store was consumed by the melodious sound of Bollywood covers, featuring the vocals of Polly Sookraj with a distinct Indo-Caribbean flavor. It was brilliant. It was apparent that the man standing across from me was a very good record producer.

However, this realization was quickly followed by another. His record would never sell. Even though it was of high quality and had all the elements which I believed could make it a hit record, it would never sell.

His record would suffer the same fate as the ones collecting dust in his grocery store and in those grocery stores in New York City.

This fact was as apparent to me as the wind was cool or the sky was blue.

This man was a good grocer and possibly a good record producer, but he was not a record man. It was apparent he would go down the same path of producing quality records, then fail to market, promote, and distribute them effectively because he was not a record man.

The life of a record begins immediately after its production. What happens at this point determines its legacy. And if this man was not a record man, a man who understands and knows all aspects of the recording industry from production to marketing and distribution, should he be allowed to have a business relationship with BWIA, to the detriment of Windsor Records?

I saw this as a potential threat to Indo-Caribbean music and by extension, to its people.

With an even greater resolve, I knew I must take responsibility in my hands for the future of Indo-Caribbean music in this world. Should it fall into the hands of those — even with the best of intentions — who kept it on the dusty shelves of grocery stores, this music would face extinction in the important expat markets.

At that moment, I knew what I needed to do next. Instead of asking him about his relationship with BWIA, I decided to take one step at a time.

I navigated the streets of Toronto, found Queen Elizabeth Way, and drove straight back to New York. It was time for me to take responsibility in my hands for Indo-Caribbean music, and to do that, it was time to contact the mecca of this music. It was time for me to make that phone call to Trinidad. I was ready.

86

CHAPTER 15

Belief is uncertain. It changes in accordance with the facts placed in front of us. Purpose is certain. Belief is the branch of the tree, while purpose is its root. Branches will grow, evolve, then fall off, but not the root. It remains planted.

The mistrust which divides the political, cultural, and economic strata within the Caribbean nations also divides its music. I knew that if I were to successfully market and distribute Indo-Caribbean music in the United States and Canada, I would have to bridge these barriers of mistrust. These barriers went back a long time in history.

European planters saw a commercial opportunity in planting sugar in the Caribbean. They envisioned an industry that supported a growing demand in Europe for molasses, rum, and sugar.

European planters brought millions of people from Africa to labor as slaves on sugar plantations. This labor system would continue until the 1830s, when it was abolished, and Africans were given their freedom within the colonies.

However, the demand for sugar did not abate because free labor was no longer available. So European planters invented a new form of labor in these colonies. They called it indentureship. They searched throughout the world for workers to support this new system. In 1834, the first ship filled with Indian laborers arrived in Mauritius, an island nation located in the Indian Ocean, off the southeast coast of Africa. This was a test of sorts to see if this new group could handle the brutal conditions of plantation life. The planters quickly learned the Indians were acclimated to the weather and hard labor, thus perfect for the work. The Indian indentureship system was born.

Under indentureship, over a million Indians, and others, were brought to Mauritius, the Fiji Islands, and the Caribbean to work on plantations. My grandmother and her parents were among those on voyages across the high seas.

The timing of this influx of cheap labor from abroad coincided with the large population of African descent being freed and looking for opportunities. They searched for better pay and working conditions in their new employment. However, the move by European planters to bring in new labor from abroad diminished any bargaining power the Africans might have had.

The African descendants believed the Indians — the largest group of people arriving by ship — had come to take away their long-awaited opportunity. A seed of resentment was planted and grew for many generations. In fact, it still grows today.

This was not the only seed of mistrust to be planted among the peoples of the Caribbean nations. In the 1970s, the Guyanese government declared a large number of food items banned from import and sale across the country, causing many in Guyana to travel to neighboring countries to purchase these items and "illegally" bring them back to feed their families. Some saw the potential to build a business out of this activity, acting as middlemen or distributors of these goods across national lines, but this dangerous activity only further escalated prices and tensions within Guyana and between her neighbors.

Many Guyanese took to sitting on the pavement beside local markets in Suriname and Trinidad, selling the few items they had planted, made, or purchased in Guyana. They sold brooms handmade of coconut branches, pineapples, and small gold rings, chains, and broaches purchased in Guyana with Guyanese currency. They sold the items for Trinidadian and Surinamese currency and then used their proceeds to purchase food and items to bring back with them to Guyana for sale. And the cycle continued.

This activity further escalated prices and tensions within Guyana and between her neighbors and created the perception the Guyanese were living hand-to-mouth. It also fueled a perception of rich Indians and poor Indians, the dividing lines clearly drawn at national borders.

It was in this environment that I, a Guyanese, one of the poor ones, was about to contact Windsor Records in Trinidad.

The owner of Windsor Records, Moean Mohammed, was an icon in the Indo-Caribbean entertainment industry. Through Windsor, he produced and distributed the biggest selling records in the Caribbean region and was the host of the most popular radio show in the land. He produced his first record in 1969, a 45 RPM titled *Nana and Nani*, with a young singer from Barrackpore, Trinidad, named Sundar Popo, backed by the-BWIA Orchestra. This single was a massive hit in the Caribbean.

The record was not sold anywhere outside of the Caribbean, except for in those few grocery stores in New York and Toronto at the astronomical price of $3.00.

This record had jump-started chutney music, later popularly called Indo-Caribbean music, and put Windsor Records on the regional map. I hoped this same record and label would help me jump-start Indo-Caribbean music on the global stage and ultimately build a global distribution platform for Indo-Caribbean music.

Moean Mohammed had three children: Sadro, Aruna and Safi. His youngest son, Zack, was not yet born. Sadro was the host of two highly rated radio shows and an up-and-coming record producer. As the assistant to his father in the recording studios, he oversaw the recordings of some of Indo-Caribbean music's biggest hits at the time.

Aruna was an up-and-coming broadcaster in her own right, and Safi was still in primary school.

Moean Mohammed's wife, Hansrajee, was a brilliant and scholarly minded woman. She had a good grasp of the business of music and the effect music had on people. She also hosted a popular show on the radio.

Moean Mohammed's nephew, Rafi, was one of the country's most popular radio and television personalities. Moean's brother, Mr. Kamaluddin, was a founding member and a government minister of the ruling party, the People's National Movement, under Dr. Eric Williams. Another brother, Mr. Shamshuddin, was a member of Parliament. Mr. Shamshuddin, along with his sons, Khayal and Jamal, produced the highest-rated television show in Trinidad and Tobago — Mastana Bahar.

The Mohammed family was so powerful that a street, Mohammed Ville, was named after them. And there, the entire family lived.

I was a Guyanese, and therefore, of the poorer class in the eyes of Trinidadians. And with the full weight of this history, I finally picked up the phone and made my long-awaited call to Windsor Records.

A gentleman answered and introduced himself as the manager. Recognizing my accent, he asked if I was Guyanese, then without missing a beat, he warned me that he very much doubted that Windsor Records would be interested in doing business with me. He informed me, this time with greater emphasis, that many calls had suddenly started coming to him from New York looking for distribution agreements to represent Windsor Records there.

Many wealthy entrepreneurs of Indo-Caribbean heritage living in New York, having noticed that an Indo-Caribbean record, my record, had grabbed the people's attention, were now interested in the record business themselves. Most of them were Trinidadian expats.

The call continued with a few more repetitive warnings, but one last thing he said lodged itself in my memory and remains there today. He ended the call by sarcastically saying, "Well, maybe you can try your luck."

Of all his words, sarcastic or not, these were the only ones I heard. I engraved them into my fertile young mind, hung up the phone, went straight to a nearby travel agency, and purchased a ticket to Trinidad and Tobago.

CHAPTER 16

Never does the heart feel so warmly as when a bad expectation others wished upon you is disappointed. It is then that gates open and bridges form.

With my record in hand and a shoestring budget in my pocket, I boarded an early morning flight out of JFK Airport with service to Trinidad and Tobago the next day.

I didn't know where I would be staying once I arrived, nor how I would travel around in this foreign country, but those thoughts never crossed my mind — not even once. I recall noticing the name of a hotel in the in-flight magazine and mentioned it on the immigration form.

Upon arriving at Piarco International Airport and exiting the terminal, a taxi driver approached me. He offered to carry my bag.

"No, thank you," I said, unaware of the custom.

He looked up at me and squinted his eyes for a second, then said, "You are Guyanese," as if his ears were specially trained to detect such things.

"You will have to pay me before entering my car," his voice now grew stern and demanding. And there was a hint of something else in his expression, like I had somehow been rude, not warning him I was Guyanese.

I held to my purpose, then asked him how much it would cost to be taken to Windsor Records in Port of Spain. He informed me that by the time I got there, they would be closed for the day.

"Let's try," I said.

Open or closed, I wanted to see this mecca of Indo-Caribbean music, to be in that environment and feel its vibrations — even if it meant going there only to touch its closed doors.

We arrived at Windsor Records shortly after 5:00 p.m. and found that the taxi driver had indeed been correct; it was closed for the day, and the steel bars that adorned the entire front of the business, tightly securing it, warned against any breach.

"See, I told you," the driver said. "It's closed. Now you will have to pay me more to drop you off somewhere."

His words were not important. I was staring intently at the building that represented so much in the life of Indo-Caribbean people.

I had imagined this moment since the day when I saw those records in that oriental grocery store in New York. I visualized this moment within my mind's eye and was now in its presence. I opened the door to the taxi, stepped out, and walked toward the doors of Windsor Records.

Behind those steel bars, a mix of Indo-Caribbean and Bollywood records decorated the display inside the tall glass windows. And then, a thought struck me. The Bollywood soundtrack to the film *Dharmatma* — the movie in which I first heard her voice and that had started me down the path which had ultimately led me to this place — could be among those staring back at me. I looked away. I decided that I didn't want to read any of the titles. Not now, not with that man waiting by the taxi, standing and watching my every move. I did not want to discover her album in his presence.

The taxi driver seemed puzzled as he looked at what must have appeared to be strange behavior. But at that moment, being Guyanese became a great asset for me. During the drive from the airport, he had told me how Guyanese people were a strange lot, and now that I was proving his assertion, he must have thought my behavior perfectly expected. And with this, I was free to be completely in my element, and I milked the moment for a long while, just standing and observing this new world around me and taking it all in.

After some time, he said, "What do you want to do? I can't just wait here all evening."

I paused for a moment more, then without saying a word, walked toward his taxi, opened the door, and stepped inside.

He regained his position in the driver's seat and having realized that he was again in control, demanded that I pay him another $20, for which he would drive me to what he described as a low-cost hotel. He informed me, in what I'm sure he thought was a polite manner, that "many Guyanese stay there when they come to Trinidad to sell on the streets." And as I was calculating my budget in my head, he added, "Some of them also sleep on these pavements. What do you want to do?"

He started to drive slowly.

I held to the path of my purpose and asked the taxi driver whether he knew where the owner of Windsor Records lived.

He slammed on the breaks, quickly turned around in his seat and looked at me with incredulous eyes. He looked at me for a long moment, clearly trying to understand what connection there could be between this young man from Guyana and the destination I was requesting.

Perhaps he was also waiting for me to reveal that I had only been joking and to change my request to the low-cost hotel. Not receiving this change of request, he closed his eyes for a moment, and when they opened, they were resigned.

"Listen," he said, "in case you don't understand, let me tell you, the owners of Windsor Records are a very powerful and influential family here in Trinidad and Tobago. You cannot simply show up in front of their house like a feather in the wind and expect to be welcomed inside. Besides, I can get into a lot of trouble if someone sees me dropping a Guyanese there."

I was not concerned, and I knew I didn't have to convince him I had a right to go there. I simply gathered my calm, pulled another $20 out of my pocket, and handed it to him. He turned around and continued driving without another word.

After some time, he slowed to a stop in front of a sprawling bungalow at the very end of a long street. He got out of the car, knocked on my window as he approached the trunk, flung it open, then dropped my suitcase on the side of the street. By the time I exited his car, he was already back into his seat and sped off as quickly as he could. A cloud of dust swirled up onto my clothes and into my eyes, and as I finished dusting myself off, I caught the last glimpses of his tail lights as they turned onto the main road and out of my sight.

My transportation gone, I felt for a moment as if I were the only person standing in this unfamiliar country. As the last of the Trinidad sun was setting, I stood next to my suitcase and studied the house and grounds in front of me. The property was announced by two large decorative iron gates, resolutely shut. A wall extended in both directions and behind it, and I could see a garden rising on one side of the property.

My eyes searched for a street name and found none. I then turned around to face the opposite side of the house, where I noticed a tall wooden post standing in a lush undergrowth. It was a street sign. It read Mohammed Ville. I had finally made it here.

In situations like the one I found myself in, we as humans tend to have any number of doubting thoughts. Having experienced firsthand how the taxi driver, the first person I had interacted with in Trinidad, responded disdainfully to my being Guyanese, gave all the more reason to doubt.

There I was, standing at the crossroad of my journey. Do I walk away, down this street and onto that main road the taxi had just disappeared down? Do I take to heart the taxi driver's words that I could not simply show up in front of their house?

As I sit here, some forty years later, writing this book, I realize what I have always suspected. Had I left, had I walked the way of the taxi, I would never have been able to tell you the rest of this story. I don't mean to say that I wouldn't have had more opportunities; more would have come. However, I'm not sure I would have seen any of them. Had I walked away from Mohammed Ville, I would have been walking away from my heritage and my purpose.

That is not what I did. Like so many similar situations that preceded this one, I remembered the teachings and wisdom of my parents and grandmother, and I focused on all that wisdom as I thought about what my next step should be.

With my eyes affixed to the street sign, I remembered I must create and feel the next moment to be what I wanted it to be. After creating it, I must make it perfect, one step at a time.

I took a deep breath, stretched my fingers over my palms and closed both of my hands tightly. And as I did, I heard the sound of a woman's shoes punctuating the silence, coming from inside the yard behind me. I exhaled.

I turned slowly toward the sound of the oncoming footsteps, allowing them to reach closer to me before my turn was complete. And before our eyes could meet, I felt that now-familiar sensation between my brows, announcing this was what I had been hoping to see.

"Are you looking for someone?" the woman asked in a voice expressing sincere concern, not for herself, but for me.

"Yes," I answered, careful to match the care expressed in her voice. "Good evening, ma'am. My name is Rohit Jagessar, and I am looking for the owner of Windsor Records."

Like the taxi driver, she too, was able to recognize my accent. Unlike that man, there was no disdain in her voice when she said, "You are from Guyana." She simply stated it as a pleasant fact and continued on, telling me her name was Hansrajee. She was originally from Jamaica, and now, together with her husband, owned Windsor Records here in Trinidad.

As we spoke, I felt the presence of someone appearing on the verandah of the top floor beyond, observing from a distance.

The lady shaded the last rays of the sun from her eyes as she turned and lifted her head to look at him, then called out, "He is from Guyana," as though it were nothing more than a bit of information. The man on the veranda raised his hand and waved to me. Before I could return the gesture, he was descending the stairs.

Hansrajee turned back toward me and smiled warmly, and in that smile, I could see the way forward. And from the veranda on which I was now symbolically standing, I saw the future of

Indo-Caribbean music for the people of the United States, Canada, and beyond. Her smile was a torch illuminating that path forward.

Her hands reached for the chains that held the gate. I held the gate steady as she unlocked the chains, then I gently opened the gate, revealing the gentleman already extending his hand toward me from the other side. With a kind but powerful voice, he said, "Hello, my name is Moean Mohammed. Welcome to Trinidad and Tobago!"

CHAPTER 17

The manner in which you serve, the impression you create, is how those who come in contact with you will see your country. You are an ambassador of goodwill for your country.

"Hello Sir, my name is Rohit Jagessar."

I saw surprise in the man's eyes as he stood opposite me, just inside the gates to his property.

"Rohit?" he puzzled for a moment. "Are you the gentleman who called my manager yesterday from New York?"

I think my heart nearly doubled in size in the span of that single moment. There I was, a teenager, a poor Indian from Guyana, and a stranger with no right to be standing where I was according to a taxi driver, in front of the most powerful man in the Indo-Caribbean recording business. Not only had he remembered my name as told to him by his manager from the day before, but he had also just addressed me as gentleman. This, I knew, was the measure of this great man. Kindness and courtesy were the elements from which he was made.

"Oh my God!" his wife exclaimed as I nodded my answer, not trusting myself to speak just yet. "Rohit! You traveled all the way from New York? You must be so tired and hungry, I'm sure."

I turned back to address her and her kind words and saw with surprise and a little embarrassment that she had picked up my suitcase and was brushing the dust off of it. I had not heard of this being possible of wealthy people; however, there it was right in front of me. Before I could respond to the situation, Mr. Mohammed walked past me with a smile, took my suitcase from his wife's hand and brought it with him into the yard.

"Come Rohit," his wife said as she followed her husband. "We are nearing dinner and would love to hear more about your journey."

I followed their footsteps as they led me up a large stairway and into their house, every step further solidifying my future and the path I was on.

The staircase not only allowed me entrance into their home but an entrance into the world of Indo-Caribbean music I had been hoping for since the day I saw this man's name printed on those records in that oriental grocery store. I also knew it was another step toward someday soon finding and recording *her*.

There must have been something about me that struck a reminiscent chord in the minds of both Mr. Mohammed and his wife. Perhaps they saw something in me that reminded them of themselves at the beginning of their journey into this world of Indo-Caribbean music.

Our conversation flowed easily from the moment we sat down at the dining table. Their kindness went over and beyond any social expectations. A Guyanese was welcomed with open arms into a Trinidadian home.

A woman wearing an apron appeared and placed a glass of water in front of me.

"Please take Rohit's suitcase to his room," Hansrajee said to her and turned to me with a gentle smile.

His room, my hostess's words echoed between the brows on my forehead. In that moment, everything I had heard about the people of this country and their perceptions of the people from my birthplace, every fear expressed to me, faded away.

As I opened my eyes the following morning, I woke to what felt like a familiar reality. Like waking up to the sound of the rooster crowing in Black Bush Polder, I knew this was a new day for me, for our people, and for our music, and it felt like it.

Soon, I heard music flowing from somewhere in the house — utensils clinking, pots clanging, and steam hissing. It was the music of the kitchen. The familiar fragrance of home cooking floated into my bedroom to accompany this wonderful tune. The sounds and smells were all so familiar, exactly the same as from my parent's kitchen when we were in Black Bush Polder.

It was then that a thought came to me. As broken as the relationships of these countries and their expats are, we still listen to the same music, eat the same foods, breathe the same air, and share the same history. With so many rich commonalities, it cannot be long before we rise together.

Dinner the previous evening confirmed this belief. We spoke nothing of business throughout the evening, only of food, family, friends, and shared experiences. My hosts were gracious throughout our dinner, and after many insistences I try something from yet another plate, I knew I had made not just an important relationship for my path forward for Indo-Caribbean music, but also lifelong friends.

CHAPTER 18

Silence is the lyrics of the wise.

Immediately after breakfast, Sadro, the eldest son, and I drove into Port of Spain, the nation's capital. The streets were bustling with activity. Busy shoppers darted in and out of storefronts. Street vendors were busy plying their trade. Breakfast foods steamed out of food carts lining the sidewalks. These sights, sounds, and flavors were the perfect setting as we made our way from the car to the iconic address I had stood in front of the day before: 55 Queen Street. Knowing that I was entering the home of Indo-Caribbean music — Windsor Records — I exhaled deeply.

Sadro ushered me through the doors and started giving me a tour.

"Take your time and look around, Rohit," he said. "We will catch up later."

I was happy to oblige.

Windsor Records was a large record store. Like at Sam Goody, records were displayed prominently on stands from the polished marble floor to the very high ceiling, and music lovers moved about from record to record and from area to area. On one side of the store, glass cases displayed some blank cassettes, which at the time were not of any interest to customers.

Vinyl records were spinning on turntables, showcasing the latest releases, and with every turn of the records, there seemed to be a corresponding ring of cash registers. The place was almost full, the customers were happy, and this made me happy.

Knowing that I had a little time to myself, I took the opportunity to collect some data. I conducted a rough calculation of the approximate number of records for sale. I calculated there must have been well over twenty-five thousand Bollywood records. There were even more Indo-Caribbean 45 RPM records. Perhaps over fifty thousand pieces. It was truly a marvelous sight to behold.

After about two hours of absorbing every last detail of the place I had so longed to visit, I heard my name being called by a now-familiar voice. Turning, I saw an open door, and through it, sitting behind a desk, was Mr. Mohammed. For over a year, I had waited to have this meeting, this moment, and this conversation. The time had finally come.

I approached and stood in the open doorway. "Good morning, sir," I said.

"Good morning, Rohit. Please, come in and have a seat. How are you doing this morning? Did you have a good night's rest?"

His manner was as free and easy as it had been the night before. I stepped inside and took a seat. "Yes, sir. I am well-rested. Thank you for your hospitality."

"Oh don't mention. You are most welcome." He smiled and looked up to greet his wife, who had now entered with three cups of coffee on a tray. She placed the tray on his desk, gently closed the door, and sat next to him.

As the door closed, another was opening. Mr. Mohammed took his glasses off, looked at me, and said, "From now on, please call me Moean."

From now on, I thought. Those words gave me hope, a clear indication we would have more meetings.

I nodded, and he put his glasses back on and reached for a stack of files sitting at the far side of his desk.

It was a thick stack. It seemed clear to me then that while I had been spending my time in his record store taking in all the details, Moean was preparing for our meeting. He grabbed a folder from the top of the stack, brought it in front of him and opened it. He scanned the first page inside. After a moment, as he continued to read, he reached into his shirt pocket, his fingers searching for a pen. There were six. He brought one out and drew a circle on the page. He then turned the folder toward me.

"Rohit, I would like for you to please read what I have just circled on this page," he said.

I leaned slightly forward and began to read the typewritten words. It read:

"As I am hereby confirming my interest, in writing, to do business with you, please be forewarned that a Guyanese teenager named Rohit Jagessar recently started out in the record business here in New York. I believe that he made a small record, and I am sure that he will be approaching you with regard to the distribution of Windsor Records. From what I heard about his background, he was sweeping the floors at a factory and certainly does not have the means to handle such a major record label as yours. Be aware that he is from Guyana."

I finished reading the encircled words, and gently returned the folder back to Moean. I had no urge to extend my fingers over my palms. There was no need.

The letter writer had correctly summarized my humble background. He had also, without realizing it, given me a very important opportunity.

He had clearly been seeking the business of Windsor Records, but in the process, had given Moean my name and my story. This man must have been concerned about me being a competitor to have mentioned me, and Moean would have been keenly aware of that. The letter writer's words had opened a door for me by confirming I was in the record business. The record I made before contacting Windsor Records had served its purpose.

Knowing I did not need to address the typed words or any reason to defend them, I remained silent and composed.

Having felt and witnessed firsthand the sincere kindness of this family's hospitality and generosity, I knew there was no point talking about the letter writer. The decision of what's best for Moean and Windsor Records must be realized by him.

I waited for my host to guide the conversation forward. He sat back in his chair and said, "You see, Rohit, many people are calling and writing from New York to do business with Windsor."

Hansrajee, obviously hearing about this letter for the first time, leaned forward. "Rohit, you must be careful. This is a very tough business," she interjected with almost the concern of a mother, not a businesswoman.

I remained silent and calm, only nodding to acknowledge and accept her caution.

"Do you know that this man," Moean gestured his head to the still open folder, "offered me $50,000 as an advance payment to distribute Windsor Records in New York?" He then added it was U.S. dollars for greater emphasis.

"All of a sudden, we don't know why," said his wife, "so many people are asking us for the rights."

I smiled at the mention of this. The fact my little 45 RPM record, the first Indo-Caribbean record advertised on television, had been the cause of this stir of interest in the record business was not something I would mention. Moean and Hansrajee were intelligent people and would soon realize for themselves what had spurred the sudden interest if they had not already suspected.

Moean leaned forward, took the open folder in both hands, and began to push it across the table toward me once more, this time saying, "Rohit, you can read the entire letter, if you wish."

I placed both of my hands on both of his, and together we closed the folder. In that one gesture, I had answered all of his questions.

Smiling, Hansrajee turned to her husband as though answering a question they had both been silently pondering and whispered, "Might as well." He smiled and nodded in return.

The very next moment, Sadro opened the door, popped his head in, and said, "Lunch is here." He joined us, leaving the door ajar. The sounds of a completely packed record store were the perfect backdrop to a pleasant lunch.

Until that moment, I had probably spoken less than one hundred words to Moean and Hansrajee that day. During our lunch, I was long with my answers about my life in Black Bush Polder and our transition to the United States. I learned my life had not been much different from theirs and that they had built their lives from humble beginnings as well and they, too, treasured all the experiences of their youth.

Our lunch confirmed that business — and the record business in particular — could be equal parts life, travel, business, and pleasure. I saw firsthand it was important to be a businessman but more important to be a gentleman.

CHAPTER 19

Don't be afraid to show your mistakes. Mistakes are rehearsals. They prepare you for taking the big stage.

Later that day, Moean told me that we would be going to Maraval Road, where he would host his radio program on the country's only radio station.

His wife told him, "Make sure you include Rohit on your show. I know he does not have any experience in radio as of yet but still, put him on your show, you must teach him." He responded with a broad but playful smile.

Although I suspected he was up to something, I knew from all of their actions that whatever this might be, it would be in my best interest.

It was widely known that while some Trinidadians were doing business with Guyanese on the pavements, they were careful to hide these business relationships. Here, it was about to be put on public display.

Although I had done a little work at both television and recording studios, I found the idea of visiting a radio station fascinating.

The medium of radio, unlike television, communicates to an audience who sees no part of it. In that way, it has no boundaries — nothing to limit their imagination. Much like the written word, radio allows the listener to create whatever world they desire within the parameters of what is spoken. On radio, the focus is on the words. It is, in my opinion, the perfect medium, and I was intrigued to see the master at work and learn.

As the sun began to set during our drive, it dawned upon me I had, at that point, been in this country for twenty-four hours. Life had changed for me in such a short time. Purpose is a timeless thing.

The words of my father came back to me. "What doesn't happen in a year can happen in a day."

The man I had waited to meet for well over a year not only welcomed me into his home and place of business but was also driving me around, showing me his country. And what a beautiful country it was.

"Rohit, this is Trinidad," Moean said with joy as he sped down another scenic road. "I am going to make a detour to show you parts of our beautiful twin island."

Then he banked around a sharp turn, and the vista opened up. The most amazing expanse of lush green landscape extended before us, tumbling out into a great valley between foothills. Long shadows stretched out, dancing between golden rays of the Trinidad and Tobago sunset. Tall trees stood in silhouette high up on hilltops where homes could also be seen, their lit windows punctuating the growing twilight.

One last turn sent us back onto a flatter area of the country once again, and minutes later, we pulled into a parking lot.

"Rohit, this is Radio Trinidad. It is from here that this country gets all of its radio. Let's walk in."

It was minutes to six o'clock when we walked into the station. Moean offered me a seat behind studio furniture affixed with a microphone. This was the third studio I had been in, and like a recording studio, it was compact.

Moean took his seat across from me, and to my right, a large soundproof glass wall separated us from an adjacent room, where a sound engineer sat behind a large control panel. At seconds to six o'clock, the engineer began his countdown, and in those final seconds before the show began, Moean completely transformed. The man who had been the gracious host was now a man of business again. His playful smile was now a face of focus and pure determination. As I observed, I soon realized this was a king taking command of his kingdom, a showman in his element. I couldn't allow myself to miss a single detail of his creative process.

A sign lit up in front of us, "On Air."

Moean opened his radio show with an Urdu couplet that he reminded his listeners was his regular opening theme. He followed it with the English translation, "If people do not speak so well of you, it cannot do you any harm. The only thing that can happen to you is the true will of God."

Our eyes met as he spoke those words. I knew he had found a specific truth in the words of his opening. He had realized the meaning behind my silence regarding the words of the letter writer earlier that day. He nodded his head in acknowledgment.

He continued on with his show. Through silent gestures of both his hands and his head, he expertly guided the sound engineer. I could hear it all through my headphones: the music, his sonorous voice, and those perfect fades and crossfades seamlessly coordinating between the man and his music.

I keenly continued to absorb everything, quenching my thirst to learn all that I could about the music, the medium and my brand-new realization of the importance of having a personality.

I realized I might create many records and many TV shows, but all of this will only have true meaning when I have a personality and apply this personality to create. Creativity needs a home, which is best upheld when it has a personality.

Some fifteen minutes into his show, the playful smile suddenly returned to Moean's face, and this time, there was no mistaking what he was up to. I said a silent prayer, "Oh dear God, please, please, please let him not put me on the radio." But before I could complete this silent beseeching, I heard these words.

"I will be bringing you on right after this song."

I immediately amended my prayer, "Oh dear God, please don't let this song end." But it did. And as it finished its slow fade and the background music came up again, Moean began speaking again on the air, introducing the next section of his show. Me.

I used his short introduction to switch gears once more and began thinking of all the questions I could ask him. But I was not the one who would be asking questions on his show.

He looked at me and on live radio said, "Rohit, I just played a song by one of this country's iconic singers, Sundar Popo. Why not tell the listeners about this music. What is Indo-Caribbean music, chutney music, and what is its history?"

"That music, this music," I struggled, searching for an answer to a question I had not guessed.

He now showed me who was in charge, who was the student, who was the master, and who had mastered personality.

He paused and in a more confident voice said, "That is not

what I asked you. I asked you to tell my listeners what you know about this music. That was my question."

I motioned with my hands, silently asking, "What do I say?"

His smile relaxed. "Oh, I am sorry, Rohit," he said. "I think your microphone isn't working. The engineer will fix it for you. In the meantime, let's listen to another song, then we'll return for Rohit's answer."

In real-time, on live radio, with the entire country tuned in to the country's only radio station, a realization dawned on me that Moean was both drowning me and rescuing me at the same time. He had been so kind and generous until this moment, but now, he placed me in what was an embarrassing position from which only he could save me.

As the next song came on, he immediately took off his headphones and motioned for me to do the same. "You see, Rohit? This is the music business." He then emphasized, "This is what you will be up against. This is exactly what my wife warned you about earlier today. It is a tough business, Rohit. It is survival of the fittest. You will have to answer my question if you are to leave an indelible impression on the minds of the people of Trinidad and Tobago. I have asked, and they are awaiting. The entire nation is waiting. With the little time remaining, think about what you are going to say."

He then placed his headphones back on, precluding any chance I might seek his guidance. He leaned back in his chair, placed both of his hands behind his head and looked at me as if to say, "let me see how you will handle the moment," as if to gauge where I was at in my young life.

At this moment, I understood the importance of rehearsals and the adage one should know what they are about to do before doing it. In this business, one is in the plain sight of the public, and one must always be prepared. I was not.

The first time I went to school, our teacher wasted no time showing us who was in charge. I had gotten up, harnessed my inner jaguar, and ran out of that room, out of that building and onto that street. The same jaguar had traveled with me ever since.

And once I reminded myself of this, I closed my eyes, and stilled my mind. I was safe. I realized Moean could not save me, that I must save myself. I was now ready.

Trinidad and Tobago, the entire nation, was awaiting my answer. An answer that would leave an enduring impression of who I was. Should I not be able to answer such a simple question then all they have heard and believed about Guyanese would hold true.

I had made a record to start a dialogue. The record led me to this decisive moment that I hoped would begin another dialogue leading to an understanding between people of two countries.

I reminded myself that this is the largest platform in this country, with the entire nation tuned in. There could be no bigger moment than this. This is an opportunity where all can rise.

As the moment arrived, I decided I must first go back in order to go forward. Muscles pull, they do not push. Like the car stuck in mud, the rhythm of pulling backward allows the next movement forward to be strong and effective so that one can continue on their journey.

If I were to leave a good impression, I would have to go back to tell this nation who I was and reveal to it the core of my being. As far as the first bank, the Bank of Karma, was concerned, the people from Guyana are very much like the people of Trinidad. We share the same heritage — we are all the people who came by ship.

The only difference was that my countrymen were viewed through the lens of the second bank, the Bank of Money. Should we continue to see people through this lens, there would continue to be disharmony among us. These two banks must come into a balance.

The moment came. Moean looked at me, his entire posture brimming with self-confidence. It was clear this lesson was an enjoyable battle of wits for him, and the showman in him saw him winning. So much so that it gave him great pleasure to repeat his question.

I reached for my grandmother's style of storytelling, and the glaring bulb of the studio became the calming bottle lamp of my home.

"Mr. Moean," I said. "I bring greetings from my village of Black Bush Polder, my country of Guyana and the city in which I now live, New York, to you and the people of this wonderful twin island, Trinidad and Tobago.

"Now to answer your question about Indo-Caribbean music, chutney music. This is the music of the people, by the people, and for the people. It is deeply rooted in the sugar cane plantations and farmlands of this region and of Fiji, Mauritius, and every other country where there are descendants of those who came by ship from India.

"The music expresses a lifestyle once dictated to our people by those calling themselves colonial masters. And in response to the harsh living and working conditions, our people wrote and composed songs that gave them an outlet to express feelings deep within. This is the music, lyrics, and poetry of their experiences and struggles. It comes from within the core of their being. It is an outlet that comforts in times of distress and in times of sadness. It is the rhythm of lyrical liberation, to which they rose to sing and dance again."

Moean looked at me, his demeanor completely changed. His look acknowledged he knew I had it within me, but I needed it to be brought out. And for the best to be brought out of me, he needed to nudge me. And as he was reflecting, I too reflected and saw why this man was one of the greatest record producers in the world — he knew the art of bringing out talent, the best in a person, revealing the personality of the man.

A pause followed. We both took the opportunity to look at the engineer through the glass at the very same time, fully aware that whatever his impression of this moment might be, so too would be that of this entire nation.

The engineer appeared awestruck. We knew the indelible impression Moean had been aiming for had been accomplished.

Moean wanted me to succeed but the showman in him would not allow me to upstage him on his very own radio show. An air of heaviness still remained around us.

In Moean's expression, I saw the realization that I had accepted his challenge and delivered a first blow he had not fully anticipated. I had left an impression, not as Rohit Jagessar, especially since no one in Trinidad knew me then, but as a Guyanese on a Trinidadian radio program. I had made it clear, on this country's only radio station with the entire nation tuned in, that the Guyanese may be selling on pavements here, but we, like our Trinidadian counterparts, are aware of our storied history, and like Moean, we too could articulate the history of our music.

Looking again between Moean and the engineer to further gauge how this nation was reacting to this moment, I saw in their eyes that I had just established a dialogue between our two countries and the beginning of my personality, a brand for myself. And knowing full well that if I could see it in their eyes, we as people, were collectively starting to see things in the same way, in the same manner.

I had upstaged the showman in Moean, my host. This was his radio show, and he was its king. I knew I needed to correct this situation, to raise him up. But I had to wait for him to speak, and so I waited with bated breath.

But Moean was indeed the true master showman and had already transformed back to showing it. He turned to the engineer and signaled with not one, but two hands, for him to take the background music all the way down. Then he turned his look toward me, and his eyes showed determination to save, protect, and defend his personal brand.

I felt that stare, but now I was not undone by it. I continue to remain calm. I now wanted more than ever for him to succeed. It was only in his success, in the preservation of his own brand, that my words could make the impact they were poised to make on his countrymen. I knew I would need to play second fiddle.

Moean, like the true showman he was, asked another question which created another opening to uplift this music and its people.

"Rohit," he said, his words more forceful than I had yet heard from the man, though still controlled. "where do you see this music going in these changing times?"

"You see, sir, in these changing times, people from this region have already started to migrate to other countries. Indo-Caribbean children are being born in those countries. And this music needs to follow them if it is to sustain and resonate with all of the people who share this background and for generations to come. This music needs to be marketed and distributed globally. But it is not."

I knew I had dealt a personal blow to this man who had produced the music I spoke of, and this man knew my words were squarely directed at him. However, in the same manner his first question had good intent, so did my answer.

His sonorous voice now rattled my earphones. "Rohit! Let me tell you something, young man. Let me teach you some economics. Do you know that here, in my country, in Trinidad, we sell a single track, a single 45 RPM record, for well over $5.00 USD. Whereas in the United States, this same record is only $3.00? And not only that, Rohit," his voice grew slightly louder, "here, we sell a full album for $20.00 USD, whereas in the United States, this music is not even available on albums."

I remained calm, mindfully indicating to him that he had won.

Upon seeing he had now delivered the return blow, Moean's smile began to return by the end of his lecture. He was convinced of a sure victory. But in his answer, without him knowing it, he had given me my answer — the piece of information I needed to understand the greatest hurdle of distributing this music globally. He had solved for me the great mystery that had been on my mind since the day I wandered into that grocery store in New York.

Why weren't these records available commercially outside of Trinidad and Tobago? Because Moean was happy with the money he was making in his own country and couldn't be bothered with the trouble of global distribution. Now that I knew this, I realized exactly how I would negotiate with him for the distribution rights when the time came. But first, it was time for me to hand this great man, this king in his kingdom, this great showman, his victory.

"I see your point, sir. I understand what you are saying," I said in a calm voice, careful not to indicate I agreed.

Realizing his triumph, he now laughed and said, "Well, alright then, young man." He then turned to the engineer, and this time instead of waving with both of his hands, he happily nodded his head, and the next song was played.

Looking back on that moment, I believe now as I believed then, that Moean had played his part correctly. What he had done on that day was protect his brand as a showman. He upheld his importance among his listeners, validating their valuable time invested in listening to him. All while serving his personal brand and advertisers' interests and ensuring they both held on to their large audience — both show and business.

But I claimed the victory I needed as well, though it was a silent one. I had navigated the conversation to an end which helped the people of Trinidad and Tobago to better understand the people of Guyana. And secondly, I gained an invaluable piece of information that held the promise for the upliftment of the people's music, all while protecting the showmanship of Moean.

As the next song played, Moean sang along, the star of the show bathing in his glory. I joined him, as happy for his victory as I was for our people. This was also a victory for the music and for the people of our two countries.

Minutes before the show ended, an idea entered my mind. Should Moean invite me back on the air again, I would use the opportunity to further an idea with his large listenership. A powerful and wealthy Trinidadian is hosting this Guyanese in his home, and perhaps those who sleep on pavements may be looked upon with a bit more understanding, perhaps a bit more kindness.

As hoped for, as Moean went through his wrap-up, he graciously invited me to join him again on the air. I thanked him and his family for being such gracious hosts, not only on his radio show, but also in the warmth of their home.

He immediately saw the greater significance of this detail, and like the true showman that he was, he told his listeners, "Oh yes. It is my pleasure to host my good friend Rohit in my home.

And Rohit, my friend, I hope that you are going to stay with us for some time more and continue to join me again on my radio shows while you are here in Trinidad."

The closing music came up, and the engineer entered the studio where we were now standing. Moean introduced us, and the man embraced me, welcoming me to Trinidad and Tobago. Togetherness was definitely in the air. Music, our music — the music of those who once toiled on the sugar plantations, the music of the people whose ancestors had come by ship — had caused that togetherness.

And although earlier on his show, Moean had quenched his thirst for showmanship and a shade of perception might have existed that he had broken me, his closing invitation had totally diminished it and all that was broken was rising.

Soon, the news traveled back to New York to the expats that a Guyanese was on the radio and was welcomed in Trinidad.

CHAPTER 20

The manner in which we navigate our lives determines the manner in which we realize our purpose.

After his radio program, Moean invited me to dinner. The restaurant was in a lush garden of coconut trees with overhanging branches and a stream on one side. A waitress followed us to our table, balancing two locally brewed beers on a tray, and within a short time, dinner was served. Our order was never taken, and it became clear that this was a place Moean frequently visited after his shows.

"What did you think about my radio show?" he asked as soon as we were seated.

"Brilliant," I replied.

He was pleased to hear that, and for the next hour he took me through the journey of how he became a showman. I learned how his family rose to become the pioneers of both Indo-Caribbean radio and music in this region of the world.

In the short time I had been in Trinidad, it was clear I had made a good impression on the most powerful figure in the entertainment industry of the Caribbean. We were having a delightful evening, and the only thing he had not yet conceded was any indication that we would do business together to provide Indo-Caribbean expats with his music — their music.

After our dinner, as we sat below the stars sipping our beers, he asked me how I got interested in the record business.

"I am on a journey to bring our music and people together by setting up a global distribution platform for our music. I want people to access it wherever in the world they may live. And I want someday to record our music with a female singer from India."

"What? Did you say you wanted to record this music with someone from India. Did I hear you correctly?"

"Yes, sir. You heard me correctly," I replied.

Astonishment covered Moean's face, and he looked up to the moon as if searching for some reason the man across from him was now talking such nonsense. He looked back and forth from the sky to me a few times, then turned back toward the table.

"Rohit, how well do you handle your drinks? You have only had a few sips of your beer, you know?"

I held my bottle and took another small sip. He picked up his, leaned back in his chair and emptied it. He then snapped his fingers, and the waitress brought him another one.

He held it in his hand and said, "Here in Trinidad we have thousands of singers, not to mention Guyana and Suriname, Fiji and Mauritius. And you are telling me that you want to go all the way to India to record someone? Don't you know the singers in India can only sing Bollywood and disco-style songs? They cannot sing this kind of music. They cannot pronounce our local dialect. I mean, you should know this by now. Anyway, who is this singer? Do you know her name?"

"I don't know her name."

Moean, recognizing the awkwardness in my answer, held in his laughter. Unable to contain it, he burst out laughing so uncontrollably that he began hitting his fists on the table.

"Rohit, we may have to cut you off," he said through his continued laughter.

By that time, I had begun laughing as well and soon found the silliness of my answer even funnier than he had. In the midst of our laughter, the waitress appeared with more beers on a tray. One for me, one for Moean, and now one for her, signaling it was the end of her shift.

Now there were three.

Unaware of why we were laughing, Moean explained it to the waitress, "He is a mad man thinking to make a record of our local songs with a singer from India."

"Wait," she said. "You know, he may be onto something here. That is a brand-new idea. It has never been done before."

It was then I saw another dimension of this great man and perhaps the side that made him so successful. The words from the waitress had resonated. He knew her opinion represented that of the people and the record-buying public. He repositioned himself on his seat, and I did too.

I sat back in my chair and rested my head against my palm. She had understood. Her words had confirmed what I had been thinking all along since the day when I first heard her voice.

In a calm, composed, and completely serious voice, Moean asked, "Do you know of any song this singer from India has recorded?"

"*Dharmatma*," I replied. "She recorded songs in the Bollywood movie, *Dharmatma*."

"Wait," he said, and his eyes searched for my next answer. "Is her voice very different from the other Bollywood singers?"

"You got it! How did you know?" That's exactly what it is! And I drew my chair closer to the table and almost as if choreographed, the waitress too, drew hers.

Moean held my gaze silently for a moment. I could see in him a new interpretation of the idea I had spoken about several minutes before. It swirled around in his mind.

He remained completely composed.

A moment before this one, the table was slightly shrouded in darkness. A small patch of cloud had momentarily hidden the moon, and as it drifted off the moon reappeared.

Moean's gaze followed mine and the waitress's up to the moon, and then he lowered his voice as he nodded to the waitress and said, "Yes, you are right."

Then he turned squarely toward me and said, "The singer you are looking for, her name is Kanchan."

CHAPTER 21

Knowing is knowledge.

It was past 10 p.m. when Moean revealed the name of the voice I had been holding on to for so long. Kanchan, the name filled my being.

The restaurant was now closed, and yet we remained seated in the tranquil garden, discussing the night away with our audience of one, the waitress.

"What I am about to tell you will surprise you," said Moean. "Last night, when you ate dinner in our house, do you remember the chair on which you sat?"

I nodded. Both my hands were tightly closed as I awaited his next words.

"She sat in the same chair not so long ago."

This was nothing short of the most amazing discovery I had yet made on this journey. It was all I could do to keep my attention focused on the rest of what this man had to say.

"A friend of mine," he continued, "Rashid Pierkhan from Suriname, had brought her along with her husband, Babla, and some musicians. He brought them all from India on a small concert tour to Guyana, Suriname, and Trinidad and Tobago. As a favor to my friend, I organized her shows here. I don't know how well you can get her to sing our songs, but from what I know, they are a very talented pair."

He maintained his steady exterior, and in a calm voice said, "Come, I want to play something for you."

We thanked the waitress for sharing her thoughts with us and said goodbye to her.

Moean then reminded me again of the words his wife had spoken.

"You will have to be careful," he said. "Her shows in Trinidad were very small. Only a few hundred people attended. She and her husband were paid only $250 per show. There is no doubt she is a good singer, but I'm not sure you can make the numbers work. You see in this business, although their fees are hardly anything, you will have to take into consideration major costs such as airline tickets, hotel accommodation, etc. These are the big expenses."

But I felt no worry about the numbers he was referring to.

As we sat in his car, he pulled a few cassettes from his glove compartment and said, "Here it is. Here is the live recording from her shows in Trinidad. I too, like her voice."

A short musical interlude began the recording as we drove off. That was followed by Kanchan's voice, the voice that had stayed within me for so long, and I recognized it as if I had just watched that movie the same evening.

Her voice rose up in the car and filled the spaces of the Trinidadian night as we navigated toward Moean's home.

Once home, we settled in for an after-dinner conversation and were joined by Hansrajee and Sadro. Moean brought out a few cassettes from a large display, and as the first began to unspool, the brilliance of Babla became the perfect background to our conversation.

It was Sadro who described the genius of this great composer as the music continued on. He explained how Babla was also a rhythm musician who played many different instruments throughout the performance. The roto tom, the bongo drums, and the tumba were among them. Even more impressive and that particularly caught my attention, he played the timbales, the Latin American instrument. The man was truly brilliant.

As the tape kept playing, my sense of imagination continued stretching, and I soon realized the possibilities for the people who came by ship within this fusion of music.

In this music was the power to celebrate every heritage — African, Indian, and others — and unite them as one. I felt this music could tear down all barriers. The broken will rise.

The proof of this fusion of music would be in how it was packaged and marketed.

Soon into the tape, the voice of Kanchan, once again, cut through the rhythm, rising to its great heights and flowing smoothly through her impressive vocal range. And what a range her voice had. The average human vocal range is about three and one-third octaves. Hers, my young and developing musical mind calculated, effortlessly scaled no less than five. I made a note of this important observation. It would be my first production note when I finally prepared to record Kanchan.

What a great privilege I had been gifted. What an honor, good fortune, and luck it was to be sitting with this family in their home and listening to her voice.

This powerful family had been in the record business for well over a decade. And even longer in broadcasting. They had everything at their disposal to now go and record Kanchan, should they choose to. They knew her and had already staged her concerts of Bollywood songs here in Trinidad and Tobago. They could easily, at any time, pick up the phone and call Rashid Pierkhan in Suriname and get in touch with her. I sat there in awe.

This family built bridges. They were not like the taxi driver who had shown me such disdain. Nor were they like the letter writer who was afraid of his own fate. This family, instead of coming in the way of aspirations, paved the way.

I spoke that night of my intentions and aspirations for the record business for the people who came by ship and the music that belonged to those people all over the world. I told them of how I intended to make a record that would be so compelling it would create an event in and of itself.

And they listened. They listened intently to every word.

When I finished, a few minutes or a few hours later, I was not sure, Hansrajee looked at her husband and spoke.

"Moean, you know what?" she said. "Rohit must go to Suriname. Let him meet directly with Rashid and discuss how feasible it would be to record Kanchan. He will learn how to negotiate everything, and that will help him when he is ready to make his record."

CHAPTER 22

Find your unique way of learning and understanding. Uniqueness lives in your interpretation.

The next evening we arrived at Piarco Airport, where Moean handed me a ticket to Paramaribo, Suriname, as well as an envelope, with instructions for me to give it to his friend Rashid the minute I saw him. He told me to return to Trinidad within a few days to discuss something important.

I had been in this great country for forty-eight hours, and much had been accomplished.

By eight thirty the following morning, Rashid Pierkhan and I were parked in front of his record store, Acme Records. Like Windsor, Acme was a large space with thousands of records for sale. Mr. Pierkhan introduced me to his staff, then led me to his plushly decorated office.

I was mindful that he would need a little time to settle in, so I picked up a magazine and began browsing through it. A woman entered with two cups of coffee and placed them before us. Much to her and Mr. Pierkhan's surprise, without even touching the one she had just placed in front of me, I immediately requested another. She began to take the first. I stopped her.

"No," I said. "I would like one more, please."

Puzzled, she soon returned with it and paused for a moment, perhaps expecting me to then ask for yet another. I nodded and smiled my thanks, and she walked from the office, closing the door behind her. Now, there were three — my two and Mr. Pierkhan's. This was a lucky number for me and the basis I hoped for a good meeting.

Mr. Pierkhan took off his glasses, wiped the lenses with a yellow cloth, then put them back on and produced the letter I had handed him the night before at the airport. The man now seemed fully settled into his element. I saw a man of business — extremely serious and astute. I had already rehearsed the scenario with Moean, and I was ready as well.

As he read the letter, he paused for a moment, lifted his head and studied me with a puzzled look, said nothing, then continued reading. As he continued, I saw his pace had slowed.

"Moean writes that you are in the record business," he said as he looked up from the letter a final time and set it down on the desk in front of him. "What records have you made?"

I reached into my briefcase, pulled out a few pieces of the 45 RPM record I had produced, and handed them to him. He carefully studied the label, then asked me two questions, both of which Moean had never asked.

"How did you finance the production of this record? How long did it take for you to get back your investment?"

It was clear this man was having trouble reconciling the youthful appearance of the nineteen year old from Guyana sitting in front of him with what was written in the letter. I knew I would have to get him past this, and I could only accomplish my goals here if he saw me as an equal of sorts. I had to demonstrate to this man, who was perhaps twice my age, that our meeting and the time he was investing in it was worthwhile.

"I got my money back before I invested it," I said and held a straight face.

"What?" His serious demeanor changed instantly, and he started laughing. He laughed so loud that even the shoppers began looking in at us through the glass pane.

As they looked, I studied their faces trying to read from their expressions what type of records they may like or want to buy. I wondered what type of records to make for them and if they would accept or respond to a voice from India singing their songs.

Some waved to us with curious looks, and Mr. Pierkhan returned the gesture with familiarity. He knew them. They knew him. No one knew me. Not yet.

When he regained his composure he said, "Rohit, come on, man. This is no ordinary business we are talking about. This is the record business. Very few are skilled or courageous enough to navigate it successfully." He looked back at the letter in front of him, then advised, "You have to be serious if you intend to survive it."

"But I am really serious, you know, I did make my money back before I had even invested it in the record."

"Okay," he said. "Tell me then. How did you go about doing this? Because I have been in the music business for many years, and this is the very first time I hear of such a thing."

I explained how my entrance into the record business had started with a little television show, which I had bartered for free TV commercial airtime, how I used that airtime to market this record, and how I gave exposure to a few local grocery stores in my ads in exchange for $1,200, of which, I only needed to spend $600 to make this record.

Mr. Pierkhan's eyes widened, but before I had finished my explanation, he had already grasped the bigger picture of it.

"Then you sold these records to those grocery stores and drove traffic to them," he broke in, now unable to contain his excitement.

I nodded.

"Brilliant, Rohit. I am telling you, man. This is brilliant. His eyes drifted across the room and stayed in one corner of his office. It was then I saw that perhaps like Moean and his wife, he too had faced many challenges and was reminded of those early beginnings on his journey to where we were now sitting.

He then looked back toward me, and said, "You know, for all the years I have been in this business, I never once thought about this angle, bringing on sponsors and doing cross-promotions. You know, Rohit, I am never too old to learn something new. I will speak with my advertisers and do this."

I had gained his trust and moved him past the difference in our ages. We were now, as I had hoped, equals. I had legitimized myself in his eyes as a worthy contributor in the record business and was now poised to get the information I came in search of.

"Hey, Rohit. I have an idea. Do you like fishing?"

"Fishing? Did I tell you the story about the time I fished in a pond in our rice field?" I said in response.

He got up and grabbed his keys. "Let's go," he said. "I would love to hear more. You can tell me on the way."

An hour ago, this man had walked into his place of business with a serious manner. But now, as we marched back through his store toward the entrance, all eyes of his staff wondered about his playful smile. Those same eyes were trying to decipher me as well, wondering who this guy was who could get their boss out of his office on a busy day.

We drove through the streets of beautiful Paramaribo and back to Mr. Pierkhan's home where his housekeeper packed some food, drinks, and tackle into the vehicle. We then drove straight to the rice lands of Saramacca in the northern district of Suriname where we sat on a hilly riverbank overlooking the majestic Saramacca River.

"The Saramacca River," Mr. Pierkhan narrated to me, "begins its journey in the Wilhelmina Mountains of Suriname, then joins with the Coppename River, and after some 150 miles, empties its brackish water out into the Atlantic." The colors of where the two waters meet, one blackish, one brownish. Yet they meet. Perhaps music can be the cause for the people of this region to meet too.

My new friend from Suriname now told me, his new friend from Guyana, about the Maroons of African heritage, who had once established their communities along the river after freeing themselves from bondage on the plantations some three hundred years before this day.

Around fifty thousand of their ancestors now lived here.

He pointed to their houses, made of wood harvested from the surrounding forests. They were set on high stilts to avoid the overflowing river during the heavy rainy season.

He told me of the more than seven hundred bird species, including the wondrously colorful toucans and parrots, enjoying nature's bounty in this part of the world, which extended to my country Guyana and Moean's Trinidad and Tobago, some five hundred miles from where we sat. Like in the two other countries, the Amerindians were the indigenous people of the land. Africans were brought here to work on the plantations during the seventeenth century, and around 1873, the first East Indians arrived on these shores to labor as indentured workers.

As he ventured into even more similarities between our countries, I began to drift away into my thoughts.

"Rohit? What happened, man? You seem to be daydreaming or something."

"I am awake. You know," I said, "as I am listening to you, I am sitting only a stone's throw away from Black Bush Polder, the village where I grew up. My old home is no more than 150 miles from here, just across the Corentyne River. And this land, Suriname, shares the same heritage as my country, Guyana, and Moean's country of Trinidad and Tobago.

"We are all the same people, living the same story, only under different circumstances. We eat the same food, watch the same movies, and listen to the same music. We dance to the same beat and breathe the same air. Why are we so divided? Where did we go wrong?"

Mr. Pierkhan had been listening intently. This powerful man was clearly moved. "Rohit," he said. "Not all that happens is under our control. All we can do is live as brothers, lead by example, and hopefully, someday, there will be harmony among all the peoples of these lands." Then he perked up. "Hey, Rohit. Your old home is so near. Why don't we go there for a day so you can meet with your old friends? I'd love to see where you grew up."

I would have loved to accept Mr. Pierkhan's kindness, but I knew it was not yet time for me to return to my home. "Thank you, but not now," I told him. "I must return to them with something in my hands, something more, something tangible, something that gives them a hope and belief they can scale the mountain of life, reach its highest peaks, and rise." And before I myself can do this, I myself must first rise.

"A lot is in your hands, then," he said. "A lot depends on you, now, and how you navigate this journey to Kanchan and Babla and the manner in which you present this new era of music, this fusion of African, Indian, and Latin American instruments. This could very well musically bring all of our people together."

A few days later, Mr. Pierkhan dropped me at the airport and handed me a large envelope. He told me that copies of the contracts he previously had with Kanchan and Babla were in it, along with their contact information. He had also included an accounting of every cost incurred staging their concerts in this region of the world. He told me to study everything carefully and that it should help me clearly understand every aspect of putting together contracts and staging such performances when the time came. He then gave me the same warning that Moean had. It was a big risk recording Indo-Caribbean music with someone from India, emphasizing it may sound like a Bollywood album and not like Indo-Caribbean music.

He then handed me a letter, telling me to give it to Moean as we embraced, as friends, at the airport, and he wished me a safe journey back to Trinidad and Tobago.

CHAPTER 23

Observe how one thing works with the other, propels it, and raises it in vibration.

Moean's nephew, Rafi, met me at the airport. We arrived at Windsor Records, where Moean was waiting for me. The minute his secretary told him I had arrived, he emerged from his office, grabbed me by the hand, and led me back with him into his office. "How did it go, how did it go?" he asked with eager eyes. "Did Rashid give you all the numbers you needed?"

I pulled out the large envelope from my briefcase and placed it on his desk. "Done," I said, and thanked him for his help.

"Don't worry about that," he waved a hand. "I am so happy your trip to this part of the world was successful. What are you going to do when you get back to America?"

Having seen how his business was set up, I told him that I was thinking of starting a small store with a small office space. Then he said the very words I had been waiting to hear.

"Yes. You will need to set that up as soon as you can because you are going to need it to distribute Windsor Records."

He then extended his hand to me, and as we shook, he said, "Mr. Jagessar, welcome to Windsor. You are now officially my record distributor throughout all of North America. Please make sure that you do not distribute my records to any stores in the Caribbean. I will continue to control sales in this region myself."

I smiled, and at first, said nothing. Had Moean been the one who answered the phone and spoken the words I had just heard, when I first called Windsor Records from New York, I might have been a bit overwhelmed. But not now. Having come on the journey, met and interacted with this great man and his family, those words energized me and my mission.

Although the door to his office was closed, I could hear the sounds of activity in the record store like a roar entering his office. I realized I would have to raise a significant amount of money again to manufacture Windsor Records, open my store, and have my small office.

Upon realizing this, I had an idea.

"Hey," I said. "Do you remember me telling you about the album Mohan Singh made in Toronto?"

"I don't even want to talk about that." His face immediately changed, and I could see frustration stretch across it. "Do you know what that man did to me? He came to Trinidad, to my country. He sat in the chair next to the one where you sit now. And when I refused to give him the distribution rights for my records, he went behind my back, took my musicians, and flew them to Toronto where he held shows with them and recorded that album, *BWIA Live in Toronto.*

Moean was upset by the end of his explanation. But I knew if I could navigate this properly, I could bend this situation to a beneficial result for all parties, including myself.

At the risk of bearing the brunt of his anger, I advised him that, "It's a good album, and I think you should import it. If you don't, the smaller record stores here in Trinidad and Tobago certainly will. This may give them an entry into the distribution business here."

I could see the anger rising even further in Moean's eyes. He became fiercely defensive at the mere thought of someone else laying claim to his territory. It was clear to me this was exactly what he was afraid of. I knew I would have to calm him down if I was going to make any progress.

"Moean, I can supply you with that record."

My words seemed to give him a hope that he had not thought possible. Still, he was wounded by what this would-be competitor from Canada had done to him and continued to pretend not to want his record. He was determined to demonstrate he was a tough and serious businessman, and when he was mad at someone, he meant it.

It was a tense moment for him, but knowing, believing fully how much he truly wanted that record, I smiled.

He realized that my idea was a good one.

"But how?" he asked. "Tell me. How exactly will you pull this off for me?"

Before I could give him the details of my plan, he confided that word had already reached him of Singh calling around to the smaller record shops, looking for them to import this record. These stores had already begun applying for import licenses. The only thing holding them back was the long wait for their license. I listened carefully, and when he finished, I asked, "Moean, how much would you be willing to pay for that album?"

"Any price, Rohit. Any price," was his reply. "I want that album at any price. I can't just sit back and allow the small stores to get their hands on it. My musicians! That would be a slap in the face, and I can't allow it. Six-fifty U.S. I can go as high as paying six-fifty per piece."

"Then why don't you simply pick up the phone and call Singh right now?" I asked, already knowing what his response would be.

"Rohit, don't play with me. I am serious. I don't ever want to speak to that man again."

Moean now crossed his arms and leaned back in his chair. Silence filled the space between us.

"Let me call him," I said, and on my face, I had donned the same mischievous smile he had shown the day when Hansrajee had first asked him to include me on his radio show.

Happy I had "talked" him into it, Moean picked up his phone, then reached into his shirt pocket and produced a piece of paper with the phone number of the very man he never wanted to speak to again. Realizing the awkwardness of the moment, he laughed, we both laughed.

As the phone started ringing, he hurriedly handed me the receiver, "It's ringing, it's ringing, answer, answer."

I calmly reintroduced myself to Singh, and in his voice I detected excitement.

"Rohit! Where are you man? I called your number in New York, but they said you were in Trinidad. I wanted to speak to you about my album. Can you help me distribute it?"

"Let me see if something can be done," I casually replied.

"Something? No, man. I manufactured too many. I have a lot of stock, and I need to get them sold. I don't have a big enough market."

"What have you done to market it?" I asked, knowing the answer but wanting for him to realize it.

"Nothing. I wouldn't even know where to begin."

"Have you tried selling them in Trinidad?" Again, I needed him to give me the answer I already knew.

"Well, there is a big problem there, man. None of the smaller guys seem to have an import license in Trinidad except for the big guy. And we don't speak anymore."

I knew he was referring to the man sitting across from me, and it occurred to me that he may well know that I was in this country to meet with Moean. Instead of responding to his remark, I steered the conversation in a direction that would keep us moving toward progress.

"How many pieces do you have?" I asked him.

"Well," he stammered for a moment, recovering from the minor shock at my unexpectedly direct question. "I made five thousand, but only picked up one thousand. The rest are still at the record pressing plant, and they are calling me every day to come and get them."

"And you sold those one thousand where? Only in your store?"

"Most of them," he replied.

This was a good sign. The records, as expected, were being received well, but Singh had no idea how to market them outside of his store. "Okay, Singh. I will call you right back."

"But don't you want to know the price?"

"No, Singh. I don't need the price. I just need to know how much you paid to manufacture each album."

He replied that he had paid one dollar each. I said goodbye and that I would call him right back, then handed the receiver to Moean to place back on its cradle.

This would be a solution to my need for capital. As Singh was speaking on the phone, I was calculating in my mind, not only figures, but something more. This could very well pay for my shop and provide me with my entry as a record distributor in this region.

Moean already had a powerful and well-established marketing and advertising arm here in Trinidad to make albums such as these successful. My goal in setting up this deal was to build a global distribution platform for Indo-Caribbean music. It would be a strong foundation for distributing this music between North America and the Caribbean. Indo-Caribbean music that had left this shore for North America would be returning for the first time. This could be the defining moment for the music of and for the people who came by ship. All I had to do now was have another talk with Moean.

At that moment, Hansrajee walked into the office with three cups of coffee in hand and sat to join us.

"What did he say? What did he say?" Moean asked, unable to contain himself.

"Who are you guys talking about?" asked his wife.

"That man from Canada!" he replied.

"Well, Moean. Why not let Rohit handle it for you? He is living in that part of the world. He knows how to deal with the people there," Hansrajee calmly suggested.

This was perfect timing. I had the perfect solution in mind and the blessing of fifty percent of this partnership before I even mentioned it.

"Instead of you paying Singh six-fifty for each record, as you mentioned," I said, "I will sell them to you for only four-fifty."

He cocked his head to the side. "That's a good price. But will he give you a price to allow such a bargain? Will he give them to you for three so that you can make a profit?"

I looked Moean straight in the face and told him, "No. He will give them to me for free."

"Free? Free! I told you not to play with me. You know I want that album. What do you mean, free?"

"Well, not free," I said. "But almost free. When can I start distributing Windsor in the United States and Canada?"

"Well, since you think it's best to release only albums there, it will take me around three months to compile my single 45 RPMs together. Then I will send my son to New York with the master tapes so you can start manufacturing and distributing. But, if you want to release singles, I already have those master tapes ready. You could start as soon as you get back."

"No," I said. "We should only do albums. This is where Indo Caribbeans will see the most value for their money. Singles sell for $3.00 in the United States and Canada. With ten singles on one album, the people will get a great deal. A $30 value for around, say, $9.00 at retail. This by itself will be a good marketing pitch for the music."

With regard to Singh's album, I explained to Moean what I intended to do. In exchange for the four thousand remaining pieces, I would give Mr. Singh four thousand pieces of Windsor Records albums. Money would not change hands. I would then ship Moean two thousand pieces at $4.50 per album for a total of $9,000.

"You give me a teller's check in this amount, and I will use it to set up my small store and office, from where I will operate this business while you are getting your master tapes ready."

The man and his wife sitting in front of me listened intently as I continued to describe how I would navigate this new era for Indo-Caribbean music. They saw this as the dawn of something special. This day held the promise that Indo-Caribbean music was about to breathe new life. The broken shall rise.

"Rohit, I wish we would have met much sooner," said Moean, quietly. In that moment, it was evident to me that he had forgotten my age and saw me as a peer.

Hansrajee, apparently happy with the promise the negotiations held for the future, said, "Oh my God, Rohit. You are trading music. You are like a merchant. A Music Merchant."

CHAPTER 24

Mindfulness can be achieved at any time and any place. Always be mindful to understand the process.

Within a month after returning from my trip to the Caribbean, I spent eight of the $9,000 opening my store. Located in Jamaica, Queens, it was a comfortable but not overly large 2,100-square-foot space, including a small office area.

My record brought in a modest cash flow and allowed me to put together small savings, within the next few weeks.

A few friends joined me on a drive to Allentown, Pennsylvania, where I spent $600 on my first car, a 1973 sky blue Chevy Impala. Before that day, I had been moving around New York, pulling my 45 RPM records up and down the subway steps in my mother's shopping cart.

I had been careful with the location of my store, strategically positioned only a few miles from Richmond Hill, the main hub of the Indo-Caribbean population in New York City. Brooklyn, where most Afro Caribbeans lived, was only fifteen miles away, and right across the Triboro Bridge was the Bronx, a densely populated mix of both. It was the perfect setting for continuing my goals.

The first step toward achieving my big goals was to ship the two thousand pieces of Mohan Singh's albums to Moean as promised. I drove to Toronto — this time in my car.

My first evening in Toronto, Singh invited me to a friend's house where a couple from India would be performing *ghazals* — a singing form of poetry with a fixed number of verses and repeated rhyme.

The music could be heard as we walked from Singh's car toward the house. When we stepped in the door, I immediately noticed something different about this performance. It was not like any other *ghazals* I had heard before. Traditionally *ghazals* were accompanied by two instruments, the harmonium and the tabla. But not on this evening. Added were the santoor, the rhythm guitar, and a variety of wind instruments. And it was performed in duet, rather than its traditional solo.

The musicians were good. More than good. The vocals were in perfect sync with the musical accompaniment, creating a new and refreshing sound. I knew I was in the presence of something great.

Although the traditional form of *ghazal* was of little interest to the young generation, I thought this new and innovative sound would bring them to the stores. Once there, they would see and buy the other albums of their heritage.

I noticed a brass plate in front of the two singers, and the audience occasionally added dollar bills. I thought this might be an opportunity to grow the seeds of one of my primary goals, improving the relationship between Indians who came directly from India and those Indians who came from the Caribbean.

I searched my pocket and took out a few coins, and waited for the moment when I could place them onto the brass plate. While some eyes would see I was putting coins while they are putting dollar bills, others might appreciate the symbolism.

Dollar bills have no sound, and therefore, they have no frequency.

The moment arrived. The two singers paused while the instrumental interlude continued. I tapped the coins in the palm of my hands, maintaining the rhythm of the music. Then I released them. The sound of my coins on the brass plate became like an added instrument in the musical performance, perfect in rhythm. Upon hearing the sound of the coins punctuating the music on the brass plate, both singers made eye contact with me.

Singh observed our brief interaction. He impressed upon me, only moments later, that not so long ago, he had taken these two artists to Trinidad and Tobago and sold their shows to Moean, but a misunderstanding between them had planted the seeds of disagreement.

He told me Moean made two albums with these two singers but did not have the licensing rights to distribute those albums outside of the Caribbean. He also told me EMI India held the rights for Asia. But concerning Europe and North America, he mentioned nothing. There, they had yet to rise to stardom.

I knew when marketed and distributed properly, these musicians could play a key role in building understanding and bridges between my ancestors from India and my descendants from the Caribbean.

When the artists took a break, Singh introduced me, "Rohit I would like you to meet Jagjit Singh and his wife, Chitra."

Jagjit extended his hand and said, "I noticed when you placed your coins in the brass plate it was in perfect rhythm with our music. Are you a musician? Have you heard any of our albums?"

His voice was a distinct baritone and as pleasant to listen to in speech as in song.

"He is a producer and distributor," Singh quickly intervened.

I could tell by Jagjit's words and manner that he was open to a discussion.

I asked him, "Who handles your albums?"

"EMI India has the rights to some," he responded. "Two are with a company in Trinidad. *Live at Wembley* is held by Savera in Europe. EMI holds an album called *Ghazals* in Asia, and Mr. Singh might release the same here in Canada."

We had come to the point very quickly, and I was reminded of a saying Moean was fond of expressing in his own inimitable way.

"Don't use a gallon of water to express a spoonful of thoughts."

I decided to follow this adage from my friend.

"Okay," I replied. "I will market and distribute all of your albums in every market they are not yet distributed. Let's meet tomorrow, and we'll make the deal."

I was clear in my body language that it was all I was going to say for now. We shook hands, and I walked away with Singh following.

Singh invited me to his home that evening to meet his family and talk more about the music business. On our drive through the backroads of Toronto, while I waited for him to ask me a specific question, my mind was on the freshness of the unique new sound I had just heard.

I believed it would appeal across the age and demographic spectrum of both the Indo-Caribbean and the Indian expat markets, including the difficult-to-reach, jeans-clad generation. And once they associated my label with innovation in music, it would follow that they would gravitate to my eventual fusion recordings with Kanchan and Babla.

I must find a way to negotiate this deal by paying the smallest possible advance. I had around $1,500 with me.

It was then that Singh asked the question I knew he would eventually get to.

"So, Rohit," he eased into the question. "What would you offer for these albums of theirs?"

"How well do you know Jagjit and Chitra," I asked, not entirely avoiding his question but leading to a different type of answer.

"They are like family. Soon, I will take them on tour across the United States and Canada."

"I see. Will it be like the same crowd we just saw — twenty-five to thirty people? How do you plan to bring large crowds to these shows? These singers are not well known."

As I had suspected, Singh did not have a plan. I was in the perfect position to help him and the performers, and realize my goal of bringing the expats together through their shared music.

"Singh, come on man, you should know this. The way to introduce these singers to the market is to first have their albums widely marketed and distributed. Their music is innovative. Once the people hear this music, they will come to the shows. Just make everything at prices they can afford."

I then asked him, what good are their records if nobody knows of them? The life of a record only begins after it is recorded. Thereafter, for it to live, it must be marketed, distributed, and sold, and then find sustenance in the hands of music lovers.

CHAPTER 25

You are wealthier than you might believe.

The next day, when Singh and I met with Jagjit, the singer wasted no time asking me for a ten thousand dollar advance in exchange for the rights to distribute his albums.

Instead, I asked him to explain his goals to me.

"Rohit, I want to rise so high that someday, I will play Carnegie Hall in New York," he told me.

What's the average attendance of your shows here in North America?

He paused for a moment. He then said in a lower voice, "About two hundred."

"And has that quenched your artistic ambitions?" I asked him directly.

"Not at all." Jagjit repeated, "I believe that one day I will be playing Carnegie Hall."

"Look, Jagjit, because you believe you will play Carnegie Hall, makes it true as long as you can feel it within you. I, too, believe it will happen because I can feel it within. However, we will have to put in the work. That's the best part of it all. The excitement of the adventure."

I explained the importance of making their albums widely accessible, which would impact their shows in New York. I told him as far as his records were concerned, the way New York goes, the country will go.

"With my help, your next show in New York will have an attendance of fifteen hundred people. And with that rise in New York, attendance at every show after will increase."

I continued, "After such a tour, you will have a real chance to play Carnegie Hall. Is that not worth many times more to you than a ten thousand dollar advance? Am I correct that Carnegie Hall will gross well over $100,000?"

I could now see the wheels turning in his mind as he envisioned sitting cash-rich upon the grandest of stages.

I handed him $1,000 as a good faith advance to Singh, the man who had introduced me to Jagjit and Chitra and who told me he managed them.

Later that day, Singh and I visited the record pressing plant in Toronto and picked up the four thousand pieces of the album *Live in Toronto*, and headed straight to the airport where I shipped two thousand to Moean in Trinidad, one thousand to Rashid Pierkhan in Suriname, some to Guyana, and the rest to New York. My first modest global distribution was set in motion.

As soon as the many titles of the Windsor Records albums were manufactured, I would ship four thousand to Singh and we would be even with this particular transaction. We also agreed I would distribute *Live in Toronto* in all markets outside of Canada.

Having secured *Live in Toronto* and the four albums by Jagjit and Chitra, I arrived back in New York with a brand-new question to answer. How many pieces of the Windsor albums should I manufacture for North America?

As I searched for this answer, I reflected on the words of Hansrajee, "Rohit, you will have to be very careful. Indo-Caribbean expats in North America are still a small population, and they are focused on saving, not spending. Making too many pieces could put you out of business."

To reinforce this caution, she reminded me of the eighty-seven records collecting dust across the grocery stores in New York. "Do not allow yours to be added to those," she said.

I would not be offering single 45 RPMs at $3.00 each. I would be releasing albums, giving those tight for money a better value — a game-changer for people of Indo-Caribbean heritage.

And with these separate but connected thoughts, I began to articulate in my mind what would be necessary for the next stage in the manufacturing of these albums. In addition to the small amount of capital I had, I would now need $10,000 of fresh capital. This would be sufficient to manufacture the first batch of six Windsor albums. I would make two thousand pieces each for a total of twelve thousand pieces.

This is what I was contemplating, when a gentleman pushed the door open and walked into my store. He was an American man around three times my age.

CHAPTER 26

We will achieve the desired results when we are mindful of all that we hold in our hands.

The man introduced himself as David and told me he owned a real estate office at the end of the block. He produced a stack of his business cards and handed one to me.

"Could I leave a few?" he asked.

"How is business?" I responded.

"Well, we're new to the area, so it's been hard marketing ourselves."

"And what is your target market?"

"Well, as you know, the Indo-Caribbean market has been growing. They're starting to buy houses, so we're trying to tap into this new sector. We really need to reach these people."

"And how many of these cards have you delivered to them?" I asked him pointedly.

"Well, that's the problem. We can't figure out how to reach them. There are only a few Indo-Caribbean places where we could leave these cards. We were excited to see your store open here. I was hoping you could help."

"David, you seem to know about Indo-Caribbean people. Do you agree that Indo Caribbeans from the other boroughs are looking to move to Queens?"

"Certainly! But how do I reach them? Are there stores like yours in the other boroughs where I could also leave my cards?"

"And if you were to find other stores like mine and deposit your cards, what are the chances of someone picking one up?"

"I know," he said resignedly, "but I just don't know how else to reach them. I advertise in the mainstream newspapers, but we still aren't getting any calls."

"That is because you are marketing in the same way as all of your competitors. You will never stand out if you stand as everyone else does."

"You seem to know a lot about marketing, what's your solution?"

Rather than answering quickly, I reached into my desk and pulled out the sample album covers Moean had sent for the compilation albums.

"Are you going to play me music?"

"Yes, what I'm about to tell you will be music to your ears."

I reached for the phone on my desk, put it on speaker, and called the Indo-Caribbean grocery store selling my records in the Bronx. The owner picked up.

"Hey, it's Rohit. I have something for you."

"Hey Rohit. How was your trip? Do you have any new records coming out?"

"Yes. Six. All brand-new albums."

"Full albums? Wow! What are they?"

"The biggest Indo-Caribbean singers from the Windsor label. Many of their singles will soon be compiled into albums."

"What? That's amazing!"

"How do you think they will do?" I teasingly asked.

"Do? Forget do! This market is a desert, and you will be the rainfall, my friend."

I held David's gaze through this conversation, and it was at this point I saw a realization spark in his eyes. If the man before him could navigate the marketing of something so small, so niche, surely, he could solve the problem of marketing his real estate.

David adjusted his tie as if getting ready for a solution to his desperate need.

"How many pieces should I make for your store," I asked on the speakerphone.

"I will start with five hundred of each. Bring them as soon as you can. You will advertise on TV, too, right?"

Hearing this, David's eyes widened. He picked up one of the album covers and began studying it.

"Yes. I will, again, include your store in the advertising of my records."

I concluded the call and hung up the phone.

"Wow," said David. "Five hundred of each. And you said there are six, total?"

I nodded.

"Three thousand records." His voice trailed off as he stared around the store, trying to connect this modest store with the activity.

And upon demonstrating to David exactly how long it would take for me to distribute three thousand of my albums, I asked, "How long would it take for you to distribute three thousand of your cards?"

"About three years," he jokingly responded.

"And once distributed, what are the chances they would get picked up?"

"Well, I have some at an Indo-Caribbean bakery. They are still sitting there."

"Exactly. When people are shopping, they are conducting a specific transaction. For instance, in the bakery, they are searching for bread or a dessert to bring home to their family. Your card lying around is the last thing on their minds. But what if there was a way for your cards to already be in their homes?"

"Well," he stammered, "of course, that would be great, if…"

"I am about to release not three but twelve thousand albums to the Indo-Caribbean population in all of the boroughs of New York City. How would you like to have the name and phone number of your real estate office, along with a short, written message on each of those records?"

I continued stoking the fire even further.

"David, for $10,000, I would place stickers with your message on the front and back of my album covers and on the record labels inside. Everyone who purchases them would see your message. When they pick up the album to read the front cover, there you would be, and when they turn it over, you would be there, too. When they take the record out to play it, there you would be, again and again. Your message will be delivered to thousands of Indo-Caribbean families all in one clean sweep. Are you in, sir?"

"Wow! In? I am in, big-time. But $10,000 is a lot of money. Can you do any better?"

"Yes, I can," I said. "I can do better. How long would it take for me to secure a real estate license?"

"Just a few weeks," he said. "Why, are you looking to sell real estate, too?"

"No. I'm in the record business. However, since this is an untried marketing strategy, I will get my real estate license and sell a sufficient number of houses to cover your $10,000. I will then get out of the real estate business entirely."

We shook hands and agreed to the deal.

Soon thereafter, Sadro arrived at JFK Airport from Trinidad. With a wide smile, he placed the new master tapes for the Windsor albums into my hands.

CHAPTER 27

The lotus begins life submerged in mud. It soon rises from its humble beginnings to kiss the sunlight and blossom as its petals open one by one. So too does a purposeful life.

With help from a blast of TV ads, the Windsor albums took off in this small market like a rocket ship. Indo Caribbeans across every borough of New York made their way to the grocery stores for the albums.

Within a few weeks, those albums became the rainfall that quenched the desert once barren of Indo-Caribbean music.

Some two years after stumbling upon those dusty 45 RPM records, I had sold twenty thousand Indo-Caribbean music albums in New York and Toronto. The total spending for entertainment by Indo Caribbeans in New York, which I estimated was $7,500 a year, had now surpassed the $100,000 mark.

It was an exponential growth in this small population of expats.

I had planted the seed for this music, then pushed the envelope to its limits. After manufacturing expenses, marketing, royalty payments, retailer markups, and overhead, my profit was about $2.00 per album.

There was more I could have done to increase my profits if profits were my main motivation. I saw firsthand the twinkle in the eyes of those who bought the albums. This was their music. I saw the joy as they found their identity in the music and a lasting link to their heritage. Seeing this was priceless. The joy the music provided multiplied within me infinitely. Amid the efforts and risks, I still managed to create a small profit which allowed me a modest living.

With these reflections, I began charting my next steps — my journey to *her*, my journey to recording Kanchan.

As I sat at my desk, in my small office, reflecting upon my modest success, my phone rang. The gentleman on the other end introduced himself as Mr. Ramzan, calling from Holland. He told me many Surinamese expats lived in Holland, and he owned an Indo-Caribbean record store in The Hague. He had been given my number by none other than Rashid Pierkhan. He said he would very much like to meet the man who had finally convinced Moean to make Windsor Records available commercially outside of the Caribbean. He had tried tirelessly for years, like so many others.

Listening to Mr. Ramzan's words, it dawned on me, however modest my success might be, I had created a link for Indo-Caribbean music from Trinidad and Tobago to the wider world. The dialogue I had hoped to establish with this music was forming.

A few days later, Mr. Ramzan arrived in New York City, and I went to meet him at his hotel, The Piccadilly, in Midtown Manhattan.

I knocked on the hotel room door.

He opened it, shook my hand, and then pushed his head out, looking into the hallway with enthusiasm.

"Where is your father?" he asked.

"My father?" I asked, puzzled. "Why, do you know him?"

He paused. "No. But who are you?"

"I'm Rohit."

"Rohit? But wait, I thought you were older. Is it you I spoke with over the phone?"

"Yes."

Mr. Ramzan broke out into a peal of laughter, then turned to his wife, saying, "We have come from Holland to meet with this young chap."

His wife joined in the laughter, gesturing to their two sons, who I could see were about my age. The sons began laughing as well, and soon, they were all in an uproar punctuated by what appeared to be short Dutch phrases of which I had no understanding.

I remained calm and reminded myself they were a family interested in furthering Indo-Caribbean music in Holland.

I invited Mr. Ramzan to join me for a cup of coffee at a nearby café. As we waited for our coffee to be served, we exchanged pleasantries. Once our coffees arrived, our conversation quickly switched topics to the business one we both had hoped for.

Mr. Ramzan again congratulated me on acquiring the distribution rights for Windsor Records. He reinforced that if we struck a deal for him to distribute the music in Holland, the most fabled Indo-Caribbean music catalog would enter virgin territory.

Like the lotus, life may begin deeply buried in the mud or drowned over with water, but it will soon rise from its humble beginnings to kiss the sunlight and blossom out its petals. Step by step.

Holland was a potential gateway into the European continent. Distributing there would bring me another stride closer to my goal of setting up a global distribution network.

"Rohit," said Mr. Ramzan seeing I had drifted into my thoughts, "are you sleeping?"

"Mr. Ramzan, you seem to have forgotten one very important thing. I only have the distribution rights for the Windsor label for North America, not for Holland."

He fell silent and seemed to drift off into his own state of contemplation. I offered him a lifeline.

"If you have any hit albums you are distributing in Holland, that you can license to us for distribution in North America and the Caribbean, maybe I can have a quiet talk with Moean with regard to me shipping you my Windsor albums," I told him.

His eyes sparked into life. "Rohit, I can get you all of Ramdew Chaitoe's albums. As you know, he is the biggest selling artist of our music in Suriname and Holland. But he is very difficult to work with."

I was familiar with Chaitoe's albums, having seen them in Suriname and inquired with Rashid Pierkhan about the possibility of distributing them. He had flatly advised against it, telling me Chaitoe was one of the best artists, but he was impossible to work with.

Up until that moment, neither Mr. Ramzan nor I knew exactly how difficult Chaitoe would prove to be. Neither did we know what our conversation would mean for Indo Caribbeans and their beloved music.

Mr. Ramzan drew his chair close to mine, motioning for me to lean in. He told me Rashid had spoken to him in the strictest confidence about my plan to record Indo-Caribbean and fusion albums with Kanchan and Babla from India.

Realizing Rashid was my friend and a great well-wisher of mine, I did not question why he had spoken about my idea with Mr. Ramzan. It was what Mr. Ramzan said next that caused my palms to clasp together like a strong magnet.

"Rohit, I am going to India soon; why don't I make an album with Kanchan and Babla. You can distribute it everywhere, and I will keep Holland and Suriname."

On the surface, it might appear that those words should have diminished my own long-held goal to record these artists. But they did not. I realized on my journey to *her*, I had gathered several of the most important pieces of the puzzle for the empowerment of Indo-Caribbean music.

I saw that the man before me was nothing short of a genius. He recognized the potential of making such a record. While others were only able to see the tree, he, like me, saw the forest and a beautiful bird singing at the center of it.

"Rashid told me you are looking to record some of the Windsor Indo-Caribbean songs with her. How about we include a Chaitoe song, too?"

It was then that I told Ramzan that I was planning to make two types of albums with Kanchan and Babla: Indo-Caribbean and Afro-Indo Caribbean.

We reached an agreement that he would record the Indo-Caribbean album comprising five Windsor songs and one Chaitoe song.

A few weeks later, I established my first distribution link within the continent of Europe. I shipped 5,500 Windsor Records and the BWIA album to Ramzan, and in return, received 5,000 Chaitoe and other albums from him. The 500 album difference was to help him pay for the recording in India.

Soon after Mr. Ramzan returned to Holland, another music retailer from Holland arrived to meet with me. Sunil Somair was born in Suriname and arrived in Holland as a teenager around 1971. His father sent him to London to continue his education. It was there that he noticed Bollywood records in a few outlets belonging to Indian expats.

Realizing the Indo-Caribbean population was growing in Holland, Sunil saw an opportunity to sell records to them. Soon his father started importing these Bollywood records from London into Holland. By 1974, there was an influx of Surinamese into Holland, and demand for these Bollywood records grew. His father moved the family to Hobbemastraat in The Hague, where he opened Sunil's Record Center.

It became the most popular Indian record store in the country primarily since it was located on the way to the main market in The Hague. Since then, Sunil, like Mr. Ramzan, had been trying tirelessly, but without success, to get the Windsor Records distribution rights for Holland.

This is what brought him to New York to meet with me in 1980. Having two strong retailers who doubled as distributors in Holland allowed me to establish my distribution network on the continent.

With my relationship with Sunil and Mr. Ramzan solidified, I turned my attention to the Jagjit and Chitra albums.

Yash Paul Soi, an Indian expat living in New York, had agreed with Singh to stage one of their concerts at the Colden Center for the Performing Arts at Queens College in New York.

As I had promised Jagjit that I would help create awareness and increase attendance at his New York show, I scripted a marketing plan to release their albums ahead of the show.

I identified two tracks on their albums that would resonate well with both Indian and Indo-Caribbean expats, but most of all, with the younger jeans-clad generation. It was the younger generation I had in mind, and was counting on, when I made the commitment to Jagjit that his New York tour would attract a larger audience.

These two tracks were *Kiya Hai Pyar* and *Woh Dil Hi Kya Tere Milne Ki Jo Dua Na Kare*. Both were masterfully written by the twentieth-century poet Qateel Shifai and musically interpreted by Jagjit.

My promos were broadcast on Vision of Asia, and as expected, both Indian and Indo-Caribbean expats awoke with excitement at this new sound. At the same time, I gained an entry into five new stores in New York — all owned by Indian expats — and together with the Indo-Caribbean stores, nine stores now carried my records.

Jagjit and Chitra's concert drew 1,600. Their popularity and record sales continued to grow, and a few years later Yash Paul Soi presented Jagjit at Carnegie Hall, fulfilling his lifelong dream.

The *Ghazals* album had so effectively excited both the Indian and Indo-Caribbean expats, that it sold more than double every other album I had released up until then. More importantly, it brought the younger generation into the stores for music.

Ghazals was also popular in Holland. It allowed me to geographically leverage my label and my distribution to Belgium and Luxembourg.

Soon, it was distributed to the United Kingdom and subsequently across the entire European continent, where Indian and

Indo-Caribbean expats lived. My global distribution platform for Indo-Caribbean music now stretched and reached both the North American and European continents.

A seed was planted, bringing together Indo-Caribbean and Indian expats. My next step — what many called the belly of the beast — was to bring together expats of both Indo and Afro-Caribbean descent.

A few nights later, I drove across the Queens-Brooklyn boundary line, deep into Brooklyn.

CHAPTER 28

There comes a moment in our life that defines our purpose.

Like Indo Caribbeans, Afro Caribbeans had started arriving in some numbers in the United States in the 1960s. They came mainly from Guyana, Trinidad, Jamaica, and Barbados. Their economic experience was similar to all immigrants coming at the time.

It was near midnight when I crossed into Brooklyn for the very first time. I drove to an area where I heard a few Afro-Caribbean record stores were located, and although they were already closed, I parked in front of one and turned my lights off but left my engine running. I sat observing this brand-new environment.

The street was dim with many non-working streetlights, causing patches of complete darkness. One hundred or so feet away, men emerged into an area of dim light. There was another man leaning against a building. The first men, maybe three or four of them, grabbed the man leaning against the building by his coat, and a scuffle quickly ensued.

My first thought was a feeling of relief that I had not invited anyone else along on this scouting mission. I decided it would be best for me to get out of there. When the traffic light turned green, I blended in with the two or so cars making their way through the intersection.

I turned onto Fulton Street, where I noticed another Caribbean record store and parked across from it, again, turning off my lights but leaving my engine running. I continue to observe the surroundings.

The sign on the store read: The Home of Calypso, Soca, and Reggae Music. There was no mention of Indo-Caribbean music. Clearly, I was the intruder here, not those men in the scuffle.

I noticed what appeared to be a concert poster pasted on to a large garbage bin next to the store. The poster was yellow with the silhouette of an artist. He, too, was strikingly yellow. A yellow artist! What a marketing idea. I was curious.

Men were lurking down this block at a distance, dodging in and out of the shadows. Realizing that the purpose of my visit and personal safety were equally important, I calculated the time it would take to reach the poster, study it, and return to my vehicle. When the right moment came, I went for it.

The poster read "Yellowman Live in Concert!"

Thoughts came back to me of the day I had first walked the streets of Richmond Hill and ended up at the oriental grocery store, where I had discovered those Indo-Caribbean records laying around. On that day, alone on those streets, I felt as if I had owned the place. I felt the same way now.

I touched the poster and found it was still wet. It must have been pasted here only moments ago. Surely whoever was pasting them might still be in this area.

I went back to my car and started driving, following those posters like a trail of breadcrumbs left for me. Garbage bin to garbage bin, post to post, and block to block, I followed them. I must have driven fifteen blocks when the trail came to an end. There I parked and found that the poster came off easily. Nearby was a large bucket standing next to the door of a small café. A brush lay on top of the bucket.

I stepped inside the café and saw a stack of the very same posters lying on a table next to a few men sitting in casual discussion. They also noticed me.

"Hey little Indian man," said one of the men. "What are you doing here at this time of night, man?"

I immediately recognized his accent as Jamaican, and a thought came to my mind — safety first.

Moean's wife had told me that her brother-in-law, Dennis Marajh, was the lead prosecutor in Jamaica and that he was well-liked by the country's citizens.

These looked like hardworking men before me, and I reasoned there was a good chance they would be on the right side of the law back home. Perhaps I could try using his name.

"I have heard a lot about your country from my friend in Trinidad," I said.

"Really? Who is your friend?"

"Her brother-in-law is the lead prosecutor in Jamaica."

"Oh you mean Mr. Marajh! Dennis Marajh."

"Yes," I said. "He is like family."

"Dennis is working hard for the people, man. Have some coffee with us. Who knows, maybe someday, we may need a favor from Dennis."

These men led me into a world that was, until then, completely unknown to me — the world of the artist known as Yellowman.

Winston Foster, better known as Yellowman, was abandoned as a child and dropped off at a foster home in Kingston, Jamaica. There, he was shunned by many because of his albinism. Despite his adversity, this broken one rose to the Top 10 Caribbean music charts on the Afro-Caribbean radio station, WLIB, in New York.

As I listened to the story of this artist's climb, a wide gate of possibility opened before me. I shared it with my hosts.

"How many songs has Foster recorded so far?" I asked.

"A few, but he is soon to be signed to CBS Records."

"And ticket sales for his upcoming show? How are they coming along?"

"Very good. The place can only accommodate a thousand people, though. We wish it were bigger."

"Bigger as in The Forum at Madison Square Garden?" I asked, holding a straight face.

"Wow! Our hands cannot reach there, man. That's a world stage you are talking about."

They laughed, thinking my mention was only a distant and unreachable dream.

I thanked them for their hospitality and started my way back to Queens. What had felt like a boundary between two disconnected places was now an inviting gateway in my mind.

CHAPTER 29

If you cannot create a convincing marketing campaign, rework your idea.

Yellowman embraced the legacy and filled the void left by the sudden passing in the previous year of the iconic reggae artist Bob Marley. If he succeeded and I could bring him further into the spotlight, this would be my opportunity to bring together those of African and Indian heritage who came to these shores. Artists representing reggae, dancehall, soca-calypso, island flavor, and Indo-Caribbean music had never shared the same stage.

In the days following, I asked customers at my store and elsewhere what they thought about the idea. From a small sampling of the responses, it appeared a great risk. Diehard fans of reggae did not want to sit through calypso and soca sets and vice versa. Moreover, reggae fans had very little connection with Indo-Caribbean music. The responses reflected what I already knew as the separation between the expats, a separation stretching back to their home countries.

My goal was to take them all into the unknown. I would create an event where they could breathe collectively and share in a blend of music that represented them all. I was convinced such an event would enable me to produce a fusion album eventually.

To mitigate the potential risk, rather than marketing the show as a concert, I reworked the idea. I branded it as a festival, *The Caribbean All-Star Festival: Live at The Felt Forum at Madison Square Garden.*

I knew the festival would be a success and knew the album someday would too. I believed and felt it within, and put in the effort to pull it off.

My theme and marketing plan were set, and it was time for me to start putting together the acts, pick a date, and stage the festival. Yellowman was the drawing card that would help mitigate the financial risk. I bought a subscription to *Billboard Magazine* and began closely following CBS Records and their soon-to-be new star. With each passing day, Yellowman continued his rise in popularity as WLIB radio, in response to listeners' requests, continued to give his songs extensive airplay.

Having decided on Yellowman, from Jamaica, for my reggae-dancehall headliner, I signed Calypso Rose and The Mighty Sparrow from Trinidad and Tobago, two of the biggest acts of the soca-calypso style at the time.

Next came the Tropical Waves, an Indo-Guyanese expat band. I first heard of them from two customers chatting in my store. I asked them about the group, and they told me about a club the band would be playing at on Saturday evening. I checked them out and signed them that same night. I later realized two of their performers, John Drepaul and Dino Dilchand, would be the perfect fit for an Indo-Caribbean recording.

The following week, a second Yellowman song, *I'm Getting Married in the Morning*, entered WLIB's Top 10 charts. It was time. I paid a visit to the rising star's booking agent at Magna Artist in Manhattan.

As I was making a case for the festival at Madison Square Garden, the agent interrupted me.

"Rohit, let me ask you something," he said. "How old are you?"

He spoke these words with a sense of authority to give this newcomer an education in the business.

"Twenty-one," I said with quiet confidence.

"Twenty-one. Okay, so let me see if I get this right. You are barely older than my son, and you think you can pull this off? You think you can pay for not one, but for two shows, and at the Garden? That's a big risk, not just for you, but also for me. A large venue with an up-and-coming artist who is only just now beginning to break. Rohit, let me be blunt with you. In all the years I've been in this business, I have never seen anything like this. I just cannot put my agency behind it. The risk is too big. How do you even plan to pay me?"

"And now, let me be blunt with you, sir. I am not going to pay you."

He broke into laughter, and I let it stretch on and for him to have his laugh.

"CBS is going to pay us both," I calmly said, and what was left of his laughter ceased abruptly.

His eyes squinted, and he leaned his head toward me.

"CBS, as you know," I continued, "has recently signed Yellowman. Their public relations machine has already begun churning out ads and articles, one after another, in *Billboard* and across the mainstream media. All said and done, they will spend well over a million dollars promoting their new artist. Do you think they will spend all of that money without knowing exactly how he handles a large crowd? Yellowman lives in Jamaica. This is New York. A mile away from the Garden is the CBS headquarters, and this will be the first opportunity for all of their head honchos, their marketing people, and the rest of their staff to see the latest addition to their roster perform live on a world stage. Do you think they are going to miss it?"

I could see the spark of my idea beginning to ignite in the agent's mind, but it was not yet fully lit.

"Here is what we are going to do," I took control of the conversation. "I am going to put tickets on sale to the general public at a modest rate, affordable to the people of say a fifteen-dollar average. Assuming forty percent of the seats are sold, the festival will break even."

"Okay, but how are we going to make any money then?" he asked.

"Simple. I will create a VIP section of about three hundred seats at $100 each and wait for CBS to call me to grab them quickly. You know, they are only going to buy the best seats."

He paused for only a brief moment, and the spark ignited into a blazing inferno in his mind.

"Rohit, I love it. You are going to scalp your own tickets. And it's perfectly okay. You're the promoter. You can price your tickets however you want. You're going to make a $30,000 profit aren't you? I'm in."

He extended his hand, and we firmly shook on the deal.

We formalized the deal that day for $15,000, half of what CBS would pay me for those tickets, for Yellowman to headline the event. On October 31, 1982, *The Caribbean All-Star Festival: Live at The Felt Forum at Madison Square Garden* was successfully staged with back-to-back shows.

Before the first show, I greeted Yellowman backstage amid a sea of CBS brass. Their enthusiasm to see their artist perform live at the Garden was palpable. Yellowman was gracious and thanked me for his first opportunity to perform on such a prestigious world stage. I told him I would someday be distributing his albums. Of course, the CBS cohorts all laughed at this, knowing that it was their label and not mine which had signed the most prized artist in the reggae-dancehall genre at the time. I was serious.

That event was the first coming together of artists representing all major Caribbean music genres on the same stage. A mainstream journalist described the event as "the perfect blend of world music that truly represents all Caribbean expats."

Witnessing firsthand the enthusiasm of expats sharing each other's music, I completed my rehearsal as a concert producer and promoter. It was time for me to live my purpose of creating the record which would someday become an event in and of itself. It was time for me to journey to Kanchan.

CHAPTER 30

*Be mindful that you understand
your goals and your purpose.*

A few months later, my phone rang. It was Mr. Ramzan calling from Holland. He spoke a mix of Dutch, Hindi, and English, all in one long, unending breath. I had a fairly good idea what was causing his excitement. He had not cleared the rights to record the songs on the new record.

He told me he had returned to Holland from India with the album we planned, and it was played on the radio. Upon hearing his song was covered, Ramdew Chaitoe threatened to take legal action, among other things, if Mr. Ramzan released the album.

He was afraid if Chaitoe was coming after him for one song, how would Moean react since all of the other songs on the album were covers belonging to Windsor Records.

Mr. Ramzan and his family had traveled from Holland to meet with me in New York. We had shared a constructive afternoon over coffee discussing our music, and I had helped him conceptualize the production of the album. Now he needed my help again. I decided, in the interests of Indo-Caribbean music and our people, to again help him out.

To release the album in Holland required the stamp of approval from the organization in that country protecting the copyright of composers and performers. Only when the artists or producers gave permission would record manufacturing plants go ahead and manufacture the record.

He was extremely upset, and to calm him down, I told him I would look into it for him. I then asked him to play the album over the phone for me.

The minute the music started, I recognized two things: this was exactly the concept we had discussed, and Mr. Ramzan had earnestly followed through with it.

Kaise Bani, originally sung by Sundar Popo and produced and published by Moean for the Windsor label, was uniquely articulated by *her* voice. Kanchan singing an Indo-Caribbean song in her inimitable style was exactly how I had envisioned it seven years before this day.

I immediately recognized the album was good. The sound was crisp and Babla's interpretation of the Indo-Caribbean covers was a breath of fresh air. Kanchan was outstanding. I sensed her voice rising above and beyond the sugar belts. A Bollywood singer was now sharing our legacy.

During the call, Mr. Ramzan reminded me I was like a son to him and reiterated his request, to have a talk with Moean regarding the rights for the five Windsor songs on the album. He told me that based on how Mr. Chaitoe was reacting, he was afraid Moean may not grant him the license to release the Windsor songs in Holland and Suriname.

I assured him I would speak to Moean, but first I wanted to listen to the entirety of the album. I had not gone to India, and yet this album with her voice was realized.

I got Moean to give the necessary clearance for the Windsor songs for Ramzan to release the album in his markets of Holland and Suriname. He subsequently managed to get the same from Mr. Chaitoe. I released the album in the markets I represented.

However, from his experience dealing with Mr. Chaitoe, Mr. Ramzan got out of the production business, remaining a music retailer.

Kaise Bani, Kanchan's first Indo-Caribbean album, was released on both vinyl and cassette and outsold every Indo-Caribbean album until then. Within weeks of its release, ten thousand copies were sold in what was once a small Indo-Caribbean market in North America, firmly establishing her as the new craze in Indo-Caribbean music.

The movement for Indo-Caribbean music that started an upward trend in international markets some two years before had firmly placed this music on its way to a brand-new day.

After settling Mr. Ramzan's problem, I was ready to reach into the large envelope Rashid Pierkhan had handed me. I brought out *her* contract, noted her phone number, and reached for my phone.

CHAPTER 31

Those in the business of entertainment must be mindful that entertainment is an art that reflects the poetry of the people. It is, therefore, a human story.

"Is this the music maestro?" I eased into the phone call.
"Yes hello, this is Babla."
"My name is Rohit Jagessar, and I am calling you from New York. It is a beautiful day with the spring season about to set in."
"Rohit? from Rohit Records? Oh my gosh! Thank you for releasing my album there. I heard it did very well."
"Hey, how is everything going? Have you recorded anything since?" I asked him.
There was a pause.
"Well," he paused again, "we did a few things for this market over here in India. What do you think of *Kaise Bani*?" he asked.

"It's good. We now need to go further. We need to do more. We need to make the next one better," I told him in no uncertain terms.

"What do you suggest?" he inquired.

"We need an album that will bring all the people from the Caribbean together —Indo, Afro, and beyond," I told him.

"Rohit, we are on the same wavelength. It would seem that while you were thinking of such an album, we were getting it ready for you. I think I may have the album for you. Can I play something for you?" he asked.

Realizing we were gravitating toward a mutual goal and understanding, I said, "No. Don't play it. Bring it."

A few days later, I had someone pick Babla up at the JFK Airport and check him into a Midtown Manhattan hotel, where we met later that evening for dinner.

As I approached, a small-framed Indian man rose from his seat and extended his hand, and we shook warmly.

A fragrance steamed from the spread of food on the far side of the lobby and drew us toward it. It was so tantalizing that we soon became enthusiastic connoisseurs, guessing what was being served, as we walked toward the buffet area.

We brought our plates to our table, and as we sat down, Babla once again asked about *Kaise Bani*.

"Babla," I paused, "think about it, man, since its release, no one has contacted you to do any shows right? This is why I told you over the phone that we need to do more. We need to be more compelling."

"Rohit, are you a musician, too?" he curiously inquired.

I replied, "Everyone is a musician, my friend. Everyone."

People listen to music; people dance to music; they interpret music as musicians themselves do when recording music.

The difference between these two musicians is that only one can make a hit record. The one who listens and dances is the only one who can make a record into a hit.

An album may enter the Top 10, but it doesn't mean that it does anything more than that. Some albums on the Top 10 create a dialogue and have their own set of rules. This is where the marketing and positioning of a record, artist development, and touring come into play. And this thought brought me to another point.

"Moean and Rashid Pierkhan discussed your numbers with me. They told me you were paid $250 per show when you toured that region a few years ago. They told me you had small crowds."

He listened intently, then conceded, "Rohit, what to do? This is how the market is. We accept what comes our way, hoping for a chance, someday."

"Well today, your chance has come. And when your time has come, you must hold it in both of your hands."

At that moment, the waitress stretched her hand across the table to refill our water glasses. Her presence reminded me of the waitress in Trinidad who had once prophesied, "you know, maybe he is on to something." That something was now here.

It was around midnight when we finally got to the tapes in his room. I called room service for a pot of coffee and three cups, while he took a few cassettes from his bag and handed them to me, one by one.

The tape recorder sat on a chair nearby. I noticed the chair back was made of wood. I moved the tape recorder to the sofa and took a seat on the chair. I rested my arm on the wooden back of the chair just as I had done in that cinema hall back in Guyana when I first heard *her* voice.

The tape unspooled, and the first song played. It was a Hindi song recorded to a disco beat. While this would do well in India, it would not work in markets where disco had by now run out of steam. More significantly, it was not the music represented at the music festival I had done at Madison Square Garden.

Babla searched for my response to the first song. I showed him none.

There was silence, and as it was stretching out, it was interrupted by a sudden popping sound. The steam within the coffee pot had risen and caused its lid to click open. My eyes followed as the steam hit the window steaming it up and obliterating the wintery night outside.

I reached over to the tape recorder and pressed play again. I settled back in my chair as the sound filled the room. Then I heard a sound that had the potential to stretch out of this room and to the wider world.

The more this song unspooled, the more Sadro's words of the brilliance of this composer and rhythm player held true. He was nothing short of a genius, and Kanchan's voice was nothing short of brilliant.

Kuchh Gadbad Hai is based on the massive hit song *Hot Hot Hot*, originally composed and made popular by the soca-calypso recording artist Alphonsus Cassell, known to the world as Arrow. Although the original song was amazing, Kanchan and Babla's interpretation could take it to another level. And as the song played, my mind searched for how I would make this song a better record.

And as I listened, I thought about all that I had learned about music production and reminded myself it is the public that makes a record a hit.

I reached over and touched the pause button. There was no need to listen further. The song was found.

I handed Babla an envelope with $5,000, an amount that far exceeded what he or his counterparts or Indo-Caribbean artists were being paid. And a few days later, he left for India.

CHAPTER 32

Think of purpose as clay. Hold it in both hands and mold it to your liking. Have it your way.

I continued with my planning for the production of the album and the creation of a record to bring Afro and Indo Caribbeans together.

Recorded in India in a small studio, the recording had its limitations. Synergizing what was recorded in India with the modern sound and recording technology available in the United States would create what I hoped for.

I reached for my phone and called a few New York-based Afro-Caribbean session musicians who played at my show in Madison Square Garden.

A few days later, I mounted the recording onto a twenty-four-track reel at a Times Square recording studio and began tweaking in the elements. I walked across town to the Frankford-Wayne Mastering Labs, where I handed the tapes over to the award-winning engineer Herb Powers to cut the album. It is here, at this step of the process, where a record is made.

Herb had cut his way to superstardom by masterfully crafting and cutting albums for hitmakers like Michael Jackson, Whitney Houston, and Madonna. Very few men had shaped the sound of modern-day music in America as he had.

Indo-Caribbean music, with a fusion of Afro-Caribbean flavor, was about to have the markings of his excellence.

As unique as this sound was, so too were its creative talents. Babla, one of the most talented of Indian composers; renowned session players; Arrow, a popular soca-calypso musician; Kanchan, a refreshingly vibrant voice; and Herb Powers, one of the world's most sought-after mastering engineers, all assembled to create the world's first Afro-Indo-Caribbean album in Hindi.

Soon, Herb called me into his lab to have a listen. My first impression was that the album had the elements that would take it across the boundary line. The final cut of the album was then done for music lovers in the United States.

I then asked Herb to do another cut, trimming the base and the high ends of the sound for the developing world, countries such as Fiji, Guyana, Jamaica, Mauritius, Suriname and Trinidad.

Around eight that night, I drove the album across the Hudson River to New Jersey to have stampers made.

During the drive, I reflected on the events of the past few days. A world-class recording engineer had imprinted his creative impressions onto the grooves of a Hindi Afro-Indo-Caribbean album — a first of its kind. The Hindi lyrical content driven by soca rhythms would inspire a future generation of artists to climb and rise to the upper echelon of Afro- and Indo-Caribbean fusion music.

For now, a record with a fresh voice was about to become the anthem of the Afro-Indo-Caribbean world and, perhaps, beyond. A unique listening experience awaited them.

The listening experience, however, depended on the playback devices used by music lovers — jukeboxes, tape recorders, or stereo systems. At the time, in North America and Europe, the available playback systems were more sophisticated and listening to a record was a different experience than in the Caribbean, where the record was played on less sophisticated systems.

I created a dual-cutting approach for the music. Maintain the exact studio sound for North American and European devices but trim the base and the high ends of the sound for the Caribbean devices. The middle frequencies, where a more neutralized sound exists on a record, remained as is. Soon this would be put to the test. Will this album cause relations between Afro and Indo Caribbeans to neutralize, as with the middle frequencies of the record?

CHAPTER 33

Deep within the raging ocean, there is calm and peace, and if we are to find ours, we too, must go deep within.

New York, the city that never sleeps, does sleep in late on Sunday mornings after a week of hard work. Sleeping in on Sunday mornings meant being deep asleep or laying awake cozily in bed. After a long winter, the beginning of this early spring day felt toasty and invitingly satisfying.

Indo Caribbeans from across this great city awakened in the comfort of their beds and reached across to their nightstands to turn on their radios. They tuned in to WLIB.

This radio station had an Afro-Caribbean format. However, on Sunday mornings, from six to ten, they played Indo-Caribbean music.

The Indo-Caribbean segment was hosted by Clyfee Madhu, a Trinidadian immigrant and his daughter, Ann. Their segment was listened to by every Indo-Caribbean expat in the greater New York market.

Until then, no one had heard my new record. I was careful to keep it a secret to create the element of surprise.

I left home early Sunday morning to arrive at WLIB around seven. As I entered the studio, the record playing on air was about to come to an end. Clyfee Madhu was queuing up another one on a second turntable. The moment he saw me, his eyes lit up.

"Rohit, I have been waiting for you," he whispered.

He noticed the records I held in my hand and asked, "Is that it? Is that it?"

I calmly placed three copies into his hand and quietly left so as not to interrupt his flow. It had been more than a year since his listeners had first heard Kanchan's Indo-Caribbean album, *Kaise Bani*. With no other album from her, this new release would take them by a complete surprise.

Knowing full well it is the public that can turn a record into a hit, I held on to the moment. I turned on my ignition and the radio. Soon enough, Clyfee Madhu's distinctive voice introduced the song. The man who commanded all Indo-Caribbean expats on Sunday mornings was into the groove of my record. It was the last time it would be my record. It now belonged to the public and I was one of them — a listener. It now belonged to all of us.

As I made my way back from Manhattan into Queens, the early New York Sunday morning roads felt empty, like no one was around, not even another car.

As Kanchan's voice played on my radio, it rose to greet the New York Indo-Caribbean skyline. My hope was that her voice would extend to greet Afro Caribbeans as well.

I arrived at my store where I had three thousand copies of the album, *Kuchh Gadbad Hai*, that I planned on shipping to

Guyana, Trinidad and Suriname. Another three thousand were for the New York market. I planned on looking for other world markets as well.

The record awaited its place in history. I waited as well. I waited for the people to push through the doors of my store and doors belonging to other stores, to make this record into a hit.

The clock in my store said it was 8 a.m. It was still two hours to the opening of my store.

I flipped on the radio in the store. I heard the phone ring in the store and above in my office. In the midst of the ringing, Clyfee Madhu gave his enthusiastic impressions about the album.

Amidst the music coming from the radio and both phones ringing, I heard a car pull up in front of the store. The sound of the car door slamming shut punctuated the silence of the quiet Sunday morning outside.

Who was arriving some two hours before the store opening? Upon entering my store, I had left the shutter halfway down, indicating the store was not yet open.

There was a knock and someone bending under the shutter, trying to look into the store. It was happening. I turned on the remaining lights, and I could see a man peering in under the shutter. I unlocked the door, and he rose to help me lift the shutter, taking the weight off my hands.

As we stood on the pavement, he enthusiastically said, "Rohit, we just heard Kanchan's new album. We want it. We came to buy. Give me one."

By this time, a string of his family members flowed out of his car, one by one, to greet me.

His wife immediately intervened, "Make it two. Make it two."

He then turned to me and said, "Three, three. I will give one to my brother."

"What's your name?" asked their little daughter.

"He is Rohit," her mother replied.

"He is the guy the man on the radio was talking about," her father interjected. "He made this record."

"Can I have your autograph?" the little girl asked. I teasingly signed her forehead. She laughed heartily.

As they happily drove off with their new favorite album, I stood on the pavement and waved to them, knowing this was an indication of what ten o'clock would bring.

During the Indo Caribbean Sunday morning segment on WLIB, all the listeners were Indo Caribbeans. All except for one. He owned a small record store on Flatbush Avenue in Brooklyn. He was of Afro-Caribbean ancestry, and he sold Afro-Caribbean music.

He phoned me, telling me that he had heard the song on the radio. He had called WLIB and Clyfee Madhu gave him my store number. He asked me for directions by train from Brooklyn to my store.

Something that had never happened before to an Indo-Caribbean record was now happening.

An Afro Caribbean would soon be crossing the boundary line from Brooklyn into Queens because of an Indo-Caribbean record. He was crossing the boundary of historical mistrust sown in another century between our two communities. And now in this century, an Indo-Caribbean expat awaited an Afro-Caribbean expat.

As it neared ten o'clock, we sat together in the office above my store where he described the moment when he first heard the song *Kuchh Gadbad Hai*. He was enthralled with the crisp, fresh new sound.

"Rohit, you don't know what you have done. You have done something that hasn't been done before. I want to be the first to tell you that this record is for everybody."

"I have been selling records for a long time now. Believe me, I know what I am talking about. This is why I have come from Brooklyn on this early Sunday morning. I want to take this record back with me to Brooklyn to sell it for you in my store. You may not know it, but Brooklyn is full of Afro-Caribbean people."

As he was speaking, I sensed an urgency in his voice. He confirmed this urgency by reaching into his pocket and emptying out the contents onto the top of my desk. There lay a small pile of crumpled-up bills.

His fingers started stretching and flattening the bills out on my desk. Realizing I was watching him straightening them, my new friend felt a tad bit embarrassed. Little could he have imagined that the man sitting in front of him, the album's producer, had himself once counted and stretched coins.

I realized then how much people are alike; how similar we are on this journey called life. I knew his path. I had traveled it myself. And this is how I knew I could trust the man sitting before me. Should I not trust him, then I will not have trusted my own path, the path I myself once walked.

"Mr. Rohit, the minute I heard this song, I got up from my bed. My wife asked me where I was going, I told her I am going to call the radio station to find out where I can get this record. She said she was thinking the very same thing. There is something about this music that touches me. I can feel it, which is very strange because I cannot understand a single word. But oh my God, her voice, she can sing. I wonder where she is from? I wish we could meet her."

"I want to tell you something in confidence. As I was traveling on that train, I kept thinking, is someone ahead of me? Did someone call ahead of me? Am I the first one from Brooklyn to get to this record? I kept hoping the train would hurry up. I want to be the first one to sell this record in Brooklyn, Mr. Rohit."

"Okay. Tell me about your family," I requested.

"Let me be honest with you. My wife and I struggled a lot. We don't have much. We are immigrants; we came here with our children from Trinidad with nothing. We believe that our little store in Brooklyn provides our music to our people in ways that no other store can. Don't get me wrong, we are not like those big record stores in Brooklyn. We are small. However, we treat our people like family."

The words coming from a seller of records, one having his fingers on the pulse of record buyers in Brooklyn, told a compelling tale of this family and what lay ahead for the record.

He counted out the bills that added up to $60.00 and as he was handing them to me, I requested that he give me only $1.00 for good luck. I wanted the record to succeed.

I placed the records in a box and handed it to him, requesting that he sell them for $10.00 each and pay me $5.00 a record after he sold them. I then wished him happy selling, and we shook hands.

By then, it was a little after ten o'clock. As my guest and I descended the stairs from my office and cleared the front door, I noticed unusual activity for a Sunday morning. Cars were parked along the road, stretching for a block — some were even double-parked. The sight told the story of something big happening while reminding me, however big it was, the Indo-Caribbean population was small.

I watched as my friend, holding his box of records, walked toward the subway. Could he and his customers in Brooklyn be the ones to help me break the barrier? Not so long ago, I had been the one who crossed the boundary from Queens into Brooklyn.

Shoppers came out of my store clutching the album. Some were carrying more than one. Others were making their way into the store. All were greeting me with happy enthusiasm.

Among this activity and bustle stood a man in his Hindu priest attire. He held a stare so strong that the grooves the great American engineer had cut into this Afro-Indo beat record with his lathe now seemed immovable. His eyes spoke of his meaning even before his mouth could open.

"Mr. Rohit, I am here for one purpose. I heard your record on the radio. And speaking on behalf of all Indo-Caribbean people here in Queens, I do not like it one bit. As long as I am an Indian priest, I will make sure that it doesn't sell." He then stood there while shoppers kept buying the album, and store owners arrived to buy it for their shops.

The next day, I went to the cargo section of JFK Airport, where I handed them three thousand albums to ship to Guyana, Trinidad, and Suriname. Then I boarded a BWIA flight to Port of Spain and checked into the Holiday Inn.

CHAPTER 34

All that is broken will rise.

Trinidad held one of the largest and most colorful carnivals in the Caribbean region. It was also the most lucrative market for both soca-calypso and Indo-Caribbean records. My new album, having both soca-calypso and Indo-Caribbean flavors, had the potential to be at the epicenter. It was an album with a purpose for all. For all but one.

As I was traveling from the airport to my hotel, I studied the music coming from the taxi's speakers. Later that evening, as I sat alone over dinner, I again paid close attention, this time to the sound of the music coming from the steel band playing at the far side of the Holiday Inn pool. Music coming from the adjacent parking lot intermittently blended with the band.

The next morning, I called Moean and told him to meet me for lunch in the lobby restaurant. He was surprised I was calling him from Trinidad.

"Oh so you are a big man now, you're taking a taxi directly to the hotel, even passing the house on the way? I see."

Soon we were both sitting over lunch at the Holiday Inn.

At the time, the restaurant area extended out from the lobby toward the pool area. As the air conditioning from the lobby mixed with the natural temperature of the outside atmosphere, it created a business setting mixed with tropical island. I hoped it was a good setting to discuss a record holding both purpose and business — both karma and money — the perfect balance of the two banks.

As we discussed the music he was currently producing, Moean didn't realize the real reason I was in Trinidad. And I wasn't in any hurry to tell him.

The prolific record producer reflected on the rhythm section of his current production, enthusiastically telling me he was trying out a new drummer for the first time. It was then, speaking of a drummer, that he led our conversation to the rhythm player, Babla, and with it, Kanchan. He asked me when I was going to release another album with them.

"It's long overdue you know," he said.

"What kind of rhythm is this new drummer doing for your album that's so different from your other rhythm players?" I asked him.

"Well as you know, our music has mainly two styles, it's either chutney with the basics or Indo-Caribbean with the added orchestration."

I pulled my chair closer as if to let him in to a secret.

"The reason I asked you is because I heard someone was going to do an Indo-Caribbean song with Afro-Caribbean beat."

"What? I never heard that. Let me tell you this, whoever is going to do that will be in plenty of trouble. Big, big trouble."

He sat back, now leaning on the strength of his chair and spoke, one word at a time, "The Hindu organization here in this country, will never ever allow that to happen. You mark my words. Never ever are they going to allow that."

Recognizing that I was holding on to each of his words and knowing me so well, he sensed it. He sensed who was going to get into plenty of trouble.

"Don't tell me, Rohit, no. You can't do that. The Hindu organization here will never allow us to live in peace again. I am begging you. Please let's not release a record like that."

I knew what he was talking about, but instead of acknowledging his words, I took his challenge and said, "Don't worry, it's a Hindi song."

"That's exactly why we should be worried. Can't you see it? A Hindi song with music the Hindu organization doesn't want our songs to get mixed up in. They don't like it when our things get mixed up with others."

There was silence. After the pause, Moean, realizing he might have been a bit too harsh, offered me an olive branch. "Ok let's go and listen to it. Let me see what you have made."

It was perhaps our most heated exchange since we had first met some four years ago in 1980, and as we rode the elevator, the silence remained. I allowed the silence to stretch out. I was sure Moean was eager to hear Kanchan's new song and to have a hit album, but the prospect of plenty of trouble caused his silence.

As we sat across from each other in my suite, I reached for the phone and ordered a pot of coffee. I also requested three cups with it.

"Are you expecting someone, or is this your three cups thing?"

"Yes. You are right on both counts," I replied.

"Who is it?"

"I will know when you call him."

"Rohit, do they still serve drinks on the flights?"

I settled in my chair and reflected in a calm voice, "You see, Moean, you are not wrong. I agree with you there are unspoken issues here in this country as in all other places.

"As you know, silence speaks the loudest. Therefore, we should let it be heard in the best way we can, and we have the medium for it. How long can the people live in this silence? You may remember the words of a great man who said, 'we may have all come on different ships, however, we are all in the same boat now.' It's time to change the dialogue if we are to get a better result. And what better dialogue is there than music?"

"Well, you are speaking to the choir. You know full well that what took place here in this country, and Guyana and Suriname and elsewhere, in these colonies, a very long time ago is causing this rift even now.

"How long can we hold on to that, Moean? How long can people hold these things among themselves? You see the cereal our people in this country ate for breakfast this morning? There is a good chance that it was made by the hand of another kind, one different from their own. That didn't bother them. Everybody happily ate their cereal. But the music made by another hand? That bothers them?"

I continued, "The hand that played this music is of one kind and the genre is of another kind. Yet, it is one record. It is the same record. So this album, the music, the beat, is of the fusion of the people and our collective heritage."

There was a knock on the door. A pot of coffee and three cups were placed in front of us. The third cup reminded us both that someone would be joining us.

"Who is it that you wanted me to call?" Moean asked.

"Radio Trinidad," I replied.

He looked at me with surprised eyes, knowing he controlled more than twelve hours per week of important Indo-Caribbean radio time on Radio Trinidad. He, his wife, Hansrajee, their daughter Aruna, their son Sadro and his nephew Rafi were a team that was powerful enough to successfully market a record and still I was looking past his shoulders. While the others went through him to have an Indo-Caribbean record played on the radio, I with full access to him was looking beyond him.

It was then that he asked, "Do you think they will play it on their Afro-Caribbean program? I mean, don't get me wrong, they know me well, and you know I can always ask them. However, it should be a reasonable request. Why don't we listen to it first to see how much it sounds like the music they play on their program, then decide how we are going to handle it?"

"Are you wishing that the record has enough soca-calypso now?" I teasingly asked him and we shared a laugh.

"Okay, let's listen to it," Moean replied.

"How, though? There is no record player here. There is only a radio." I pointed to the phone and said, "If you want to hear it there is only one way."

He shook his head in disbelief and laughed as he picked up the phone and dialed.

A short time after, one of the assistants overseeing the soca-calypso segment at Radio Trinidad arrived and joined us over coffee.

CHAPTER 35

Music cannot be heard unless it is held by the trust of those who listen to it.

Pat was in his early thirties, a Trinidadian with roots stretching back to Africa. Like Moean, he too was a strong nationalist, ready to defend his country and his music. Pat lived and breathed for soca-calypso. He lived on one side of the boundary line.

Calypso was widely known in these lands. Its heritage stretched back to Africa, and its lyrical content was deeply rooted in a long struggle.

And this struggle left far behind in this now progressive country was celebrated as a reminder of the history of the people who once came by ship from Africa. Pat was born into this history.

What Pat saw for his heritage, was what the Hindu organization saw for their heritage. This is why the twain had never met.

And this is what caused Moean to now understand why I chose this hotel as the middle ground to have this meeting instead of going "home."

He turned to Pat and said, "Pat look, I know you help at the station to make the playlist. This is why I wanted to have a talk with you. You see my friend here, who you have seen with me many times at the station, has produced a new album."

"Of course, I know Mr. Jagessar. I have seen him cohosting with you at the station many times."

"Congratulations on your success Pat," I said. "Moean told me ratings at the station are at an all-time high."

I got up, and started walking toward my production bag sitting on the far side of the suite and opened it. As I looked into it, I continued telling him, "I have been listening to your programming since I arrived here yesterday."

I took out a few pieces of the album from my bag, and walked back toward them.

In keeping things in the order of who introduced me to whom, I handed them to Moean, who keenly examined the cover, seeing it for the first time.

Pat, sitting opposite him, still wondered what role he could have in what seemed to be an Indian album. I stood there and observed them both.

Moean lifted his eyes from the album cover and looked at Pat. He handed him the copies of the album and spoke with great calmness.

"Pat, I am sure that you must be wondering why I wanted to see you. Just between the three of us, I want you to put this record on top of your playlist. Just add it in so the DJ can play it as soon as you get back to the station."

Pat appeared confused.

"Moean, this is an Indian record. You are the best man to push this record on your Indian shows at the station," Pat replied.

"Pat, you are right," I spoke. "Kanchan and Babla are Indian artists. You don't have to play the record. Just have your DJ put the needle on it and take it off if you don't like it. Just give it a little touch, a slight nudge, that's all I am asking. And if it doesn't work, take it off. No hard feelings."

Pat took another look at the album, then looked at us and said, "Ok Mr. Jagessar. Ok Moean, I will try."

While Pat was on his way back to the studios of Radio Trinidad, Moean and I now sat back silently in our chairs, deep in our thoughts.

After some time, I leaned forward, poured some more coffee into both of our cups.

"Rohit, are you thinking what I am thinking? Do you realize that we have never asked anyone to play our records before?"

Moean and I were record producers and distributors. He more powerful than me. Between us, we had well over sixty albums in distribution by then.

We also had full access to the Indo-Caribbean media. Having our records played on Indo-Caribbean radio programs — here, in Surinam, in Holland, in New York, anywhere — was a given.

This was the first time we found ourselves sitting anxiously waiting to know if someone would play our record. We were like the artists and producers who sat by the radio for hours, for days, at times for weeks, to hear if their songs would play on the radio.

And we understood Pat's predicament. Exactly how much damage can be caused by playing an Indian song when his listeners are expecting the biggest soca-calypso hits. Losing listenership causes program directors and radio jocks to lose their jobs.

Both Moean and I were asking Pat to do the unthinkable at the time — play an Indian song on the country's most popular soca-calypso program. From what I understand today, playing Indian songs on such programs has now become the norm. It is so because of what happened on that spring day in 1984.

On that day, we waited to see if our "same boat" would start its journey.

I walked across the suite to pull the blinds open. The panoramic view of Port of Spain revealed bumper-to-bumper traffic. The late afternoon rush hour traffic had started. And as I stood by the window, the rhythm started coming from the radio and filling the room. I turned in its rhythm, to the movement of music.

Seeing the change in my expressions, Moean exclaimed, "Is that it? Is that it?"

And before I could give him the affirmation he sought, her voice answered to the man who first gave me her name. *Kuchh Gadbad Hai*, she sang.

Moean got up from his chair, grabbed my hand and pulled me back toward the window.

He pointed down toward the cars, "Look, what's going on, look how they are dancing in the cars."

In the drive-time traffic jam, a few ladies opened their car doors and took the rhythm to the sidewalks. A few men joined them. Who they were didn't matter, for moments like this had no boundaries.

What we had earlier proposed to Pat, to give it a short try and take it off if he didn't like it, stretched to the full six-minute length of the song. An Indian song had just completed its full rotation on the turntable on Radio Trinidad's soca-calypso show. And just as Clyfee Madhu had done on the radio in New York, the DJ returned the needle to the first scrapings of the record.

"Let's call the station, let's call the station!" Moean excitedly said.

I calmly replied, "Let's wait."

And before he could respond, the phone rang. He grabbed it. He must have made five attempts to speak. However, it was apparent to me the caller wasn't allowing him to even get in one word.

Occasionally, he would place the receiver to my ear then quickly pull it back to his, a showman not wanting to miss out on a single stir.

He ended the call by saying, "Okay we will. We are on our way. We are leaving the hotel right now."

He then turned to me and asked, "Guess who that was? Let's go."

On the drive, Moean not only took control of the gears of the car but the grooves of the record.

"Rohit, you don't know what we have here. You don't know."

In the midst of Moean's excitement, it dawned on me that whenever he released a record in this country, it was on his shoulders to debut the record and popularize it. For the first time, he was in the audience.

As we listened to the public's impressions and reactions live on the radio, The Mighty Sparrow, the iconic exponent of calypso, suddenly appeared on the air and expressed to the DJ that "this voice, is a breath of fresh air."

"Alright! You see, Rohit, that's what I wanted to hear. What the other side has to say about it."

I asked him, "And what about your side, your Hindu organization side?"

To which he replied, "Rohit, don't play with me, that's none of my business. If music be the food of love, play on."

He then turned up the volume, opened the windows and like a symphony, the song flowed and blended together with all the other cars.

Upon seeing him, drivers and passengers waved to him in excitement, all having the same question, "Is it out yet? Can we get it at Windsor tomorrow?"

After some time, we pulled into Maraval Road. Pat was standing in front of Radio Trinidad, waiting and waving at us.

And like a true trouper, he walked us through the familiar hallway, leading to the station, teasingly telling his colleagues, "You guys know my friends right?"

Everyone laughed and clapped in appreciation. They made it clear this was a brand-new day for music and for all the people of this land who came by ship. All that was broken was now rising.

The engineer who had worked the controls the first time I had appeared on the radio some four years back, shook our hands excitedly. That evening, he once again sat behind the controls, just as he had done the first time when Moean and I took our seats behind the studio furniture.

The engineer began his familiar countdown, the lights came on, indicating "On Air." Moean held onto his earphones, pressing them even closer to his ears. He recited the familiar couplet that formed the opening of his show and then announced to the country, "Get ready for a recording event like none this country has ever seen before."

CHAPTER 36

Purpose is a profound power.

The excitement stretched into the next day.

It was around six in the morning when the phone rang in my hotel suite, and Moean asked me for the umteenth time, "Rohit what are we going to do? I know you told me yesterday you made six thousand pieces in New York. How fast can you get me even one thousand to start? Anything to feed the fire."

Hansrajee came on the line and calmly said, "Rohit, don't listen to him, you go ahead and ask your New York office to send as many pieces as they can spare right away. We'll discuss the inventory strategy at the office. We'll pick you up at the hotel on the way. I am bringing breakfast for you. We'll be there soon."

As we traveled from the Holiday Inn to Windsor that morning, I noticed the difficulty Moean was having, and he moved around in his seat impatiently. At times, he anxiously tapped the steering wheel with his fingers.

It was then I told him we would have to go to Piarco Airport later in the day.

"Piarco?" they both exclaimed in chorus, as they turned their heads in unison, looking at the back seat to find me sitting calmly.

Realizing how calm I was, Moean immediately caught on.

"Rohit, you've my mind fetching records from New York to Trinidad ever since I heard the record. Man you are something else. You mean to tell me that you already got the records into the country and didn't say even one word?"

"I just did. I said Piarco."

The moment we arrived at Windsor that morning, Moean sprung into action, calling his staff together and putting in place a release-day strategy. He instructed his staff to keep the anticipation high and to tell shoppers to listen to us on the radio that evening for the release date. He instructed Sadro to accompany me to Piarco to make arrangements for the records to be cleared from customs and delivered to Windsor.

He then picked up the phone and started calling the media.

It was an honor to watch him orchestrate the release of the record and to learn from him.

On release day, the following morning, as we were making our way into the midst of the crowd of shoppers, we noticed that many were already there in front of the store. Moean, Sadro, Rafi, and I had promoted it on the radio the previous night. Pat's team continued playing it across all of their programs. Listeners from across the country were there early on this day, anxiously waiting for the doors of Windsor to open.

Familiar faces from the media — newspapers, television, and Radio Trinidad — had already arrived. Some were getting comments from the eager crowd.

"I work right here in Port of Spain, but I am not taking any chances. I want to be the first one to get this record."

"You see, by lunchtime this place won't have any room to stand up. It will be even more jam-packed. That music is hot!"

"I am from the south, and I traveled all the way here this morning to buy ten records to take to my friends and my family."

"I sell in the Chaguanas market, and I came early to get as many as they would allow me to get to sell at my stand."

As Moean led the Windsor team into the midst of this crowd, I stood a slight distance away. I could see the top of the closed doors behind the crowd.

There was a day when I found myself waiting for the doors of this iconic Indo-Caribbean music store to open.

I joined Moean and the team, and we collectively walked through those doors. The crowds rushed in behind us. *Kuchh Gadbad Hai*, the album, lined the record displays leading from the door and stretching deep into the store.

Hands stretched and grabbed the record. The tireless work by Hansrajee and her staff the evening before, while we were out promoting the release date elsewhere, was eye-catching. It felt like the American record stores I often frequented, admired, and held within. A record that bore my imprint now adorned the display. Purpose had revealed itself.

A TV cameraman, unable to freely move about the crowded store, climbed up on one of the counters; pointing his lens downward, he captured a shot of the record spinning on a turntable. I asked him to keep that shot in his edit for the evening news.

All turntables were fired up, and the record played on rotation on multiple counters. Cash registers rang to the rhythm.

In this market, a new promising Indo-Caribbean release would sell around three hundred copies on release day. Not on this day. On this momentous day, the fifteen hundred records I shipped to Trinidad were all sold.

Kuchh Gadbad Hai was bringing people together.

CHAPTER 37

Giving is receiving.

Where people meet, the broken will rise.

The bridge was built, and people were crossing it. *Kuchh Gadbad Hai*, became a musical anthem for an entire nation.

To keep up with the demand for the album, Hansrajee suggested I talk with West Indies Records Ltd (WIRL), a record manufacturer based in Barbados within the CARICOM. This was the common market of Caribbean countries, and products manufactured and shipped within these countries were exempt from exorbitant import duties.

Manufacturing within CARICOM would make the album more affordable to the people, and a more affordable price made the picture complete — balancing the two banks.

I gave the green light to have the record manufactured there and shipped to Moean in Trinidad. In the midst of the impending success of the record, I reflected on my grandmother's words of wisdom that wherever we may go and however far we may have gone, no one really ever leaves their home; our thoughts always bring us back to our home.

One of my homes was here in Trinidad — the home of my friend, Moean, and his family. In Suriname, there was the home of my friend Rashid Pierkhan, the man who gave me Kanchan's number four years earlier. And before I could call Rashid to ask him about release day there, he called Windsor to give me the good news that the album was creating a similar craze in his country. Much to his delight, and mine, he told me the supply was exhausted in Guyana, and some of my countrymen had bought copies directly from him and crossed the Corentyne River, taking it back to Guyana. He told me that both countries would need more stock and was delighted to hear the record would be manufactured in Barbados and made available in the Caribbean at a price to suit every music lover's pocket.

On my way back to New York, I added Barbados to my itinerary to meet with the CEO of WIRL Barbados, at the time, one of the very few record manufacturing plants in the CARICOM market.

As I waited for my flight, Sadro and I sat at the restaurant at Piarco Airport, overlooking the tarmac. While we sipped on our coffee and chatted away, we lost track of time. Suddenly, I noticed his eyes widening.

"Jag, Jag, look your plane is leaving."

As I looked, I saw that he was right. The jet bridge was pulling away from the aircraft.

Sadro took off like a jaguar. I gathered my production bag, and followed him to the departure area. The ropes were drawn.

As I was approaching, I heard the ticket agent ask, "Who is traveling?"

To which Sadro replied, "It's Mr. Rohit Jagessar."

"Don't worry, we will hold the aircraft for Mr. Jagessar," the voice calmly said.

As we lifted off over the island on that afternoon, my spirits were high. The goodwill I spread across this land had been reciprocated by the people.

I was met with great enthusiasm in Barbados. They, too, had followed the stir the record was creating in the region and promised to swiftly manufacture and ship the album to keep up with the demand. In addition to Guyana, Suriname, and Trinidad, they would also manufacture and ship the album to the other countries throughout the Caribbean region.

I arrived back in New York, where ten thousand additional copies had been manufactured at the U.S.-based plant and delivered to my office. I headed straight from the airport to the office. My record store friend from Brooklyn was eagerly awaiting me.

"Rohit, I came here to tell you that the news is now all over Brooklyn. I am here every single day to buy your record for my store. Every day it keeps selling out. We cannot keep up with the demand. Yesterday they told me you would be returning today. I brought my friend. Look, he has a van. Brooklyn hasn't seen anything like this in a very long time."

My Brooklyn record store friend told me the record was all over WLIB like a wildfire in a sugar cane field. Once the Trinidadian expats in Brooklyn heard from their families back in Trinidad that this song was being played all over Radio Trinidad, they started demanding WLIB play it on all their programs so they could hear it too.

"Rohit, *Kuchh Gadbad Hai*, I hope I pronounce it properly now, is a game-changer. This record has blazed the trail. And mind you, it's not only WLIB radio, but all the Brooklyn clubs are playing it too. They are playing it wall to wall."

My record store friend continued excitedly explaining to me, "This music got us grooving. I saw it in clubs with my very own eyes. The minute I give it to the DJs to play, they jump on it. My people do not understand the words, but they are dancing to your Indian song. And they are singing the title, *Kuchh Gadbad Hai*."

One thing was clear to me, having gone to Trinidad, the home of soca-calypso, and lit a fire perhaps as deep as the Caroni sugar fields, the news had reached the expat shores.

Within days, the entire second pressing of the ten thousand copies of *Kuchh Gadbad Hai* was sold in New York and was selling at a much faster pace than Kanchan's first Indo-Caribbean album.

Having felt the pulse of the broken ones, it was time to keep rising.

CHAPTER 38

When thoughts are in balance, beings function to their fullest potential — as individuals, and as a nation.

As popular as the record was, it was clear it would have to outsell and outpace all other soca-calypso records by a large and compelling margin before being allowed to take its rightful place on the WLIB Top 10 chart — the most coveted soca-calypso music chart in the New York market at the time.

On the 31st day of May in 1984, the West Indian cricket team was scheduled to play England at Old Trafford in Greater Manchester. The match was set to beam across the Commonwealth and to some of the expat markets. It would also be broadcast on WLIB, and I saw an opportunity there.

Rej, a Jamaican expat and an avid cricket enthusiast, was an up-and-coming record distributor based in London. He had been trying for some time to bypass my distributors in the United Kingdom to buy directly from me. I reached out to him.

He traveled to Old Trafford with a small tape recorder and strategically positioned himself at the point where the players were interviewed live on air. There he sat quietly. I sat in New York with my radio tuned to WLIB.

As an interviewer started his interaction with one of the players, Rej started his. He pressed play, and the song seeped into the interviewers' microphone and was heard on WLIB.

It felt like it was the game's theme song, and many took notice.

Although WLIB were playing the record, they had been playing hardball when it came to their Top 10. It became more and more apparent that they reserved their chart for Afro-Caribbean songs. World-class cricket was a different matchup altogether. WLIB took notice of what happened at the game.

The following Saturday, I accompanied my nephew, Den, from Queens to Manhattan to buy fresh vegetables. Saturday was also the day WLIB introduced their new Top 10 chart.

Den and I planned our drive to coincide with when the tenth song of the week was getting ready to spin. Number ten was not *Kuchh Gadbad Hai*.

Despite outselling all other soca-calypso records, some doubted that a Hindi song with a soca-calypso beat would get its fair due on the chart. My nephew sensed it might not be on the chart at all. Not on this morning, not ever.

He expressed this dissatisfaction to me, which gave me reason to do some silent reflection.

I could hear my Brooklyn record store friend's voice, "I know you haven't been given a fair chance for so many weeks. The record is selling strong, but sales went through the roof after it was played during that cricket match. I am telling you they have no choice now. The evidence is in plain sight for all to know."

By the time the Saturday morning traffic eased on the approach to the Williamsburg Bridge, WLIB had already drawn the countdown to number three with no *Kuchh Gadbad Hai* in sight, causing my nephew to grow even more impatient.

What seemed a huge disappointment to him, gave me hope. I found myself hoping not to hear it in the number two slot.

As we were crossing the bridge, I noticed where the tides of the Hudson and the East River met. In this confluence, they rose to bear witness to a momentous feat that took place in their presence. The rivers witnessed the collaboration of people who first met more than a century ago amidst great mistrust in colonies far away.

A Hindi song rose to the top of an Afro-Caribbean chart in the greatest city in the world. *Kuchh Gadbad Hai* debut at number one.

CHAPTER 39

*In the company of the great ones,
no one will ever see you as weak.*

The song held momentum right through Labor Day weekend of 1984, when the celebration of calypso's most colorful carnival this side of the Atlantic, the West Indian American Day Carnival and Parade, took place on Eastern Parkway in Brooklyn.

The day before the big event, I ventured out to see the preparations. I walked the parkway and except for a few people casually walking along the sidewalks, the streets were empty. Barricades anticipating the next day's event were already up.

A familiar melody filled the air, and I followed its trail to notice someone whistling while walking with his bicycle. His Walkman strapped to his waist with *Kuchh Gadbad Hai* on his lips. His lungs filled the quiet streets.

The following morning, I arrived with my friend Dino Dilchand on the parkway. From many blocks away, we could see the wave of colors. Nearing the colors we realized people had come from near and far to be among their own to take a dip in the oasis of the Caribbean culture, song, dance, and food.

"Rohit, Rohit," came a familiar voice.

There he was, my record store friend, trying to get my attention, shouting out and above the decibel of the crowd.

At that very moment, we heard the familiar melody. He heard it before me. His eyes lit up, and he placed his hand on my shoulders and pointed me toward its source.

"Look, look what is going on over there."

A young woman standing on a carnival float was singing. As the vehicle drew nearer, I realized that indeed, a young woman of African heritage was singing *Kuchh Gadbad Hai.* Backing her was the guitarist, John Drepaul, and the brass band, The Tropical Waves.

We waved and John quickly returned the wave and without missing a beat, he continued to strum the sound that reflected the collective heritage of the Caribbean.

"That's my friend, John. He used to lead an Indo-Caribbean band in Queens, and this is my friend Dino. They played in my show at Madison Square Garden."

As the float passed us, and another approached, my record store friend grabbed me by the hand and walked me over to media stands. They all recognized him; he knew everybody. He introduced me as the producer of the song, and all camera lenses suddenly shifted on us.

The next morning, I was woken to the sound of the phone ringing.

I answered to hear the sound of newspapers rustling, followed by that familiar voice.

"Rohit, I know it's early and you haven't received the Trinidad papers in New York yet. I just saw it. My friend, you have made all the papers. The news is all over the country. Pat from the radio station was the first man to call me this morning, telling me that an Afro-Caribbean woman sang the song at the carnival in New York, and it created a media craze."

"If the song can make such an impact at a carnival in New York, just imagine what it could do at a real carnival, here in the land of the steelpan, soca, and calypso. Plus, keep in mind Trinidad and Tobago is a major market for Indo-Caribbean music. We now hold in our hands the best of both worlds."

I listened to his words — the words from the most prolific proponent and pioneer of Indo-Caribbean music.

"Rohit, a man must strike when the iron is hot. I'll meet you at the airport when the next flight arrives from New York. I will see you then."

The very next day, we both took our familiar poolside chairs at the Holiday Inn in Port of Spain.

Had I gotten up early and gone to my store or office on that morning when Moean had called me at home, I would have missed his call. Had he then tried reaching me at the store or office, where the phones were almost always busy, he might not have reached me at all. He might have then gone on with his daily routine. But I was home that morning to take his call.

And here I was in Trinidad and Tobago, sitting comfortably with my friend. It was as if the day had been choreographed to happen with the song coming from every direction — from the Holiday Inn parking lot to cars passing by on the roadway to the steel band right across the pool from where we sat.

Moean raised his coffee cup as if in a toast.

"Rohit, we are now kings."

Ordinarily, moments like these are toasted and cheered with alcohol. Instead of putting bottles on the table, we placed the faith the people showed in us and in our music, in front of us and honored it with more planning and work.

Moean and I found our intoxication in the way we collaborated with the people. This was the pinnacle of our high.

And I thought to myself, all of us can rise.

It was then, as if seeking counsel, Moean asked me, "Rohit, where do you now see us going from here?"

"Indo-Caribbean music now has its chance to finally become an industry. And as you know, a successful industry has to empower all of its participants, meaning that the pay for artists can no longer remain $10, $20, or $50. Look at Sundar Popo, he is the most in-demand artist of our music here. He sometimes gets only $20 a show. The last time Kanchan toured this region, as you and Rashid Pierkhan told me, she was paid $250 for her Bollywood shows."

I believed the way for us to establish Indo-Caribbean music as an industry, was to continue creating events around the music. The world was seeing that this music could be economically viable and stand on its own. Well-attended concerts would attract many new artists, producers, and technicians. This was how successful industries were raised. We must inspire and welcome others to it. I believed this was how the broken would rise.

CHAPTER 40

The journey is to the self.
Within lies the kingdom.

We started creating such an industry; it was the next stage of our collaboration. Our purpose.

On Moean's part, his purpose had its roots stretching back to 1947. As India became a free nation that year, thousands of miles away from the motherland, an Indian family was about to make strong inroads in Trinidad and Tobago. That year, Moean's brother, Kamaluddin Mohammed, had debuted on radio with an Indo-Caribbean program. Later, as Kamaluddin became involved with national political affairs in the country, Moean was given full control of the programs on Radio Trinidad.

By 1970, another brother, Shamshuddin Mohammed, started the people's program, *Mastana Bahar*, on television. It became one of the longest-running programs on television and the most popular Indo-Caribbean TV show in the nation.

In this environment, and with a strong commitment to his heritage, Moean became a record producer and distributor.

Over time, the next generation, his sons Sadro and Safi, daughter Aruna, and nephews Rafi, Jamal, and Khayal, among others, would take up and assist in these responsibilities.

They, like my family, had started in life as farmers.

Knowing full well the album could help us to jump-start the Indo-Caribbean entertainment industry, and celebrate the lives of all of its people, all who had toiled on the plantations and farm lands, we searched the calendar for the next Carnival Monday in Trinidad. We found it would be five months later, on February 18, 1985.

Carnival in Trinidad and Tobago is a competitive time with hundreds of promoters and artists vying for the public's attention. I personally never saw what others were doing as competition. I kept my focus on what I needed to do.

If this music could be celebrated in the midst of the African history of carnival, then this new music would forever find its place in any environment.

The envelope had to be pushed. We were so driven by this purpose, by this commitment to see the music continued to find its way into the fabric of this and other countries and ultimately emerge an industry. We decided to include Rashid Pierkhan from Suriname and Ramzan and our colleague Sunil Somair from Holland into our plan.

Instead of holding one outdoor stadium show in Port of Spain, Moean proposed that we go countrywide with fifteen indoor shows and a nationwide tour of Trinidad and Tobago.

Having set the first draft on the table, we then started the discussion.

"Moean, what's the average attendance for Indo-Caribbean shows in Trinidad?" I asked him.

"Well, as you know, it's around three hundred people."

The way Moean expressed the word "well," told me that my question had struck a chord. He sensed that things, the way he knew them, were about to change forever and perhaps would never be the same again. I was looking at a man whose past was at the precipice of change, and he was a participant in this change.

Knowing that people are more comfortable with things they are familiar with, I realized that if we were to make history, we would have to change the dialogue within which this music would rise.

When Moean was growing up, people attended Indo-Caribbean shows in small gatherings, by the roadside or under tents, calling it local music.

This was the history he knew. This is the history I lived growing up in Black Bush Polder. In this way, we were no different. Perhaps I was also leaving behind the same past.

However, culture, like the branches of a tree, is never a static thing, it keeps changing, it keeps evolving. And we are responsible for building bridges so those who would come after us can more easily cross.

Moean and his family had been advancing, changing, and growing. In this manner, they managed to grow the audience size at the shows. Hence, Moean's number of an average of around three hundred people per show was the number they were accustomed to.

My father had told me a man afraid to die is already dead. If I am afraid the past will kill the future, my future is already dead.

I must change the dialogue. I must bring him to his proverbial pedestal when he declared: "we are kings."

I asked, "And outdoors? Stadiums?"

Moean got up then sat down again. When he spoke, this time, he omitted the word, "well."

"The *Mastana Bahar* finals are the biggest. Although it is staged for television, it is held at a stadium, and it attracts a few thousand people. It is the biggest Indo-Caribbean show in the country, but it happens only one night a year."

As he spoke, it was as if a switch was turned on.

"Therefore, instead of one, let's do two. Two stadium shows; staging them back to back," I said.

And upon returning comfortably to sit upon his pedestal, Moean boldly added, "Yes, I agree, let's have two stadium shows and five countrywide shows."

CHAPTER 41

*The intuitive Being is a synergy
of the awakened senses.*

A few days later, I arrived in Bombay and checked into the Taj Hotel overlooking the Gateway of India.

Checking in at the Taj, I requested breakfast and the morning papers to be sent to my room by six. Although I had phoned Babla a few days before and told him that I would be in India to meet with him and Kanchan, I did not tell him exactly why or when that would happen.

As I was thumbing through the morning newspaper, I felt a sudden sensation in the palms of my hands, and upon turning to the next page, I found the reason. In the entertainment section one of the ads read: BABLA ORCHESTRA TODAY at 1:30 p.m.

I had first heard Kanchan in a cinema in Guyana thousands of miles from where I now was. Soon she would be performing in another cinema here in Bombay.

A small signboard on the pavement outside the cinema had the ticket price written in chalk. I calculated it to be around $1.00.

This prompted me to remember the words of my friends Rashid and Moean, "Rohit, you will have to be careful. They were paid around $250 for each of their Bollywood shows when they toured the Caribbean region some time back. You may not get much more than that should you bring them on a tour of the Caribbean. Be careful."

I asked the man at the ticket window what the capacity of the cinema was and he informed me it was four hundred seats.

In his answer, I could hear Hansrajee's words of wisdom, "Rohit, it's a tough business. You must be careful."

Even with a forty percent take of the gross, their pay here, on their home turf, would be around $160 per show.

My goal was to bring Indo-Caribbean music from where I had found it when there were only eighty-seven 45 RPM records in all of New York to an industry with sales from records and tours of one million dollars in a twelve-month period.

When this was accomplished, it would encourage many more potential producers, promoters, and artists to come into the Indo-Caribbean entertainment business. More entrepreneurial opportunities would become available to those with the ambition to enter the business and provide products and services such as lighting, sound and stage productions as well as the development of more venues for concerts. Such an industry would also attract more businesses to market and promote their brands. Seeing the potential of a new revenue stream, governments would also sponsor and encourage these talents.

Together, the broken, the Indo-Caribbean music industry, can rise.

I asked the man at the ticket window to send a message to Babla that someone would like to see him.

A few minutes later, Babla, in a light blue jacket, appeared with surprised eyes.

"Rohit you are in India," he exclaimed as we shook hands and embraced.

We started walking through a dimly lit area to backstage.

I noticed her first, standing and looking into a mirror.

"Kanchan guess who?" exclaimed Babla.

I walked into the frame of the mirror. There, our eyes met. Recognizing me by my picture on her album cover, she turned and our eyes met again as she took both of my hands. I had anticipated this day for many years.

Here she was, a unique talent that took rise in lands where music once stood behind boundaries.

"How was your journey?"

"All went well."

I then told her that I didn't want to disturb her while she got ready for her show.

She turned around to face the mirror and took a little step back to reveal a bit more of her dress and asked, "How is this color? Do they wear black on stage in the Caribbean?"

"Kanchan, the dress is fine. The color of light is black."

Her smile reappeared in the frame of the mirror, and she softly repeated, "The color of light is black."

"We must now turn on the switch for the light to reflect and shine upon it," I replied.

There was a momentary pause. She then insisted I have a seat, saying it was better for her to stand as she would soon be taking the stage to perform.

"I am so afraid," she said, "I don't know how I will be able to match the dance steps if I were to perform in the Caribbean again."

I looked up at a light bulb and said, "Kanchan, to turn on the lights, what do you need?"

Her eyes followed mine to the bulb and she replied, "We need a bulb."

I then told her of an old Caribbean saying, "Turn the bulb, and you will turn into a Caribbean dancer."

She laughed heartily then asked, "Is that it? Is that all that I need to do?"

"Yes, keep it simple, that's all you need to do."

At that moment, as if on cue, her name was announced for her to take the stage. She mimicked the action of turning a bulb. It lit a path for her to see, perhaps to the sugar belts of the Caribbean and even into another cinema.

CHAPTER 42

When people have a similar purpose, their thoughts fall in line.

I returned to Trinidad in November 1984. Some three months from then, Carnival Monday would take place.

Moean and I met around the clock. We brought in the Windsor Records team to our inner circle — people who were never afraid to voice strong opinions.

I broke the news to them we would be touring Kanchan across the country during the carnival season. Moean would pay me $75,000 for the rights to have the tour of the country. Further, it would cost at least that amount to cover other costs such as air travel, first-class accommodations, ground transportation, security, and meals, in addition to venue rentals, sound and light technicians, and government taxes. We would import the special effect laser lighting from the United States.

"We will have to keep tickets at a price to cover these expenses and make a profit," Moean told the team.

I noticed deflation in the eyes of the Windsor staff.

One of them said, "It's such a big opportunity to stage Kanchan in the country, why risk this opportunity by bringing her during carnival? Look at the great Bollywood superstar Amitabh Bachchan. He was paid $50,000 for his show, and look what a large crowd he got when he came here many months away from carnival. No Indian artist can do well here during the carnival."

Another warned, "Look, carnival is not an Indian thing and Indian people in this country will not want to be seen going to a show that seems to be part of the carnival."

Another continued, "And the very few Indians that do go to carnival will not pay exorbitant prices for a ticket when they can pay $10 or $20 for shows featuring many of the big soca-calypso artists."

We had carefully studied the manner in which both Afro and Indo Trinidadians came together and bought this album. While those on the outside may have seen a tree, Moean, Hansrajee, Sadro, and I saw the entire forest. The four of us saw a new Afro-Indo-Caribbean frontier.

In February 1985, the Windsor team and I arrived at Piarco International Airport to greet Kanchan and Babla along with their one-year-old daughter Neisha, Kanchan's mother, and their entourage of musicians.

The campaign on radio, television, and in the print media that started the month before had raised anticipation. This anticipation spilled over to the large, enthusiastic crowds that made their way to see Kanchan's arrival at the airport. An artist from India set foot in the land of soca, calypso, and the steelband. And she came for carnival.

The following evening, Kanchan, Babla, and I departed the Trinidad Hilton for a much-awaited press conference at Moean's sprawling residence. Every media personality in the country had requested a press pass to attend.

As we were making our way to Mohammed Ville that evening, large crowds and media personalities were already there ahead of us. The crowds, both Afro and Indo, were so large that they overflowed from the street to the balconies of neighboring homes. People were chanting, "Kanchan welcome to Trinidad."

The outpouring from the people of this country was so pure that Kanchan was overcome with emotion. Her tears flowed as she answered the questions from the press. Babla and I sat silently. Not so long ago, she had toured Trinidad, and these streets were empty to her, and the venues where she performed had only a handful of people in attendance. This was her rising moment.

Kanchan Dinkerao Mali was finally having her moment. Her journey to this moment was filled with a strong determination and unrelenting trials. I could very well relate.

Entertainment may be called show business. Its light may be glittering and bright. However, I was mindful of my responsibility, and that entertainment is an art reflecting the poetry of the people of a country, and it is, therefore, a human story.

When the people of a country come together to celebrate this poetry, as they did on the evening of the press conference, all burdens are lifted, and the path forward is lit by purpose.

CHAPTER 43

The joy we provide for the many multiplies within us infinitely.

A week after the press conference, around 5 p.m., a few feet were seen walking past the turnstiles and shortly after that, the foot traffic developed into a slow tempo.

The switches were soon turned on, and the dark bulbs that hung hundreds of feet above the Jean Pierre Complex in Port of Spain reflected bright lights.

Two hours before showtime, the line of concertgoers extended and curved around the corner from the venue entrance.

Moean walked from the center aisle directly to the stage where I held discussions with the stagehands, settling last-minute details and finishing touches for the production.

He whispered into my ear, "Rohit, it's happening."

At 9 p.m., the baritone voice that held the nation still on the radio for many years resonated through the speakers at the

Jean Pierre Complex. Moean recited the couplet that he always started his radio show with.

Moments after that, I walked with Kanchan out of her dressing room. The second the crowds caught sight of her, the complex erupted into an electrifying welcome. Babla and his orchestra picked up the tempo on stage, and the sound of the crowd was deafening.

They cheered to the rhythm of her walk, serenading her long journey to the stage. The special effects fog from the stage of the complex lifted to rise to the sky carrying with it traces of laser light beams to illuminate the Trinidadian skyline.

Nearby at the Holiday Inn car park, the bright lights of the show of soca and calypso stars performing there also took rise. The lights and sounds from the two venues rose and reflected the heritages and people of this island — the descendants of the people who came by ship.

As intermission neared before the climax of the show's first half, I walked onto the stage and whispered something to Kanchan to which she nodded in response. Upon my walk back across the stage, a gentleman got up from his front-row seat, stretched over and shook my hand.

He started speaking but realized he couldn't hear his own words over the deafening sound in the complex, so he motioned that he would call me. I had never seen this man before.

Early the following day, the Hilton front desk rang my room, informing me a gentleman from the advertising agency McCann Erickson was at the front desk inquiring about the earliest time he could have a meeting with me.

As I exited the elevator, a man extended his hand to me. It was the same gentleman from the front row at the show.

Over coffee, I learned the agency he represented had its roots stretching back to the beginning of the century. By the 1930s, McCann Erickson had grown to a full-service advertising agency in the United States with offices in many other countries.

Over time, McCann Erickson helped shape the lifestyle campaigns for iconic brands such as Coca-Cola, "It's the real thing," MasterCard, "There are some things money can't buy. For everything else, there's MasterCard," and Esso, "Put a tiger in your tank."

In 1973, among other campaigns that featured celebrities, they came up with the "Because I'm worth it" campaign for L'Oréal, featuring three well-known women personalities: Meredith Baxter, Joanne Dusseau, and Cybill Shepherd.

Should we make a deal on this day over coffee, Kanchan would join the illustrious elite roster of McCann Erickson personalities.

The McCann Erickson executive advised me they paid $500 to well-known Caribbean personalities appearing in their regional campaigns. He asked me if I would consider having Kanchan appear in one of their advertisements. I calmly told him no.

He then offered me twice as much and received the same response.

At that moment, one of our musicians walked by. I invited him to join us and asked the waitress to bring a third cup of coffee.

The executive appeared slightly baffled that I randomly invited someone else to sit in on our meeting. Perhaps he thought I was not taking his offer seriously. Little did he know that the third cup of coffee could help him accomplish his goal.

"You know, Mr. Jagessar, although I am an Afro Trinidadian, with no understanding of Hindi, I sat through that entire show last night — from the very beginning to the very end — and I can't stop thinking of what an electrifying experience it was. I have never seen such a broad cross-section of people at any show in this country before. People from all walks of life just love her."

"Let's do a deal for $10,000," I told him.

Within the space of a few hours, they shot the ad.

Under the terms of our agreement, McCann Erickson showed me the final cut of the ad for my approval. There she was on the screen smiling while changing the diaper of her little daughter, Neisha. She then picked her up and sang the words reflecting the country's most popular song *Kuchh Gadbad Hai*. Johnson & Johnson appeared across the screen.

"Approved!"

A Fortune 500 American company was now officially invested in the music. With the resounding success of the first show at the Jean Pierre Complex, there was now a real chance for Indo-Caribbean music.

After our show at the complex, word spread like wildfire across the country and by the time we arrived at Skinner's Park in San Fernando for our second show, crowds even larger than the night before made their way into the stadium. That night, Skinner's Park recorded one of the biggest crowds in its storied history.

Over the next several days, we toured the countryside and concluded the seven shows that we had set out to accomplish.

It was time to go home.

At the end of the tour of Trinidad and Tobago, Moean and his family sat with me, reminiscing about all we had accomplished over the last five years. That evening, as Moean was taking me back to the Hilton, I suggested we make a short detour to the Holiday Inn and take our familiar seats poolside. It was here we had sat and set our goals. We now returned to determine how those goals were progressing.

Album sales across the entire Caribbean region and revenue from concert tickets across Trinidad and Tobago had brought us across the halfway mark of our goal of one million dollars in twelve months.

A few days later, I bid farewell to my family in Trinidad and boarded the BWIA aircraft with Kanchan and Babla for New York.

After spending time in rehearsals for our next album, *Ab Na Jaibay - Live 1985*, they all boarded an Air India aircraft and returned to India.

CHAPTER 44

You are a reflection of your inspiration.

Fueled by complete faith and belief that I could create an Indo-Caribbean music industry and that all would share in the music, it was time for me to return to my home for the tour of Guyana.

I had moved from Black Bush Polder to the United States when I was fifteen years old. I was now a twenty-four-year-old record producer and promoter with the number-one album in the region.

The album had topped the charts in many countries since its release in 1984, and a year later, our tour brought us to Guyana, where we would perform four shows at three different outdoor venues.

The first show was scheduled to be held at Albion, a well-known sugar belt. Some thirty minutes from there was where I grew up in Black Bush Polder. Just a few minutes away was the Corentyne Education College in Rose Hall Town where I went to high school from ages twelve to fourteen. The Roopmahal Cinema, where I first heard her voice was only a few miles from Albion.

On the day of the show at the Sports Complex in Albion, I scheduled the soundcheck for nine in the morning before the intense heat of the midday sun. Under the influence of the full nostalgia of my not-too-distant youth, I arrived three hours early and sat in the wooden stands.

From that perch, I saw the early morning sunrise as it opened its panoramic view of Albion and the sugar belt beyond. As I sat there in the cool morning air, I thought back on my life in this part of the world.

My mother was born at the nearby Number 19 Village in the Cumberland area of this very county of Berbice. My father was born here in Albion and moved with his parents and the rest of his family to Friendship Village and later with us, his own family, to Black Bush Polder.

How different would my life be if I had never left Black Bush Polder? Would they still accept me as one of their own?

My mother once told me some plants could not grow forever in a single pot. They must be uprooted and placed in new soil. This way, they can continue growing and thriving to their full potential. She told me only those who risk the unknown are courageous and that luck favors the brave.

My life had truly been one of great luck. I had risked much in my young life and knew what it was to be brave. As I sat in the stands, these thoughts swirled in my mind.

The show was scheduled to begin at seven that evening. The county had declared the day a holiday to allow students and workers from and around the sugar belt to attend the show.

As the morning progressed, the sound of *Kuchh Gadbad Hai* came floating up into the stands from cars driving by on the main road nearby.

The atmosphere appeared festive. Although it was now a year since I released it, it became apparent the song remained their favorite song.

I took this as a sign of confirmation it would be the perfect homecoming.

Shortly after noon, long lines formed in front of the makeshift ticket window, and by 4:00 p.m. the lines extended from the entrance and stretched around all the way to the main road. Soon, there was no space left to stand in the cricket ground where the show was scheduled to take place.

One of the promoters of the show, Anand Persaud, the owner of Strand De Luxe cinema, came backstage and told me that there was no room even for one more person to stand in the venue. One of the groundsmen informed me that this was the largest crowd the Albion Sports Complex had ever seen.

Many of my former neighbors, classmates, and teachers from Black Bush Polder and the neighboring Rose Hall Town were among this crowd. They had gathered at the front of the performance stage, waiting to welcome me back home.

Although my life was now so different than theirs, the welcome they gave me was pure love, joy, and happiness. They looked the same as I remembered them nine years earlier and gave me a glimpse of what my life would have been like had I remained in Guyana.

They, in turn, witnessed the change in me and saw that despite all adversity, it was possible to scale the highest of mountains. One could rise even from the backlands of Black Bush Polder.

I asked them to wait where they were, that I had a surprise for them, and walked calmly back to the dressing room, bringing the shining stars of the night — Kanchan and Babla.

The excitement of my friends was overwhelming. The huge crowd across the grounds looked at them with envy. It was a moment and experience I will always remember. After we embraced and said our goodbyes, they took their seats in the crowd.

Nothing more was needed. They had shown me what life would have been had I not climbed the mountain, and I had shown them what life could be once they take the first step toward it.

That night, as I lay in bed in my hotel room, I reflected on the many fortunes of my life. The intuition that had risen in consciousness that had connected me to the voice in the cinema nine years earlier, the journey to her and the purpose for all to join together through our music.

After that night, I would never again wonder about my home. In truth, I had never left it behind nor been forgotten by those who still lived there. I was still that little boy from Black Bush Polder, and these were still my friends.

The other memory I carry from that trip was my first meeting with President Burnham's number two, Guyana's then Prime Minister Hugh Desmond Hoyte. Anand Persaud had requested that I pay a courtesy call to the prime minister's office. I invited Kanchan and Babla to accompany me. He welcomed us warmly.

"Mr. Jagessar, I heard you now live in the United States. Where exactly in Guyana are you from?" he asked with an outstretched hand.

"Black Bush Polder, sir," I responded and felt the grip of his handshake tighten.

The statesman momentarily reached deep into his thoughts then turned to his assistant, realizing this was an opportune moment to show him that all was possible.

He then turned and looked me in the eyes and proudly said, "See, a boy from our backlands has risen this high at such a young age. Thank you Mr. Jagessar, your music is bringing all the people of our country together as one. Thank you for this."

Within three months of this conversation, President Burnham was dead, and Prime Minister Hoyte was sworn in as the new President of the Cooperative Republic of Guyana.

Over the next several days, we toured the country far and wide. The tour of Guyana attracted tens of thousands of people.

CHAPTER 45

The next time you look up to someone, look higher and you will see yourself.

A few days later, we arrived in Suriname, where Rashid Pierkhan and his team awaited us at the airport in Paramaribo.

As a security detail escorted us from the airport to the Torarica Hotel in Paramaribo that afternoon, people enthusiastically lined the streets. Kanchan regally returned their waves.

It was then, the full meaning of Moean's words, we are kings, dawned on me. What he foresaw was that a queen was about to reign. His vision had been realized.

A few days later, we continued the journey, this time from the hotel toward the venue. Having been caught in the traffic leading to the Albion Sports Complex, when the motorcade to the show was held up for more than two hours by crowds lining the streets, this time I decided we should all leave the hotel early in the morning and stay closer to the venue.

Fans standing in front of their modest homes waved as the motorcade moved slowly along the Paramaribo roadway.

"Kanchan, we will see you tonight. We will be there to see you," they chanted.

Like Guyana, Suriname was a country with a small population of around half a million people, of which half lived in and around Paramaribo.

There were great challenges for promoters looking to bring people to their shows when a population was as sparse as this. For an event to be successful and have a sizable crowd, a promoter had to bring people from far and wide.

It was a time when even the mail was extremely slow. The turnaround time for sending a letter from the United States to Moean or Rashid in the Caribbean or to my distributors in Europe or Asia and receiving their response could be as long as two months. Communication by telephone was expensive, and international calls had to be prebooked as long as forty-eight hours ahead of time.

More specifically, people in this region had to travel long distances to a show venue and risked facing a lack of transportation in returning home after the show, especially late in the night. Blackouts in the night could pose a danger to patrons returning late at night after an event. This was especially true for those traveling back to distant rural areas of the country.

Soon the motorcade to the venue banked a smooth turn, causing the sight of the modest homes with people lining in front to fall away. Ahead of us, we saw a sea of people.

It was ten hours before showtime. Kanchan looked at me.

"The show is sold out. They must be looking for tickets," I calmly settled her mind.

To avoid the crowd of fans, security exited the main road and detoured onto smaller back roads to arrive at the bungalows that Rashid had prearranged for us.

The show was scheduled for eight that evening, and at four I left the bungalows and started walking back to the main road. As the wind blew through the lower branches of the trees lining the road, I could spot people and hear the commotion. In the short distance ahead were thousands of her fans, all continuing to try and buy tickets for a show that had been sold out for many weeks already.

Two hours before showtime, I directed security to go to the bungalows and carefully escort Kanchan, Babla, and the musicians to the venue.

Many years later, I spoke to a neighbor from Black Bush Polder who had been there. He was hoping to meet me so I would get him into the show. Once there, he soon realized that in order for him to do so, he would first have to get my attention.

He described the forty security and police personnel surrounding our group, trying with all of their might to prevent the crowd from crashing the barriers as Kanchan and Babla made their way to the backstage door.

He told me that because he knew me, he felt a sense of responsibility for our safety in the country where he now lived. He leaped over the barriers, trying to pull people away from us. He was quickly returned, even further from where he had started, as security picked him up and tossed him back.

The last time he had seen me, I wore rags, working on the farm in Black Bush Polder. It was hard to fathom, he said, how a man could rise from the backlands of Guyana to create a shining night like this in Suriname.

That night, Kanchan took to the stage and rewarded the audience with one of the best performances on the tour.

After the show, we returned to the bungalows. As the team unwound and had dinner, I stood quietly by a window, looking out far into the darkness and said a silent prayer that all who came from near and far would return home safely.

The day after the next show, we arrived at a school for the blind. Kanchan's mother, the wisest of us all, led the way. She approached the students with extended arms, gently touching their faces. Soon they all grew quiet, almost in a trance of admiration from the feeling of a motherly touch.

Kanchan followed her mother. Her touch brought smiles to their faces, and the children started clapping their hands. Kanchan signaled for Babla to play the drums and to join in their rhythm. Those who saw the brightest, danced the afternoon away to their heart's delight.

CHAPTER 46

*Happiness is at the doorstep of observation.
Open the door and let it in.*

I n May of 1985, we arrived to play to my home crowd in New York City. It was the first show of the North American leg of the tour.

This was a time when many new arrivals to North America were earning minimum wage or less.

The newly arrived were not new to struggles. Their ancestors had been enslaved or indentured, shipped to colonies far and wide, and forced into labor. In countries such as Guyana and Suriname, they themselves were shackled under authoritarian and dictatorial regimes. They were left fighting for survival.

They were now immigrants to yet another place. This time, it was one of their choosing. Perhaps it was for the first time they were given agency over their lives. And they weren't going to allow this chance to pass them by. They held the opportunity with both hands. They held steadfastly to it.

It was either buying a record and going to a show or stretching every coin to save for their newly founded American dream — educating their children and owning a home.

Therefore, Afro- and Indo-Caribbean shows at the time were attended by very few, numbering between fifty and three hundred people.

"Rohit, wherever you may go, always remember should you want something to continue growing, you must keep on cultivating it," my mother would tell me.

That is exactly what I was doing, and now it was growing and blossoming to see this new day. But I did not know how much growth I had awakened in the expats from our recent tour of the Caribbean. Had the Caribbean wind reached the expat shores?

As it turned out, both Afro-and Indo-Caribbean expats in North America were closely following the news of our tour of the Caribbean through their weekly newspapers from back home. The news was so compelling that they were eagerly waiting for their turn.

Until now, they had yet to experience a sold-out Indo-Caribbean show in New York. Would I be able to deliver the experience of a sold-out show to them?

Many months earlier, I had booked the Colden Center at Queens College, an upscale venue with a capacity of 2,143 seats located in Queens, where most Indo Caribbeans lived.

Days leading to the event, I made a round of calls to stores selling the tickets. I reached eight of the nine stores selling tickets.

Their response was in the same tone of excitement, "Mr. Rohit, we have been trying to reach you. Your phone is always busy. We don't have a single ticket left. We need more."

I sat back in my chair, realizing what this moment meant for this music and its people. This day would be a monumental accomplishment if I got the same response from the one remaining store.

I reached for my phone and made the call. "Mr. Rohit, we have sixteen tickets remaining, and we are holding them for a family that's on their way to pick them up. We do not have any more."

A few days later, I walked up the steps leading to the doors of the Colden Center some eight hours before showtime, and that's when I saw it.

ROHIT JAGESSAR PRESENTS
LIVE TONIGHT
KANCHAN & BABLA
SOLD OUT

The environment at the Colden Center that evening was electric. Before the show started fans were talking among themselves.

"We have never seen a crowd like this for any Indo-Caribbean show."

"This is history."

"Wow. Look how many people. This place is full."

"Look how everyone is dressed up."

"Kanchan, she did it."

At eight sharp, a trace of music started, it took rise, and filled the auditorium with increasing volume. The curtains parted and an Indo-Caribbean show started on time — a new experience for all in attendance.

Babla led the musicians through a short warm-up with the theme music followed by a few Bollywood songs, all performed by our warm-up act.

As this short set got underway, I waited knowing the audience would soon be searching the sides of those curtains. The emcee, at center stage, thunderously announced her name; yet she was nowhere to be seen.

The music stopped. There was a silence. The anticipation grew. Still, she was nowhere to be seen.

The emcee tightened his grip on the microphone, loosened the knot of his tie, and motioned for the spotlight to be shown through the crowd. All heads turned, following the spotlight far into the darkness at the back of the auditorium. The spotlight found her. Her shining gown glittered as she walked from the back toward the stage bathing in the spotlight.

She smiled, waved, and greeted them in their uproarious cheers and applause while I walked with her making our way to the stage.

Many years later, I am told those in attendance still feel the excitement of that magical moment. Over the course of five shows we staged in New York that month — the one at the Colden Center, three at Madison Square Garden and one dance party — more than sixteen thousand people attended.

The tour continued to play before sold-out audiences at the prestigious Roy Thomson Hall in Toronto, followed by a stopover in Montreal.

CHAPTER 47

The one who listens silently has potential.

We returned to India, and it was time to record again. These recording sessions yielded four best-selling singles released for Christmas 1985.

Tiny Winey
Ai Ai O
Kuchh Kuchh Baby
Bolo Bolo

In the new year, I recorded B sides in New York then compiled them with the best-selling singles into an album. Demand was so strong that I decided we should tour this album and continue finding ways to expand Indo-Caribbean music.

While Kanchan and Babla had now risen to stardom in Indo- and Afro-Caribbean markets, Babla continued to be popular in India with his Dandiya recordings — a dance form celebrating the festival of Navratri. Although Navratri spans nine nights, the Dandiya festivities can last for as long as three weeks, and during these weeks, Babla played to sold-out audiences in India, year after year.

At the time, Indo-Caribbean expats in the United States lived mainly in New York, with a few in New Jersey, Georgia, Minnesota, and Florida. How could I expand the Indo-Caribbean music market across the United States when few Indo Caribbeans lived outside of New York?

With Babla's Dandiya sensation in India, I saw a path to expand the audience for Indo-Caribbean music in America. I had in mind the wisdom of my father's explanation of Einstein's theory of relativity how one thing works with the other. I intended to market the show as a Dandiya and variety music show to the Indian expats scattered across America and introduce them to a segment of Indo-Caribbean music.

With a few Indo-Caribbeans also scattered in some of the same cities and towns, I thought I could scrape together people from both communities and make something happen. I knew for sure that the people scattered in these towns longed for anything belonging to their heritage.

The Indian expats who moved to these smaller towns across America were professionals — scientists, doctors, nurses, and engineers. In addition to these professionals, a few Indian expats owned hotels and other businesses. How would I, a Guyanese, reach these Indian expats, now living across America?

India Abroad, the leading Indian newspaper, was published weekly from New York by Gopal Raju, a visionary expat from India. Each week Indians across the country eagerly anticipated receiving it and news from the motherland.

I placed an ad in *India Abroad* informing readers across the country that Kanchan and Babla would soon be touring America and the show was available to them should they be interested in hosting it in their town.

A few days later, my phone rang. It was a gentleman from Nashville, Tennessee. After exchanging pleasantries, he asked where I was from.

"I am from Guyana."

"Guyana? How do you know Kanchan and Babla? Are you sure you have the rights to sell this show? I mean don't get me wrong. I am sure you understand my skepticism. After all, I can't just do business with someone I don't even know. I mean how does a guy from Guyana have the rights to sell an Indian show from India?"

"How long have you been living in Nashville?" I asked him.

"More than fifteen years," he responded.

"Who is your favorite Nashville-based musician?"

Oh, I love saxophone. Definitely, it's Ace. Ace Cannon."

"Do you know Ace?" I asked him.

"Not personally," he responded.

"Would you like to meet Ace?"

"No way. How will I get to meet Ace Cannon? He is a big star."

I asked him for his number and told him I would ask Ace to give him a call. I thought after a call from Ace, we might be in a better position to negotiate.

An hour later, Raman Patel, my new friend from Nashville, called me again. This time he was excited.

"Mr. Jagessar, you have made a dream come true. My wife and I were on the phone with him for almost an hour. I didn't tell you how we came to love Ace Cannon. When we got married, there were no Indian DJs here to play music, so we hired an American DJ and he recommended an Ace Cannon piece for our first dance. This is how we fell in love with his music."

"You buy the show, and when I come to Nashville, Ace will be at your show." I told him.

"Mr. Jagessar, we are now starting to know each other. Let me tell you, I can sell at least four shows for you. I have friends in the Indian and Gujarati Associations here in Nashville and in Alabama, North Carolina, and Georgia. And even in other states. But I'll be honest, there are only around 250 families in each of the Associations. However, we can get around $51 per ticket."

He wanted me to come up with a reasonable price for the shows and guaranteed he could sell a minimum of four shows.

My Nashville friend advised me that with the small population we could sell around three tickets per household or seven hundred and fifty tickets in each of the small towns.

"That would mean every family would have to attend," I said.

"Exactly. We are living far away from everything. We crave anything Indian we can get our hands on. Every one of us supports any and everything the Indian and Gujarati Associations do."

Having sensed that this gentleman was straightforward, it became easy for us to make decisions together. He was now familiar with an Indo Caribbean, and I asked him if there were people from the Caribbean in his markets.

"Yes, there are a few," he told me.

"And do they shop at the same Indian stores as you?"

"Yes," he said. "I see a few of them at the stores when my wife and I go shopping. But not many."

"Well, good then. I will send you a few large posters to place prominently at those locations so they too will know about the show," I told him.

We ended the call agreeing I would send him the necessary paperwork.

Indo-Caribbean music was about to modestly echo across the American heartland and beyond. I rented a tour bus, calling it the Indo-Caribbean Mobile, and in a few weeks, we headed for Nashville.

After the group took in some sightseeing along the way, we arrived in Nashville a few days before the show. My friend hosted a welcome party at his home with a small gathering.

We were enjoying ourselves at the small party, when the doorbell rang. Our host looked around; no one else was expected. He opened the door and there stood the great American musician, Ace Cannon. It was Ace's turn to tell him and his wife how we met and formed a business relationship. I had released two of his albums in the expat Caribbean market the year before.

The show in Nashville was a synergy of Dandiya, popular Bollywood, and Indo-Caribbean music. I had arranged the list of songs Kanchan would be performing, in such an order as to lure the audience from familiar ground to music that was until then unknown to them.

My plan was for the first forty-five minutes to be a blend of Dandiya and Bollywood. As the momentum rose, the music would lead Kanchan directly into *Kaise Bani* and climax just before the intermission with *Kuchh Gadbad Hai*.

The idea was to have the Indian expats in attendance buy Indo-Caribbean albums.

As Kanchan sang through the Dandiya and Bollywood segment, there was little indication from the audience how they were feeling. They sat attentively and clapped politely at the end of each song. I realized that for the Indo-Caribbean songs to have the effect I wanted, there would have to be some momentum and energy created.

Soon Kanchan reached a song that was set for the forty-minute mark of the show. It was the Bollywood song that lit the whole idea that day in the cinema in Guyana. She was singing it here in an auditorium in Nashville.

As the Bollywood rhythm got underway, I signaled to her from the side of the stage to make her next song the beginning of our Indo-Caribbean set, as planned. An Indian woman was about to sing Indo-Caribbean songs — music that moves to its own rhythm — to Indian expats that had never before experienced it.

We had ventured far into the heartland of America. And I wanted them to dance. I wanted this polite audience to be moved by the music, then to buy the Indo-Caribbean albums in the lobby and bring them home where this music would live and breathe. A new beginning.

Kanchan's brother, also from India, loved to dance to Indo-Caribbean songs. I pulled him aside and had a few words with him. As the Bollywood song was coming to an end, he took to the stage, and became the surprise element first to both Kanchan and Babla. They laughed at his antics, dancing before the next song even started. A man dancing without music.

Upon seeing a man dancing without any music, the audience responded. The auditorium loosened its tightly held grip, and as Kanchan got into the Indo-Caribbean set, their energy flowed freely. During intermission, they headed straight to the albums that stood awaiting them in the lobby.

It soon became evident to me that Indo-Caribbean music became the outlet that these busy, hardworking Indian expats very much needed. These were men and women who toiled year in and year out to become professionals and immediately after their education, they went straight to the workforce. Indo-Caribbean music is the music of the people who came by ship.

It is music deeply rooted in a work environment purposefully to numb the pangs of hard work. Whether you were a doctor or a cane-cutter, this was something you understood.

Indo-Caribbean music had now recorded its first income from Indian expats in a market that until then had no idea of its existence.

During the tour, Indo-Caribbean music played to small audiences in sixteen towns and cities, stretching from Washington, DC, across the Carolinas, into the American heartland, and westward to places such as Los Angeles and San Francisco.

Indo-Caribbean music crossed the one million dollar mark within those twelve months.

After nearly two exhausting but exhilarating months on the road across America, we returned to New York.

That night, as the group was checking in at the hotel, Kanchan's mother took me by the hand and said, "Rohit, thank you my son, you have done a lot for my daughter, you have made her and all of our dreams come true. I wish her father was still with us in this world. I know he is watching over all of us, smiling that our daughter met you, a brother that has helped her climb to such heights. He is watching over all of us."

CHAPTER 48

The journey is to Moksha.

Before they left for India in the summer of 1986 following our successful tour across the United States, I invited Babla for a discussion regarding the next phase of their careers.

We sat over coffee in the lobby restaurant of the Paramount Hotel. Often our meetings went on for hours as we discussed many music ideas. It was not to be on this day.

Earlier in the day, my friend Alphonsus Cassell, popularly known as Arrow, the internationally acclaimed soca and calypso recording artist, had called wondering if I could meet with him over coffee in the city. He had been working on a new album and wanted to share the demo recording with me to see if I would be willing to do a Hindi cover with Kanchan and Babla.

By then, I had released albums featuring two of his soca hits in Hindi — *Kuchh Gadbad Hai (Hot Hot Hot)* and *Tiny Winey*. Arrow himself was a big fan of these recordings especially since they helped keep his name in the spotlight long after he had originally recorded these songs. These Hindi covers also helped to extend and sustain his name into Asia. I told him it was not the right time to do a Hindi cover of his new song.

After having coffee with Arrow, I walked across to the Paramount and sat with Babla. I shared a funny story Arrow had told me earlier that day, we had a good laugh, and whatever tiredness was evident from our long tour was gone. However, I noticed, as our conversation continued, that he seemed uncharacteristically preoccupied.

"Does Arrow have any new songs we can cover?" he asked.

"He's working on new material, but I told him not now."

"Any idea what we are going to record next?" he asked.

"Nothing." I said. "We should record nothing."

"Nothing?"

Knowing that he was a big fan of the Latin American rhythm musician Tito Puente, I asked him, "If Tito was playing at the Garden would you go see him?"

"Of course. I will be the first one there," he responded.

"And if he plays every day will you still go see him?"

"Every day? How could I go every day, man? One or two times is sufficient. After that, it becomes too predictable. Don't you think?"

If the great fan of Tito, sitting across from me, would ever view his idol as predictable, he too should see recording an album similar to all we had made before would make us predictable.

After sharing these reflections, I pointedly told him that we must explore and innovate fresh ideas. We must give the people a newer, fresher, and greater experience. And this new music should be of a deeper poetic expression — music that uplifts the people.

We must look for ways to rise in poetry — in lyrical content — the next time we make a record. And to do this, we would need to take a year and a half off from tours to focus on recording to further empower and strengthen Indo-Caribbean music.

As he listened, I sensed that he was struggling and while I sensed that his struggle was about my idea, what he said next made his position clear.

"Someone was here last night. They came to see me. They are offering me a lot of money to work and record directly with them."

The room fell silent.

The poetry that I wanted was for the people who came by ship. Those people were my ancestors, not his. It was time for me to walk the path of my people — the path of my purpose.

CHAPTER 49

*I will create the next moment
to be what I want it to be.*

As I walked the familiar streets of the great city that summer day, I noticed the bright signage of my old stomping ground, the Sam Goody record store. This was the American record store I frequented while sweeping the floors at the factory.

I entered Sam Goody and was happy to see that the international section had grown. They had allocated many more record bins for it, and it now dawned on me that getting my records into these mainstream record stores may not be the challenge it once seemed. Now was the time.

But why would I want my records in a store if I did not have a way to tell people they were available there? I did not want my records gathering dust. Records on store shelves are meant to be sold, taken home and heard. So how do I market my records to mainstream America once I find a way to get them in the record bins of mainstream American record stores?

The college student demographic was hugely influenced by the rise of international music in America and this cultural phenomenon. This demographic led a new movement some two decades after the Woodstock era. Their choice of music was frequently the international genre. And college radio stations often played this music. Getting them to play my records was like asking friends.

As I reflected, I recalled that I had purchased a publication that had listed every college radio station in the United States. It was sitting in my office, and time for me to open it.

The previous year, while touring, I came up with the idea of having Bollywood soundtracks more widely distributed in the United States. However, EMI India, the copyright holder of more than ninety percent of Bollywood music at the time, was unable to back my plan.

Over the years, consumers across India have bought both records and radios made by EMI India. However, over time, imported radios made of cheaper stylish-looking plastic casings overtook radios made locally with the more expensive wooden casings. The new plastic radios were imported from China, causing EMI India, the manufacturer of the wooden radios, to find few or no buyers. In addition, EMI India was forced by the labor unions to retain all of the employees hired to make these wooden radios.

Burdened with such an expense and with declining sales for their wooden radios, EMI India soon found itself staring in the face of closing, inadvertently affecting the manufacturing of their records as well.

I phoned my friend at EMI's executive headquarters in London, and we came up with a plan to work around the situation in India. I would manufacture selected Bollywood albums in the United States for the North American market.

Soon, I had six Hamilton injection molding presses installed to manufacture records at a facility in Franklin Lakes, New Jersey. This location became my new office as well. My friend T.R. Varadachary, who was looking for office space, joined me there.

The first time T.R. Varadachary contacted me was in 1983. He told me he imported shrimp from Brazil, but the company mistakenly shipped him a strange-looking fish, and he didn't know what to do with it. The company told him it was a popular fish with the Caribbean expat population and he should explore this market. Being from India, he had no clue where to even begin.

I had a good idea of the type of fish he was talking about. The time I fished the pond in our rice fields in Black Bush Polder, I caught this specific type of fish.

"Is it Hassar?" I asked.

"Yes. Yes. How did you guess?" He grew optimistic.

"How much do you have?"

"Around one hundred tons," he replied.

"That's $300,000. You have $300,000 sitting in cold storage."

"Can you help me out?" he asked.

T.R. spent most of his working years as a banker and was appointed Chairman of State Bank of India, India's largest banking institution, by the then Prime Minister Indira Gandhi, when she had declared a state of emergency. Upon retirement in 1977, T.R. moved from India to New York with his wife, and they started a small business importing brake pads from India and seafood from Brazil.

As the three of us sat over coffee, the thought entered my mind that it was only a few days ago that I felt the need to raise capital and here I was sitting with a man who spent all of his life in the business of finance.

We spent several hours talking about our family, beliefs, and backgrounds and established a relationship of mutual respect, very much like father and son.

We agreed that I would help him unload his inventory sitting in cold storage. In exchange, he would extend to me a credit line of around $300,000 if I ever needed it. We made the deal on a handshake. No written document was necessary.

As I was going over the list of college stations with my employees, one of them who knew I once held concerts with reggae-dancehall artist Yellowman at Madison Square Garden, informed me Yellowman was free from his contract with CBS. As I allowed that information to settle in, I recalled my words to Yellowman on that day at Madison Square Garden when I told him that someday I would be distributing his records.

We identified several hundred college radio stations, and my team began the task of packaging copies into mailers of Kanchan's compilation Indo-Caribbean album that featured *Kuchh Gadbad Hai*.

Mailing records to radio stations did not mean they would be played. I needed a connection. I dug deeper into the college radio publication and found a name.

Loren Chaidez immediately told me of the challenges of getting a record into the American stores. If I could accomplish this, his team would call the college radio station DJs and program directors to push my record and add it to the playlist.

Once my record was on the playlist, I would receive a weekly report on the airplay it received from each of these stations. I would also receive copies of their Top 10 charts.

I began my efforts to get my records into American stores. And I told my new record promoter friend I would give him the green light to contact the college radio stations once I had accomplished this.

What stood out to me was not only were there no Indo-Caribbean titles on the American shelves, there were hardly any Afro-Caribbean albums in these stores as well. And almost none on the CD configuration. The one or two that existed were from the major record labels such as CBS and Atlantic records. Afro-Caribbean record labels had not stretched their dreams sufficiently either.

Should I get the American record stores' attention, then both Afro- and Indo-Caribbean records would adorn the shelves of mainstream American homes.

CHAPTER 50

Imagine your journey. It is in the palm of your hands. Feel it within.

The sales people in the record stores had become familiar with my inquisitive presence. Many were still working there from the time when I swept the floor in the factory and were friendly with me. I was the curious guy who asked about their experiences. Not only about their experience selling records but also the experience of the records themselves.

A record had a life. Its journey started from its conception in the minds of producers, poets, composers, musicians, and singers to the day of its realization.

Ultimately, consumers would hold a record and either put it back or purchase it and take it home.

With the heightened interest in international music in America at the time, people, mainly my target demographic, the college students, would crowd around this section in the record store.

The shoppers would ask store employees questions such as whether they heard a specific song on the college radio last night and if they had it in stock. I listened when they asked if the international titles were also available on the CD configuration. Employees told me the store managers made it mandatory for them to listen to these college radio stations to familiarize themselves with the songs they played.

The record store employees told me that to get my records into mainstream record stores such as theirs, I would have to go through distributors. They cautioned me since no other Indo-Caribbean records were on the American shelves, no distributor had anything to go by. No one knew if the Indo-Caribbean records would sell in the mainstream stores.

I felt a familiar tingle in the palms of my hands, one similar to what I had felt when I first heard her voice. And while she was on another journey now, and I on mine, we still had all the records we had made together. I felt Indo-Caribbean music, the music of the people who came by ship, the music of my ancestors, was now on the precipice of making its debut on the American record store shelves.

I decided my strategy would be to call the smallest distributors first to rehearse until such a time when I would be ready to call the big ones. And so I began.

"How do I pronounce your name? Is it Robit?"

"It's Rohit," I replied.

"Oh Roheet," they would continue.

"It's Rohit," I would say.

With the pronunciation of my name out of the way, I would tell them why I was calling.

"You need to speak with one of the buyers."

Buyers, it seemed, held the solution I sought.

"Okay, so let me speak with one of your buyers," I would say.

"Does he know you?" they would insist.

And to ceremoniously get rid of me, they would say, "Okay leave a message, and I will get it to one of the buyers."

I was not discouraged. I had already decided to make this a three-step process. I would rehearse by calling the smallest distributors, then go on to the midsize ones and ultimately the largest ones.

Once I got familiar with the American lingo, I upped the ante. I found a distributor that was a bit larger, located in Hawaii.

This time while the receptionist spoke American, she also spoke in a familiar manner that had strains of my background. I felt at ease, and I sensed that she felt the same and wanted to be helpful.

Perhaps, she had similar experiences when speaking with the mainstream industry personalities. As we settled into a real conversation, her heritage spoke to mine and I found the guidance I was looking for. I was ready to call the big players.

One of America's largest record distributors at the time was Schwartz Brothers, located in Washington, DC. They distributed labels such as CBS, Columbia, Warner Brothers, Elektra, Atlantic, A&M, Capitol, and many others.

My rehearsals had prepared me well.

"Does he know you?" asked the receptionist.

I then started speaking American.

"Well, if you put me through to him, he will get to know me."

She laughed. Not leaving anything to chance, before she put me on hold, I reinforced what I had just said.

"Please tell your buyer I have the next Yellowman album."

She put me through.

With a promise that I would ship the new Yellowman album when its street date became known, I arranged to have Indo-Caribbean records in 1,800 mainstream record stores across the United States and shipped across the ocean to reach mainstream record store shelves in places such as Canada, Japan, England, France, Germany, Spain, Belgium, Holland, Luxemburg, Australia, and New Zealand.

I phoned the good news to my record promoter friend, who was on standby, awaiting this call. My team shipped the record to college stations, and he and his team got into action.

College radio found Indo-Caribbean music to be a breath of fresh air, joining their international roster. Over the next several weeks, Kanchan's album sat comfortably at the top of their charts and college students and people from all walks of life and cultures flocked to record stores to buy it.

Yellowman's album, *Blueberry Hill*, soon followed. I had secured a licensing deal with Bob Marley's Tuff Gong studios, the rights holder to the album, and released it on my label.

The mention I had an Afro-Caribbean album, Yellowman's album, to the distributors was a bridge that helped get Indo-Caribbean music to the American shelves. In doing so, it helped to bring Afro-Caribbean music along.

Having built a modest sales, marketing, and distribution team, and with the American shelves now firmly secured, it was time for me to solidify everything into shaping a stronger cooperation.

Within three years, I acquired, produced, and distributed a number of Indo- and Afro-Caribbean titles — records by such great artists such as Bob Marley, Dennis Brown, Gregory Isaacs, Machel Montano, John Slingshot DrePaul, Carl and Carol Jacobs, Shelly Thunder, and Gem Myers and compilation themes such as Hot Hot Soca and Hot Hot Lambada.

While the Afro-Caribbean expats did have their own radio station, Indian and Indo-Caribbean expats did not have a station in the great city of New York to call their own. And here lay my next step and my next challenge.

CHAPTER 51

The desired results will rise toward realization, when purpose is fueled by passion.

Radio first came into existence in India in 1923 when the Radio Club of Mumbai held its first broadcast. Thirty years later, the most popular radio show transmitting across India was from Radio Ceylon in Sri Lanka.

The program was a weekly music countdown that immediately rose in prominence and took the Indian nation by storm.

By 1988, thousands of miles across the Atlantic, my friend Rashid Pierkhan continued in his father's legacy, operating the family's radio station, Radio Paramaribo in Suriname, with his son Faried assisting him. It was the only full-time Indian radio station in the Caribbean. Guyana had Indian programs a few hours a week; Trinidad and Tobago had a few hours more. New York had even less.

Almost all of the radio stations in the Caribbean featured Afro-centric programming. And in New York, WLIB did the same except for Sunday mornings when it had a few hours of Indian and Indo-Caribbean programming. Our community had very little representation on this important medium of communication called the radio.

There was a need for a twenty-four hour a day radio station. It is easier for a community to come together when they share a common communication platform. And as with everything I had done up to this time, having found a problem, I saw an opportunity to empower the community of Indian and Indo-Caribbean heritage.

And instead of thinking of where the money would come from to start a radio station in the most expensive radio market in the United States, I thought of this empowerment, and soon enough, a series of events unfolded.

On an autumn day in October 1988, in a meeting at my Franklin Lakes office with a gentleman with roots stretching back to Jamaica who was pitching a compilation album featuring some of reggae's greatest artists, I noticed that he was carrying a little radio.

"What is this radio you are carrying around? It looks different."

"Boss, you don't know," he replied.

"Tell me what I need to know."

He described that the radio had a chip to receive programming from the sideband of an FM radio station hence creating a brand-new radio channel. For people to listen to this radio channel, they would need to purchase this radio.

He said since FM radio stations are very expensive to lease or purchase, this particular radio is a less expensive way to start a new radio station.

"What are the numbers?" I asked as I wheeled my office chair around to sit on his side of my desk and closer to this little wonder.

"You will have to pay around a million dollars for a ten-year lease to secure the sideband of an FM frequency from which you can build a private radio channel, and this radio will pick up your signal. And you would need around another million dollars for overhead."

The amount was so large that it had caused T.R. who was sitting calmly on the other side of my office, to struggle swallowing his coffee.

"So I will have to sell these radios to my potential listeners?" I asked.

"Yes. That's also an investment and also part of the challenge especially since this technology is not fully developed," he warned.

"And how much will these radios cost me?"

"They're fifty each," he said.

"You leave this radio with me and take this album back with you." I told him.

He saw value in giving up the biggest selling reggae artists for a radio. He too, was a man who saw tomorrow; he too saw the forest.

I handed him $51 — fifty for the radio and one dollar for good luck.

I then asked him about his compensation, and he told me that should a deal be made, the brokers will compensate him directly.

I then pointed him to the phone to call the brokers handling an FM radio signal from which I could lease the sideband to build a subscription-based radio station for Indian and Indo-Caribbean expats in New York.

We scheduled a meeting that evening with the brokers at their office at WNWK radio in Manhattan.

CHAPTER 52

The journey to our purpose is today.
It is here and it is now.

Just before leaving my office for the meeting with the radio brokers, my mother phoned. She told me to come home early as there was a beautiful house for sale a block from where we lived and that I should buy it.

I placed the radio next to me as I drove from my office toward the George Washington Bridge. Instead of thinking about that house, I wondered if this radio could give the Indian and Indo-Caribbean expats a station. I did not think about where the two million dollars would come from to make this a reality.

I thought about how times had changed. The digital age was maturing, the innovation of the CD — the compact disc — was the music configuration of choice, and the internet had passed the infancy stage. Although not fully realized, there were innovative ways of receiving information, entertainment, and music.

In these changing times and advancing technologies, I saw the possibility that the Indo-Caribbean music I had introduced through records and concerts could continue in its legacy. It could be piped directly into homes, making it easily accessible. And if I did not keep up with the innovations, expats would drift away from any interest in Indian and Indo-Caribbean music.

These reflections reinforced my purpose, that I must continue on this Indian and Indo-Caribbean expat journey.

Soon, my car slowly rolled atop the George Washington Bridge, sitting high above the mighty Hudson. The traffic slowed and although the wind had risen and was howling with all of its might at my tightly closed windows on that autumn evening, there was a sense of a deafening silence within.

I could feel the rhythm of this bridge as it slowly stretched and flexed back in vibration.

I asked myself an important question. Who is this bridge named after? And had he been the one sitting behind the wheel of this car at this very crossroad of life, which path would he have taken?

As my car rolled toward the end of the bridge, traffic slowed to a complete stop. In front were two signs, one directing me toward Queens and the other pointing toward Manhattan. Will I go home or toward my purpose? I made a right turn into Manhattan, leaving behind my mother's dream that I would own a home, the dream of every immigrant.

I parked my car, walked over to a pay phone, deposited a few of my coins, and told my mother of my decision. She again reminded me that once I have a purpose, I should follow it.

It was her words of wisdom and her blessing that had started me on this journey in the record business in the first place. It was time for the next step, time for the expats to have their own radio station in the New York market. Although the numbers didn't make sense, the idea did.

Once again I made a calculation, as I had done when I had found those eighty-seven records some ten years earlier. I calculated that the total advertising revenue available for those few hours of Indian and Indo-Caribbean radio programs in the New York market was less than $25,000 annually. The revenue came from a small number of mom-and-pop businesses owned by expats.

The way things were, twenty hours of radio a day would not necessarily increase this revenue.

AM and FM radio stations at the time cost upwards of fifty million dollars to buy. Setting up a subscription radio channel was the less risky option for providing a twenty-four hour a day radio station for the expats.

As I examined the numbers and looked to find a way to accomplish the task, I reflected on Einstein's theory as my father had explained to me. In his words, he had explained how one thing works with the other. An idea started forming within.

It dawned on me that mainstream advertisers could help. A dedicated Indian and Indo-Caribbean radio station would be an entry point for them to this market — a market that was growing more affluent by the day.

To make the pitch to these mainstream advertisers, I would first have to sell a large number of the subscription radios and have a sufficiently large number of listeners. If I built it, they would come. First, I would have to build it.

With this realization, I walked into the meeting that evening.

As I sat there, I noticed a map on the wall indicating the signal coverage of PanAmSat. I made a mental note of it. PanAmSat was founded by Univision, a Spanish language broadcaster that General Motors later acquired.

The brokers explained they represented an FM signal from which I could build out my radio channel. It was a small signal with limited coverage in parts of New York and New Jersey. Although small, this was the perfect signal to start out with. When the time came, I would go big. But for now, starting out with a small signal was more manageable than finding two million dollars.

"Look, no one will lease this signal from you," I told them.

And as I spoke those words, I observed both of their adam's apples moving, indicating they had already realized this to be true.

"I listen to this radio. It is not a very clear signal. It works on and off. In a stable position, it works a bit better. Radio is mostly for on the go, and this signal is limited to homes and offices at best," I told them.

It was then they confided in me that instead of representing the FM signal on behalf of the owners, they had signed a ten-year deal to secure the signal so they could sublease the airtime and make a larger profit.

"Well, you are not going to make it off of me," I told them in no uncertain terms.

The room fell silent.

I looked up again at the PanAmSat map, this time carefully studying it, making sure that they noticed my curiosity.

"And PanAmSat, is it the same type of deal? You gentlemen secured a spot on it, too?" I asked.

"Yes we have a spot on it," one of them admitted.

"What's the footprint like?"

"It covers all of the Americas — North and South America," he said.

"And to receive the signal, people must have one of those large satellite dishes, right?

"Yes. That's right."

No one I knew of had a large satellite dish. But during our concert tour of the United States, I noticed a few of the hotels and motels had them on their rooftops. And who owned some of these hotels and motels? Indian expats.

The two signals would give me a perfect starting point to learn the business, develop some listenership to hone my skills as a radio personality, and prepare me for the day when I would lease a larger signal across the New York market.

"It would seem to me that you gentlemen are in a fix. You have a radio signal that's spotty and a satellite signal where very few consumers have these large dishes. How much does it cost you for both of these signals?" I asked them pointedly.

"$8,000 a month," they replied.

"Let's do this. I will lease both these signals from you for $8,000 a month. You go out and find someone to pay you more, and when you do, I will hand these signals back to you."

They also threw in one of their small studios from where I could broadcast.

CHAPTER 53

Purpose is stronger than the facts placed before us. It will change what once seemed like facts.

On March 15, 1989, Indian and Indo-Caribbean music was transmitted from my small studio in Manhattan to an earth station in Carteret, New Jersey, then rose to a satellite and was beamed in full glory across the Americas. A second feed was sent to the FM transmitter in New York to my radio signal. No one was listening to either.

The first song I played was *Jyoti Kalash Chhalke*. Its poetic symbolism evoked a divine light overflowing from an urn, heralding the dawn of a brand-new day.

If only I could find the owners of these large dishes and if only I could convince the others to buy these little radios. If only.

The following day, along with a few broadcasters from the station, we took to the streets of New York to pitch to the expats. By the end of the first month, we had sold a grand total of four radios.

The expats were delighted to have their own radio station. But the concept of a subscription radio station left them puzzled. They had never heard of such a thing as buying a radio with a chip.

"Why can't we hear the station on the radios we already have?"

Many who thought the concept was a practical way for the expats to have their own station, then thought the price of $99 for a radio was too rich. The few who bought it thought the signal was not very clear.

As the staff sat with me in a meeting, they wondered, what's next? Many saw the writing on the wall and never showed up again. Pandit Ramlall, Dino Dilchand, Dalbir Singh, Bob Singh, Issurdat Ramdehal, and Eshri Singh were among the few who remained committed to the purpose.

The following day, I drove to my office and talked with T.R., who had been planning to return to India to retire within two years.

We determined it would take at least five years for the station to sustain itself, and to achieve that three things had to happen. I needed a significant line of credit to keep the operation going. I had to find a way to devote most of my time to the radio business, which meant I had to find another record company to take over day-to-day responsibilities at my record label. And finally, I had to develop compelling and innovative programming and secure a stronger signal.

With T.R.'s experience as the former chairman of the State Bank of India, I asked him to set up a meeting with a local bank. A few days later, I secured the line of credit. We both signed as guarantors, and the first item was done.

Regarding the second item, having another record company take over my day-to-day responsibilities, I reflected on how best to accomplish this. I decided to look for a new album to release, one that would cause a sensation and create a buzz with the buyers, both those buying records to stock on record store shelves and customers taking them home. I thought this was the best way to attract another label to mine. Ultimately this would free up my time to establish an Indian and Indo-Caribbean radio station for the expats.

I made finding such an album — one that would create sufficient interest with another record company — my purpose.

CHAPTER 54

The answer you seek is already within you.

It must have been after midnight in New York when my phone rang. My friend Reg from London was on the other end.

"Rohit, do you remember that thing we talked about?" he asked me.

"Do you have anything?" I replied.

"Well, do you know what day this is? It's Bob Marley's day. It's the anniversary of his passing."

Reg and I reminisced about the life of the man neither of us had ever met.

Robert Nesta Marley had risen from the tenements of Kingston to play and dance on the stages of the world. A broken one had risen to such great heights that millions of people around the world remembered the day he passed from this life and celebrated him. The day was May 11.

Bob Marley was named the most influential artist in the second half of the twentieth century by *The New York Times*. His song *One Love* was chosen as the anthem of the millennium by the BBC, and his album *Exodus* was voted as the best album of the twentieth century by *Time* magazine.

As we reminisced, Reg reiterated the reason why he was calling.

"Boss, how would you like to be the re-issue producer and distributor of a Marley compilation album? I think this could be the answer to your goal of releasing a record that would generate interest for an American record company to do a deal with you."

"Reg, I agree with you. But as you know, since Bob's passing, over twenty compilation albums have been released out there. Think about it, the last time I went to the music festival in Cannes, there must have been that many of Bob's compilation albums exhibited there. We will have to think this thing through some more."

The line fell silent. It became apparent my friend had not thought his idea through. Not to completely deflate his idea, I offered a thought.

"Hey Reg, how about I work on a Marley compilation of recordings the world hasn't heard since the early 60s? Recordings made by the great man before he became an icon — Bob Marley's earliest recordings, the ones he did as rehearsals to get to the big stages of the world."

"Everyone has tried. Those tapes are lost — no one has ever found them. They are lost forever."

"Well then, Reg, my friend, we better go find them."

That evening, I arrived at the Norman Manley International Airport in Kingston, Jamaica, where my friend Winston (Yellowman) awaited me. Soon, he and I sat over dinner at the Jamaica Pegasus Hotel where I was staying.

As we were parting, he touched my shoulder, then lowered his voice and cautioned me, "Rohit, please be careful."

An hour later, Reg arrived from London. Our friend Striker picked him up and took him directly to his ancestral home. Later that night, they picked me up at the hotel.

With no clues to go on, we drove the streets of Kingston.

As we retraced the steps when the young Marley made those recordings that were now lost, my Jamaican friends started reminiscing.

"Rohit, the world doesn't know the mission you are on. This is the very courage that led Bob to bring this country together in one unforgettable night back in 1978."

My friends told me Marley, like the people in this country, lived the struggle. He was born in Nine Miles, and from there, his father took him from his mother and left him to live with an older lady in Kingston. Marley was ten years old at the time.

A bit later, he lived in the government yard in Trenchtown. That's how my friend Striker got to know him. They used to all meet at the recording studios. It was where Marley started recording, writing social commentaries, and hoping to bring the injustices he saw around him to the world's attention. Even if he was paid almost nothing for a song, he never complained. His focus was on bringing his message to the people.

"Rohit, should you manage to find these tapes, it will revive Bob's purpose during those very early years of this struggle."

Striker told me that following the recording sessions, producers took the master tapes to King Tubby to cut dubplates for them.

"Tubs?" I interjected.

"Yes, your buddy Tubs."

"King Tubby?" I clarified.

"Yes, Rohit, King Tubby."

There was a silence. We realized the clue we were searching for had been found. And the silence remained until we reached the gates of his widow's residence. Osbourne Ruddock — King Tubby — was gunned down three months before as he stood by those same gates.

Known to everyone as King Tubby, he was born in Kingston. He was one of the most brilliant sound technicians in the Jamaican music scene. We became friends in 1987, the year I released Yellowman's *Blueberry Hill* album. We made a deal, and I distributed selected works from his label in North America, Europe, Asia, and Africa.

Tubs used a wide range of techniques when cutting a record, insisting that no two records were the same. He brought a uniqueness to each record he would cut. This was why artists far and wide across the island took their master tapes to him.

In the early 1960s, Jamaica was in the infancy stages of independence, and people in the young nation had little money to buy records, much less to make them. Many who brought their tapes to Tubs had hardly anything to pay to him.

That night, Tubs' widow stood with us by the gates and told us, "When people brought their tapes for Tubby to make dubplates, many had no money to pay him. They would tell him to hold on to their master tapes, and if over time, they were still unable to pay him, they would give him ownership of those tapes."

I had known Tubs and his wife for some time. We reached an understanding that should I find the Marley tapes, I would release a limited edition album and pay the royalties directly to her, regardless of who may claim the rights to the tapes.

"Let me be honest with you, Rohit, I don't know where those tapes are. We moved from one place to another. Many things got lost. I don't know if those tapes got lost, too. And another thing, with the harsh weather conditions, as you know, tapes are a delicate thing. Even if you were to find them, it may be next to impossible for you to do anything with them. They are either lost or damaged somewhere."

She asked us to wait and returned shortly with outstretched hands.

"Rohit, here are the keys to the new studio. You know, I still can't believe it. He worked so hard to build this studio, and right after he opened it, they shot him down, right in this very spot where we are standing."

She handed me the keys and said, "Rohit, you and Tubby were like brothers. I want you to please be careful."

With her blessing and good wishes, we continued our drive into the night.

CHAPTER 55

When we step into the unknown,
a whole other world opens.

As we drove, both Reg and Striker continued to tell me stories about the man whose voice we hoped to find on tapes, perhaps at Tubby's previous locations or at the one we were heading toward. However broad, the search was narrowed.

Striker, who was behind the wheel, turned to the back seat to say, "Rohit, Bob too, must be blessing us. He understood that the need of the people must be first. You know he too never owned a house."

He then turned back to look at the road ahead of us as we entered what seemed to be another part of Kingston. He navigated the sudden rough, broken road, looked out the window, then steadied his hands on the steering wheel. After some time, he continued to speak.

"Do you know, not so long ago, right here in Jamaica, political tensions were so high that Bob decided he must do something to release the pressure hanging on the minds of the people. That's how the Smile Jamaica Concert came about. I know. I was a part of it."

The Smile Jamaica Concert was held in December 1976 at the National Heroes Park in Kingston, and the headliner was Bob Marley & The Wailers.

What was planned to ease tensions, placed Marley in between two of the country's most powerful forces, the country's prime minister, with communist ideologies, Michael Manley, and his arch-rival, Edward Seaga. They both demanded Bob's endorsement.

Bob Marley would have none of it. He was the people's champion, one who instead of siding with those who divided the nation, wanted to bring all of the people together. That's why he had a strong commitment to stage the Smile Jamaica event.

Two days before the concert, around nine in the evening, Bob Marley was shot. Many bullets were fired. One grazed across Marley's chest and lodged into his arm. Television cameras flashed the news around the world. The journalists who had arrived on the island to cover the concert carried the story.

The night of the concert, a determined Marley took to the stage and delivered one of the most riveting nights in the country's storied history. And Jamaica smiled. But there was disbelief that someone would want to kill him. He lived for his country and its people. The more I learned about Marley that night, the more determined I became to find those tapes.

With the thought that someone would want him dead, Marley left Jamaica and flew to London. It was there that he made his famous *Exodus* album.

While Bob was in London, back in Jamaica, the two political parties, the People's National Party and the Jamaica Labour Party, kept on widening the political divide, setting the people against one another.

There was hope that Bob Marley would one day return. When the One Love Peace Concert was announced, the nation was elated. To ensure a safe return home, overflowing crowds gathered to welcome him. Many lined the roads stretching along the path he traveled.

Jamaicans had held on to hope and took it with them to the stadium on the night of the concert. Midway through his set that night, Marley did what many thought was the unthinkable. He called out into the crowd for the two political rivals to join him on stage. The overflowing stadium waited as police and soldiers paved the way for the two politicians to join Bob. While they shook Bob's hands, he had something more in mind. They stood on either side of him, and he held their hands up. Then he brought their hands to join together into an arc above his head.

The One Love Peace Concert, held in April of 1978 at the National Stadium in Kingston, solidified Marley's life purpose.

As my friend Striker reminisced, we lost trace of the rough patches of road. Perhaps it was the stories that steadied his hands on the steering wheel.

Edward Lee, better known to music lovers as Bunny Lee and known to us, his friends, as Striker, had cut his teeth in the music business as a record promoter, plugging records on the radio. Hence, his passion for both records and radio.

He produced rock steady, reggae, and dancehall records such as Eric Donaldson's *Cherry Oh Baby*, a song later covered by the Rolling Stones, rock and roll legends. The group UB40 also covered it.

Striker produced well over a hundred records, some of which I licensed from him for distribution to American, European, Asian, and African shelves.

He was later given the Order of Distinction to honor his work in Jamaican music.

Very few record men had left such an impact in the life of music. As we drove, we were heading toward the legacy of yet another such man.

Widely known as the dub inventor, King Tubby single-handedly created the B side, the instrumental version of records. He would strip away the bass and drum tracks then recreate and refashion them before rejoining them to the other instruments on a record.

He also built and created playback systems, amplifying his sound, to bring the full effect of his studio innovations to some of the island's most successful sound systems from which these dubplates were played.

These were my friends. We understood the importance of balancing both banks — the Bank of Money and the Bank of Karma.

It was past midnight when we entered the neighborhood where Tubby's studio was. It was a tenement environment, eerie and dark with the loss of Tubs still hanging in the air.

Over the next several nights and days, we persisted. Our search for the lost Marley tapes took us from box to box, place to place, retracing Tubbys' movements. Nothing was found.

A few days later, on a Sunday afternoon, the Jamaican sun bathed the steps on which we sat at Striker's home. The voices of children playing a game of cricket echoed in the distance. We sat discussing life and the tapes.

"Are you sure that we have searched everywhere?"

After a moment of thought, Striker said in a low voice, "Rohit, I just thought of something; there's somewhere we haven't looked. Tubby used to store some boxes at my house."

"Let's go open them," I suggested.

Striker's house was built on stilts. In one corner under his house, there was a wooden enclosure. There must have been more than twenty tall boxes in this dusty room, each around four feet high, some on top of others.

Striker opened and delved into the first of the boxes. He started pulling out tape after tape. The more he pulled from the box, the more encouraging it was. With so many boxes to open and such a large number of tapes, there was a chance what we were seeking was possible.

Striker dug so deeply into one box that it appeared as if he had fallen into it. When he took his head out of the box and turned to look at me, his face was completely covered in dust.

The Marley tapes sat in the very last box that we opened, just as they were placed there by King Tubby.

We carefully cleared off the dust and saw that the boxes holding the lost recordings were taped tightly shut at the seams by many layers of masking tape. We took off the masking tape, mindful that no further dust entered the casing, and slowly opened the cover. There sat, for over twenty-five years, the first spool of Marley's once lost tapes. Tubby had secured it tightly. It was now revealed to us.

CHAPTER 56

Gold and diamonds grow and thrive deep in the earth, revealing themselves to those who unearth and see them. They are then known to the beholder as treasures.

The restoration of Bob Marley's earliest recorded works began immediately, and over the next several nights and days, I stayed the course. Songs from *I Have Got to Cry* to *Hey Happy People*, a total of ten A sides with their corresponding B sides, showcased the memorable magic of two of the world's greatest masters at work, Bob Marley and King Tubby. *Billboard* magazine would call the album Bob Marley's best since *Buffalo Soldier*.

On the day I finally left Jamaica for home with the newly restored tapes, both Reg and Striker dropped me at the airport. We had achieved what we had set out to accomplish.

Striker wished me the best, "Rohit, I think you are onto something. I wish you the very best in your radio journey, my friend."

And Reg did the same.

I sat on the Air Jamaica aircraft reflecting on the work we did over the last several days — creating an album from the lost tapes to rekindle the legacy of Bob Marley. I would soon put his lost lyrics on the shelves of American record stores, where many of his other albums were already placed by the large record labels.

I had ticked off another item on my list — finding a record that could lead to a label deal with a large record company. I placed a full-page ad in *Billboard,* showcasing some of the albums on my label, emphasizing my new Marley release and waited for a record company to call.

The same day the magazine was received by the labels across the country, the head of Peter Pan Records, known as America's first independent record company, phoned me.

He told me they were interested in the distribution of my record label. Under the terms of the deal, they would take over all of my day-to-day responsibilities — marketing, manufacturing, and distribution — and I would receive royalty payments once a month.

They wanted me to commit to fifteen hours each month for meetings with them. I now had time to focus on developing the Indian and Indo-Caribbean expat radio station under the five-year plan.

A few days later, the president of Peter Pan records and I placed our signatures on freshly minted documents and shook hands on the deal.

I drove from Peter Pan's offices in New Jersey to my Indian and Indo-Caribbean radio station on 59th Street in Manhattan, where a microphone awaited me.

CHAPTER 57

*The more we are broken,
the more light shines through.*

After some two years of broadcasting, from 1989 to 1991, I had only managed to sell around eight hundred subscription radios.

With such a small number of subscribers, I did not pitch to advertisers. However, one approached me of his own volition, Baljit Balgobin, the owner of B&R Uniforms. I told him I had a small number of listeners. Still, he handed me a check for $500 and told me to run his ad. He said to consider it as support for my efforts to make something happen for our people.

With advertising revenues of $500 and an investment of $250,000 in signal fees and overheads, everyone except for Pandit Ramlall and Dino Dilchand had by now walked out thinking this could never work.

The radio signal brokers called to inform me that they couldn't find anyone else to lease the signals to and would be winding up this part of their activities.

The very next day, I informed the bankers. They told me that since T.R. would be returning to India, they were calling up the line of credit.

All I had learned would be put to the biggest test of my life. And he who believes in purpose must now demonstrate that truly, only the broken one will rise.

That evening, I went on air to inform the expats it was time for me to get off the air. When I could find a stronger signal, and when I got back on air, I would exchange their radios with more technologically advanced ones. But for now, the station was closed.

As the station went dark, I touched the microphone in reverence and gratitude for the opportunity it had given me to communicate with the expats and for all I had learned.

What many saw as adversity, I saw as an opportunity. The expats would be willing to buy the radios if they functioned better. Two years of broadcasting had allowed me to create a dialogue with them. I viewed it as a rehearsal for the next stage of my journey to creating an expat radio station of my heritage in the greatest city in the world.

A night later, I looked up at the many album covers on the wall of my office. My eyes stopped at one. It was my Kanchan greatest hits album. Memories of our journey through music and all that we had accomplished brought a gentle smile to my face.

I walked over and touched the album cover, then sat down again in my chair. It had been five years since we last worked together.

An hour later, my phone rang.

"Rohit, where are you?" she asked.

"Kanchan, how are you?"

She spoke the words that always formed the basis for recording a new album.

"When are you coming to Bombay?" she asked.

"Get your tape recorder and speakerphone ready. I will call you in a little while."

"My Panasonic will be ready."

I walked into a room where I had boxes of tapes stored. They were the tapes sent to me by artists looking for a record deal, and tapes that I had set aside to work on personally. I searched for one tape that had songs from when Indo-Caribbean recordings were in their infancy. These were songs with lyrical content deeply rooted in the sugar belts of the Caribbean.

I had kept these songs for an album that I planned to record with Kanchan before our parting five years ago. And as I searched, a realization dawned upon me that a record is not made before its time.

As I opened a box, I saw a bundle of cassettes partially wrapped in paper. Upon unfolding the wrapping, I noticed an image of the Great Wall of China. I thought of its significance in relation to this moment. Building this great wonder of the world had been a monumental task.

I brought the tapes into my private music room and phoned Kanchan an hour later. She recorded a few of the songs on her speakerphone directly on her tape recorder. I told her and Babla to start rehearsing.

I then phoned Panasonic headquarters in Beijing and set up a meeting. Three weeks later, I checked into a hotel overlooking Tiananmen Square, where student-led demonstrations took place around the time I first went on air in 1989. I wanted to walk in the square that had become a symbol of the people's spirit of freedom.

The following day, I sat with the Panasonic R&D department and showed them a chip from one of my old radios. I wanted them to develop a more technologically advanced chip with the exact same functionality, and I wanted to install this new chip in Panasonic radios. They agreed.

The next morning, I packed my tapes and Sony Walkman in my bag, went to the hotel's tour desk, and requested a guide to take me to the Great Wall of China. I was delighted to learn no one else had shown up for the tour that day. The thought that I was going to be undisturbed with the treasures that lay in my bag on this tour of the great wonder of the world was more than I had hoped for.

"What's the purpose of this wall?" I asked the guide.

"It was built to protect the land from invaders. What brought you to China?" she asked.

"I have a purpose to preserve my heritage."

She looked into my eyes then slowly turned away, looking into the fields. I sensed she was thinking that although this land might have been protected from invaders, it was these very same protectors that invaded the minds of its people.

We soon arrived at Badaling, on the northwestern side of urban Beijing. I placed my hands and touched the great wonder that once protected this land. In that moment, I felt a higher purpose was reachable.

I climbed the steps and upon reaching a peak, I sat quietly with my Sony Walkman, overlooking the hills and a steep ravine below. It was here, on this peak, thousands of miles from the sugar belts of the Caribbean that I picked the final songs for what would become the biggest-selling Indo-Caribbean album of all time, *Leggo Me Na Raja*.

CHAPTER 58

*There is a rhythm in everything we do.
Within your rhythm, you will find
your way home.*

The album was recorded and mixed over ten days. When I was done, one person was always the first to hear my new recordings. As I changed the batteries in my Sony Walkman in anticipation of playing it for her, the phone rang. Hansrajee had experienced the occasion of birth earlier on this day and had passed from this life.

Not so long ago, she unlocked the gate that allowed me entrance into the wide world of Indo-Caribbean music. And now she wasn't there by her phone.

I took my fully charged Sony Walkman, placed the earphones on my head, and headed out, closing the hotel room door behind me. I walked the streets of Bombay that night, with Indo-Caribbean music playing. I was in the land of her ancestors, and the music stretched and traced back from the sugar cane belts of the Caribbean to this land. The genre of music that Hansrajee, along with her husband and children, had shone a light upon kept unspooling in my Walkman. With all of her success, she had held strong to her heritage and strong to her purpose.

The last time I saw her, she had visited my home in New York.

A few days later, I arrived back in New York, bringing with me the *Leggo Me Na Raja* recording — the ten songs I had recorded with Kanchan and Babla.

In a few weeks, I would release the album. It had been five years since I produced and released a studio album with Kanchan and the anticipation was high. The fans' call for a reunion album from the team that had given them such hits as *Kuchh Gadbad Hai, Bolo Bolo, Kaise Bani, Ab Na Jaibay, Ai Ai O, Tiny Winey,* and many other memorable songs was heeded.

I decided to release half of the album and hold back the rest of the songs. The weekend *Leggo Me Na Raja* was released, album sales crossed over $100,000, surpassing all Indo-Caribbean records ever made. And all that was broken now held a renewed promise.

Released a few months before Christmas in 1991, *Leggo Me Na Raja* continued to sell strongly through the Christmas holidays and by the time its sting was starting to show signs of slowing, I released the rest of it, its counterpart, *Ker Away Me Na Raja*.

The second album, as anticipated, continued the excitement without missing a beat. Kanchan's comeback was now certain.

And knowing that the broken one had risen, preparations for the 1992 tour were put into motion. I visited the Caribbean.

While in Trinidad, Moean, instead of asking me about the tour, asked about the progress I was making with the radio station. This was a reminder to me that I must get back to where I had left off. While I was giving Kanchan a voice, the expats back in New York were waiting for me to provide them with theirs.

What had prompted Moean's question in the middle of preparations for a busy concert tour piqued my interest. Here was a man who rose to the heights of the record business and had once recorded and promoted the top artists, and they were turning their backs on him. Not only that, by this time, the pirates had stolen the music of our heritage; they wiped out the entire recording business in the Caribbean, rendering Moean entirely out of business. While Moean had the overhead of rent and other expenses, the pirates had a free ride. They were sitting on the curbsides selling cassettes which were cheaper to produce than records.

The iconic Windsor Records building, once the house of Indo-Caribbean music and the address imprinted on record labels, was shuttered then destroyed during a coup attempt in the country. Moean now was working out of a modest two-story structure in Mohammed Ville. The first floor was rented out to a pharmacy, while upstairs was set up as his personal office and the operations of the final fragments of what was once the mecca of Indo-Caribbean music.

"Rohit, the pirates have finished the business. They are everywhere throughout the country now. They are not hiding. They are openly selling our music on the street," he said.

He then spoke in a lower voice, "I am so sorry I will not be able to participate any longer. As you can see, with your very own eyes, my days are now done. The pirates here have taken everything away from me, perhaps from all of us.

"However, you will always have a home here in Trinidad, and we will always be family. Nothing will ever change that. You go ahead with the business, and any advice you may need at any time, I will be here to support you. As a matter of fact, I would very much like to see my label, my Windsor Records label, end up in your hands, and this is why I want for you to take over the ownership of my entire catalog from now on."

It was then I reminded him that there were two main reasons why I was setting up the radio platform. Foremost was to give a voice, an identity to the Indian and Indo-Caribbean expats living in New York and elsewhere. Of equal importance was that the music of our heritage would have a brand-new way of distribution. Subscription radio would bypass the pirates and bring the music directly into the homes of our people twenty-four hours a day.

"I am in full agreement with you, but remember you will have to prepare yourself if that is going to become the next platform for our music in the great city of New York. It is an important global market. As you well know, and have proven over and over again, the way New York goes, the world goes."

We then agreed that after completing my upcoming tour with Kanchan we would sit together and work toward my getting back on the air with my planned, bigger radio station.

Kanchan's 1992 tour was a resounding success. We toured Guyana, where Yesu Persaud and Komal Samaroo of DDL, one of the country's largest beverage companies, sponsored us. Demand for tickets from every nook and cranny of the country was so high, we extended the tour from four to twelve shows, an unprecedented number of shows at the time.

The Trinidad leg of the tour was sponsored by Nestlé and other major brands. As Moean had correctly predicted, the tour recorded the highest attendance of any Indo-Caribbean show in the history of the country at the time.

Soon I brought the tour to North America, and at the New York shows, I was delighted to meet with some who had bought my radios. They came in support of me, and meeting them again reminded me of the urgency to get back to my purpose, radio.

The tour continued to other countries while I remained in New York. Kanchan performed in Europe and Asia, and I remained determined to travel toward my purpose, which awaited me in New York.

Our journey grew apart, but together we had charted our way to twelve number-one singles and nine number-one albums.

CHAPTER 59

*One can only grow large if one can
see and hear what is small.*

Kanchan was fully back in form. I turned my attention to where I had left off. I returned to radio and the promise I had made to those who had bought my radios. Before signing off from my small signal, I had told them what I needed to do before getting back on the air — raise additional capital, secure a big signal, and build better radios. These items would provide them with a better listening experience. They patiently waited for me to do all I needed to do.

They waited because they knew there were many wealthy individuals in our community, yet none had stepped forward to give the expats a twenty-four hour a day radio station — an identity and voice in a country far from their motherland. They knew that almost every other community had a radio station.

They purchased my original radios. They witnessed us setting up ladders and scaling up to their rooftops to connect their antennas with the small signal from my radio station so they could connect themselves to their heritage. They had bought my albums and concert tickets. Now they waited patiently.

It was time for me to return to them. But first, I must secure a signal — a big signal.

My next step was to update myself on the latest technology from the radio magazines I had subscribed to ever since I realized there was a need for a radio station for the expats. I had kept these subscriptions going and would have them forwarded to me while I was traveling. Now I had more time to catch up.

A sideband subscription radio station shares the same transmitter as an FM station. While the FM station can be heard on any FM radio, the sideband station could only be heard over specially tuned radios, subscription radio. Sideband stations were leased from the main FM station owner.

What makes a strong signal? An FM — frequency modulation — signal traveled vertically. This meant the higher the antenna, the stronger the signal. Therefore I would find my big signal on the tallest buildings in the city.

Further, the signal had to be in the middle of the FM band, and the FM station must play soft music. If it played rock or rap music, those harsh tones and sounds could easily penetrate and leak into the sideband signal, causing cross-talk.

There were two FM stations in the New York market playing such soft or classical music. Of these, only one was in the middle of the FM band. Although the New York market had many FM stations, I had only one chance of getting my big signal.

Even more, in the subscription radio market, either the sideband signals were already leased out, or their owners had no interest in leasing them out at all. These signals were owned by some of America's largest media conglomerates such as CBS, ABC, and NBC. One was also owned by the country's largest-selling broadsheet, *The New York Times*. Often there was not enough financial incentive for the conglomerates to be bothered because sideband radio lease payments averaged around $15,000 per month.

The New York Times radio signal was located at 96.3 in the middle of the FM band. Its classical music format, with soft easy tones, would not interfere or leak into the sideband signal. The antenna was located on top of the Empire State Building, one of the tallest buildings. It was the perfect station.

Securing a sideband signal did not mean one could conduct business from day one. Chips had to be installed in the radios and then tuned to the sideband signal. This was done after the sideband signal was fully built out and turned on. The sample radios would then be tested, and any adjustments needed would be made. Only then could the radios and chips be manufactured in commercial quantities. I had to negotiate that signal fees would begin after testing the signal and having radios available for sale.

I decided to bring all these points to the negotiating table. When a company the size of the *Times* gets into a situation, they can write a check to get out of it. When a small company gets into a situation, we often have to look at all angles to find a solution.

I must tell them about the challenges the expat groups faced and why the Indian and Indo-Caribbean community did not have a radio station. We were consumers of major brands, but those brands did not spend any money on our expat communities. Before the major brands spent money and advertised on an expat radio station, I would first have to sell a large number of radios. In order for me to mitigate the risk, I would need to initially pay a small monthly amount for the signal and over time increase this amount.

It was an early afternoon in 1993 when I arrived for the meeting at the 5th Avenue offices and studios of WQXR, *The New York Times* radio station, to meet with its president. Not so long ago, I was a newspaper delivery boy, and I delivered this paper from home to home.

The walls of the reception area had decorative panes of glass. The hallway had paintings of the great classical masters, Bach, Handel, Mozart, Beethoven, and Zubin Mehta, the renowned Indian orchestral conductor and music director of four philharmonic orchestras. Neatly polished cherry wood panels demarcated what appeared to be the studio sections beyond.

As I sat in the meeting, I wanted the president to see me as my true self, then he would see the programming style of my proposed radio station. This was of great importance because if the sideband radio station breached the FCC rules, the FM station owner, which in this case was *The New York Times*, would also be held responsible.

And before he could say it, I decided to address his concern by telling him that I recognized the office in which I was sitting, and by extension, its parent company, *The New York Times,* and the role it played and the symbolism it represented globally. I then assured him that it was of great importance to me that the rules and regulations of the FCC, in any radio station I would operate, be upheld to its highest standards at all times.

Following a short discussion, he reached across the desk and shook my hand saying the words I had waited for five years to hear.

"Mr. Jagessar, welcome to *The New York Times*. We will entrust our sideband radio signal in your hands. The signal is yours."

On July 6, 1993, the agreement was signed. *The New York Times* radio station, WQXR, gave me the exclusive rights to broadcast Indian and Indo-Caribbean programming to subscription radios on the sideband of their FM station. I would pay three million dollars over the next fifteen years for these rights. In addition, I estimated another three million dollars would cover the operating costs and expenses. Six million dollars would give the expats their voice, their radio station in the greatest city in the world.

The New York Times required five months for the engineering design and equipment installation to get the sideband signal ready. Thereafter, I had three months to test the signal, tune my radios, and begin distributing them to the Indian and Indo-Caribbean expats.

We agreed to set our official launch date for March 15, 1994, at which time payment of the signal fees would begin. With eight months away from the official broadcast date, I had a great deal of preparation and rehearsal before my return to the radio broadcast chair.

CHAPTER 60

He returned to his village.
It was in this familiar environment
that he found his voice again.

I arrived in Trinidad a few days later to rehearse Bollywood and Indo-Caribbean themes with the man who had first put me on the radio some thirteen years earlier. We had one hundred days to prepare for the new style of programming I was hoping to achieve and bring back with me to the expats.

Moean and I would start in the mornings over coffee and rehearse straight through to lunch. Fueled by more coffee and a short afternoon nap, we were back to the veranda for our second round of the day. Sometimes our discussions continued while going for a drive to the countryside.

By dinner time, recording artists who had worked with us in the past would occasionally stop by and reminisce about the days when we were hitmaking kings.

Moean had helped me set up a global distribution network for records. Now, he was helping me prepare to establish a more forward-thinking distribution methodology — an electronic distribution platform. Here, Indo-Caribbean music and its Indian counterpart, Bollywood, would bypass the pirates and be piped directly into expats' homes.

One of the key goals was to tell a story for sixty seconds or less in between each song, then press play, allowing the song to continue telling the story. The idea was that the full story would reveal itself within the span of four to six songs, but certainly before the next ad break, the 28th or 58th minute of the hour.

I did not want to be a radio personality who spoke more than the music. I did not want to seem loud and over the top. The music told the story; it was the poetry of the people.

The environment in which a song was conceptualized and ultimately realized was itself a story. It is a poem set to music and set to motion on the radio. Each song had its very own story. And this story would only be revealed to those ready to hear it. Stories are such a thing.

What songs I would play on the new expat radio station determined whether people would buy the radios. This, in turn, would determine what Fortune 500 companies I could attract as advertisers.

As one-time record producers ourselves, having produced several hundred recordings between us — Moean more records than I — we had a good understanding of the language of a recording. We understood how the process began, how it lived, and how it completed its journey and began a brand-new one when it reached the listener. Telling the story of how their favorite song was conceptualized, created, and recorded would help me to create this larger-than-life world of the recording studio for the listeners.

The radio personality's role was the last link in the chain. I was the link between the artists and the listeners, and as such, I believed it was an intimate partnership with the listeners. I took my role as the interpreter of the entire process of creating a song as empowerment to the listeners.

As I was going on air for the first time with my big signal on the evening of March 15, 1994, my friend in my adopted homeland, Trinidad, was doing his final show. It was a bittersweet moment as I felt the baton from the master pass to me.

From the time I was first on the radio in Trinidad, Moean had been helping me find my voice — my radio personality. It was honed in the articulation of my words, imagination, thoughts, and intent.

In the three months leading up to the launch date, as provided for in my contract with *The New York Times*, we tested the signal and completed the exchange of those eight hundred old radios in the homes of enthusiastic Indo-Caribbean expat subscribers with brand-new Panasonic radios.

Upon informing them that we were stopping by to exchange their radios with the new ones, some already had their ladders out and were waiting for us to arrive to scale to their rooftops.

Much to their surprise, instead of walking toward their ladders, we walked straight into their homes, plugged the radios into an electrical outlet, and the crisp, clear sound of Indo-Caribbean and Bollywood music filled the air.

Having experienced this big signal, the expats were now certain that they had their own radio station, and therefore, their voice in the United States. Word spread to their circle of friends and family. Within the three months, those eight hundred Indo-Caribbean homes had swollen to well over three thousand.

The power of *The New York Times* sideband signal, broadcasting from atop the Empire State Building, rose to a beautiful sound, a brand-new day, in a brand-new way.

In this world of the Indo-Caribbean expats, I finally exhaled.

CHAPTER 61

*Purpose creates what is good for us —
both around us and within us.*

When the Indian expats, those coming directly from India, found out I was Indo Caribbean, they mostly sat on the fence. Only a handful bought a radio. We shared a common heritage — Indian — but there was a boundary line.

There was a time when I crossed a different boundary line. It sat between Queens, where Indo Caribbeans predominantly lived, and Brooklyn, where Afro Caribbeans mostly lived. There was also a boundary line between Trinidad and Guyana and one between Suriname and Guyana. And here too, in this great city, there was one.

Those who came from India to New York looked down on those from the Caribbean. We were considered second-class Indians and people of the lower class.

I had heard things. And now, having returned home to give both the Indian and Indo-Caribbean expats their own radio station, I saw the Indian expats sitting on the fence. I kept trying to give them their own radio station — their voice. They kept measuring and weighing my country of birth in their decision whether to subscribe or not.

A turning point came with a phone call from a soft-spoken Indian gentleman. He introduced himself as a diamond merchant with offices in the Diamond District in Manhattan.

The diamond merchant told me he heard from his friends that I was from the Caribbean.

"Are you really from Guyana and playing Indian songs on your radio?"

I confirmed this, and he expressed a hearty laugh. While those before him would question a Guyanese offering Indian programming and music on the radio and hang up, this gentleman did not. He was happy to know that New York now had its own Indian radio station.

With this soft-spoken diamond merchant as a potential listener, I saw a pathway opening to mainstream advertisers.

But for me to pitch such advertisers, many more such soft-spoken individuals would have to buy my radios. At least twenty-five thousand of them.

I asked him what prompted him to call.

"*India Abroad*," he responded. "Having your ad in *India Abroad* makes it appear that your station belongs to us, Indians. Word on the street is that it's only after Indians call you that they realize that it's a Guyanese who has started this radio."

He went on to say, "Let me tell you the truth why I am calling you now. Although I have heard about your radio and saw your ad in *India Abroad*, it was only last night I actually heard it myself. A gentleman from Guyana who works as the security guard in the building where I live was playing your radio on the job last night. As I was going out, I heard it. It caused me to stop in my tracks. You were playing a song that my mother used to sing to my siblings and me when we were children back in India."

He told me it brought tears to his eyes and memories from his childhood.

"Mr. Rohit, Guyanese or not, once every Indian hears your radio, they will want to become Guyanese and Indo-Caribbeans too. It is clear you guys from the Caribbean are more Indian than we are."

The diamond merchant placed his first order for fifty-one radios — one for himself and fifty to give as gifts to his family and friends. Fifty plus one as my start to another fifty was his way of wishing me success.

Those fifty-one radios would soon be placed in the homes of Indian expats. With this small start, I chose a date to diminish whatever was left of the Indo-Caribbean—Indian boundary line.

August 15 was the anniversary of India's independence. It was two months away. I chose this as the day to free people from the constraints of putting a group of people into a lower class or caste.

Not so long ago, my friend, the head of EMI India, sent me a recording of the speech made by the country's first Prime Minister Pandit Jawaharlal Nehru on the night of India's independence, in 1947.

He told the nation, "Long years ago, we made a tryst with destiny. And now the time comes when we shall redeem our pledge, not wholly in full measure, but very substantially. At the stroke of the midnight hour, when the world sleeps, India will awake to life and freedom."

While many Indian expats had heard this historic speech, none had a recording of it. A Guyanese, an Indo-Caribbean, had their treasured recording in his possession.

On the night of August 15, 1994, precisely at eight, I went on air with my Indian Independence broadcast. I opened the program with the recorded speech made on the night of the country's freedom, then showered it with patriotic songs, echoing the fire that lit the Indian nation's spirit to self-determination.

The broadcast caused the Indian expat listeners, which had by now grown to a few hundred more, to stand on their heads.

They went from asking if I was from Guyana to wondering who I might be. How did I have such a treasured recording? How did I have so many Indian songs — songs even they couldn't find? How did I know so much about India?

On that night, the Indian expats, overflowing with patriotism, were calling their friends, placing their phones to their radios, and showing their friends they owned one of those radios. They explained it was a special radio that was not available everywhere, but they knew of the place to get it.

That evening with the music already queued up, I continued playing one memorable song after the other. The phones lit up with calls from the Indian expats. I put some of them on air to share their memories, sentiments, and patriotism in the Indian Independence anniversary celebrations.

All my listenership — Indo-Caribbean and Indian — was bathed in my Bollywood and Indo-Caribbean music format. It was a new day and soon thousands of subscribers added themselves.

A few weeks later, around midnight, thunderstorms caused the electrical circuits at the studios to flicker then pause. Early the following morning, I arrived to realize that the storm taken the station off the air. The only sound was from phones ringing off the hook.

After bringing the station back on air, I stretched and reached over for the phone.

"Oh, thank God it's back on," whispered what appeared to be an older Indian woman.

There was a pause after which she said, "We are depending on you."

The radio station represented the heritage of the people. It became the common ground on which Indians of all ages and walks of life — from India or from the Caribbean, Fiji, and Mauritius — stood as one in the great city.

Over the next several weeks, new radio subscriptions outpaced even those of the *India Abroad* newspaper.

CHAPTER 62

*What is in your hands,
no one can ever take away.*

This new radio station had now overtaken the day-to-day subscriber growth of a powerful and established newspaper, causing Gopal Raju, the paper's founder and publisher, an India expat, to phone me.

Six weeks after my Independence Day broadcast, we sat across from each other.

Raju, a man appearing to be in his sixties, was busy clearing the clutter from his desk. I was thinking about times not so long ago when I used to stand by the front door of this place of business to hand the receptionist my coins to place my tiny ads in this newspaper. I was never allowed to cross that line into the inner sanctum. Now I was sitting in the publisher's office.

After some time, Raju's voice broke the silence, "Has any other Indian media contacted you?"

"Like?" I asked.

"Well, you know, like my competitor, the other Indian newspaper. As you know, they have a two-hour weekly radio program themselves. I am sure that they must have contacted you even before I did, especially since you broadcast twenty-four hours a day."

"You see Raju, the expat population is growing, and changes are bound to happen. We must leverage our collective media properties to pitch to the advertisers, to collectively give them a larger audience — more bang for their buck. This is how we can acquire and reinvest resources to provide better content that will empower this and generations to come."

Raju fell into complete silence again. He held that gaze for some time.

It was then I realized that sitting before me was a powerful man living with the fear of his own assets, of his own abilities.

And perhaps sitting just outside of his office was an employee planted there by his competitor. Something seemed amiss.

Here was a man who founded the great city's first ever Indian expat newspaper. As the founder of the first expat radio station, I understood and respected the work he had done to get to this day.

Sensing I realized his plight, he asked me what I had in mind.

"Give me a day. There is a call that I am expecting from someone. There is also a call I would like to make. Let's meet again tomorrow."

"Let's meet for dinner tomorrow then," he suggested.

That evening, I went on the air with my broadcast. Even before I settled in, a friend of the other newspaper called. As expected, what had seemed amiss earlier in the afternoon was now revealing itself.

The friend was a prominent figure in India's Congress Party and a close personal friend of India's late Prime Minister Rajiv Gandhi. From his tone, I could sense his message. I also sensed that someone working at *India Abroad* had told him I had met with Raju.

He ended the call by telling me he needed to speak to me urgently and would be waiting outside my studio and that we should have coffee.

I signed off at 11:30 p.m. and by midnight, we were having coffee at a nearby diner.

"Rohit, forget about *India Abroad*. You must make this deal with the other paper. Whatever it takes to make the deal, let me know now and let's finish it here and now. We will put money on the table. I have known you for some time, and I don't want people to do bad things to you."

The threat from his phone call earlier was now more direct. But I had pulled alligators out of deep trenches back in Black Bush Polder and lit entire fields on fire. What was there to fear? I calmly got up and walked the streets, stretching my legs, leaving him and his threats behind.

Around two that night, I called Dr. Viswanath, the owner of Vision of Asia. By then, he had been slowly expanding his television programs on cable in New York and was thinking about also setting up operations in the United Kingdom. I left a message and he called me back a few minutes later.

"Doc, would you be interested in us weaving together a synergy of media properties: radio, television, and newspaper? All on one platform."

"Rohit, what an idea. If we can accomplish it, it will be a powerful force in the market and the best way to attract more advertisers. What newspaper do you have in mind, though? You know they are all fighting with each other, right?"

341

Instead of answering his question about which newspaper I had in mind, having sounded out his interest in a possible media collaboration, I assured him that I would get back to him soon.

That evening, I met with Raju as planned, at Shaan, an upscale Indian restaurant. Even before we sat down, he asked if the other newspaper had called.

"I talked with Dr. Viswanath last night. He might have an interest in joining hands with us," I responded.

"Rohit, hold on. Hold on. Not Dr. Viswanath. I found out that he is also looking to launch in England and I cannot be there because, as you may know, Amitabh Bachchan's family has secured a large judgment against me in a libel case in London."

"You mean the Bofors case?" I asked

"Yes," he replied.

Amitabh Bachchan, one of India's most iconic film personalities, like the gentleman who had called me the night before, had also been a close friend with the late Indian Prime Minister Rajiv Gandhi.

Now having all the facts, all the cards on the table, knowing who was doing what, we began the discussions of our collaboration.

"How much are you in for?" he pointedly asked me.

"Well, I did a lease for my signal, and together with the overheads, I will need to generate around six million dollars over the next fifteen years."

He flinched at the mention of six million dollars. I allowed him time to search his mind and then asked him a question to which I knew the answer.

"What newspaper are you aspiring to be like?" I asked.

"Oh without a doubt, *The New York Times*," he replied

I patiently waited for him to go on.

"Can we negotiate a better deal for the signal with the Empire State Building?" he asked.

"No. I am broadcasting from atop the Empire State Building but they themselves do not own any signals. They own the antenna which they lease to the FM station from which I lease my signal."

"Who owns it then?" he asked, puzzled.

"*The New York Times*."

"Rohit, you mean to tell me that you are in business with . . . how did you manage to pull that off?"

"Well, I am not in business with the *Times*. I lease my signal from them."

"But you know the people there," he insisted.

Under the terms of the agreement we struck, *India Abroad* would advance $300,000 to my station from which I would build out a facility of world-class studios and executive offices in a 2,500-square-foot space on the 7th floor of the same building that housed the paper. It was the perfect setting for mainstream advertisers to visit when I made a pitch to them.

In addition to this, *India Abroad* would make the monthly signal payments until such a time that revenue from advertising began.

They would make their best efforts to sell a duo advertising rate card, so that when advertisers placed ads in the paper, they could also place ads on the radio.

The paper would feature the radio station in weekly full-page advertisements and the station, in turn, would market the paper with a daily thirty-minute musical segment, called "*India Abroad*'s Classics."

I would retain full and sole ownership of my music library.

The radio station transferred fifty percent of its ownership to *India Abroad*. I retained ownership of the other fifty percent.

343

Soon after that, I brought in contractors and radio engineers and built out the facility in our new space. While this was happening, I also brought on board a staff of twelve interns and started training them to become the next generation of media personalities.

When the space was ready, I invited Raju to have a look. Immediately, as he saw the broadcast equipment light up, so too did his eyes.

"Is all of this equipment yours? How much did it cost you?"

"I bought it three years ago. It's valued at around fifty thousand dollars."

"Is it paid up free and clear?" he asked.

"Yes, it's free and clear."

"Rohit, I have an idea. I am a bit tight for money because of all the legal fights I have been having with my competitor as well as my recent legal problems with Amitabh Bachchan. Can you give me the title for this equipment? I can have it refinanced and raise fifty thousand. I will give that to you as part of the $300,000 I have to invest in the station."

As a courtesy, I gave the title of ownership of my personal equipment to the paper in good faith.

CHAPTER 63

Money is an important tool.
Karma is the true currency.

At the beginning of December 1994, with *India Abroad* handling some of the responsibilities, I focused on programming and positioning the station to achieve the large number of subscribers that it would take to attract mainstream advertisers.

Instead of selling the radios directly to consumers, I decided to sell them through retail outlets. With the Christmas season approaching, I created a holiday print campaign advertising a sale that appeared in *India Abroad*.

The minute the radios appeared in the stores, the expats grabbed them up. The holiday sale proved a success, a craze that no one had ever before seen in the expat market for a media product.

News that the radio station was fast becoming the epicenter of expat media reached the office of *India Abroad*. One afternoon, I was sitting behind the broadcast console in the studio, the lights dimmed in a preproduction atmosphere. I was preparing for my show scheduled to begin some six hours away.

As the music came through my earphones, I sensed the presence of someone standing by the door inside the studio. I lifted my eyes to see a gentleman, attired in a business suit and tie, standing there.

Upon realizing that I noticed him, he remained there, motionless. My employees noticed I did not engage with him so they escorted him out of my studio and sent him on his way.

An hour later, Raju walked into my studio with the gentleman in tow. They sat down in the far corner of my studio, an area built out for private meetings. I joined them.

"Rohit, this gentleman," he was careful not to name him, "is advising me to take full ownership of the station. Would you be interested in selling me the remainder of your shares?"

"Would you gentlemen like some coffee?" I offered and walked over to the coffee area in the studio.

Turning my attention to what the two gentlemen had on their minds, I was reminded of the words of the older woman: we are depending on you.

Raju asked again, "What do you think of the idea of selling the rest of your shares?"

I remained silent.

The other gentleman spoke, "How about we give you two million dollars?"

"No."

After some further discussions, they realized I was standing my ground. I wished them season's greetings. We shook hands, and they left.

As the wintry season continued to cast itself upon the great city, the Christmas holidays were festive, and my life was filled with music and the satisfaction of what I had achieved for the expats. They now had their own radio station.

By the following month, January of 1995, *India Abroad*, tasked with bringing ads to the station, did not bring in even one. Although I knew Raju was dragging his feet to force my hand, I sat with the *India Abroad* sales team to hear it from them.

They seemed mostly tongue-tied and a bit embarrassed.

I assured them that I understood the difficulty in which they were placed and that they should free themselves from the burden of serving two masters.

I saw both relief and disappointment in their eyes. They were relieved that they were free from hiding and told not to sell any ads for the station. Disappointed because, although they had the know-how, they could not help the station of which they were now fans.

Although *India Abroad* had made the commitment to bring in ads for the station, it was now clear that the station was left to fend for itself.

A few months later, I got a call from the president of *The New York Times* signal. After we exchanged pleasantries, he told me that *India Abroad* was two months behind in payment for the signal. He advised me that as a matter of policy, his accounts receivable department would be sending a written notice. He concluded the call by advising me that he had called as a matter of courtesy.

And before ending the call, he lowered his voice and said, "I am rooting for you, Rohit. I really hope that you make it."

It was not even an hour after the call that a messenger handed the notice to my secretary. Having noticed it was an envelope addressed to *India Abroad*, she told him to take it to the *India Abroad* floor.

He told her that he had already attempted to deliver it there, but they sent him here.

The station was put on official notice — a demand for payment within ten business days.

Those who bought the radios were now, unknowingly, exposed to a risk of losing the money they spent buying the radio, as well as the risk of losing their station. The far greater risk was to the Indo-Caribbean community. The Indian expats had looked upon us as a people of the lesser strata. The station came along and changed that perception. Closing the station would make all that they once thought of Indo-Caribbeans to be true.

I called *The New York Times* radio and set up a meeting with its president. Our offices were only a few blocks from each other.

As we met, his welcome was warm and friendly.

"Rohit, I am fully aware of the situation. I wasn't born yesterday. I know exactly what's going on. I am going to lay it all out and then I want you to tell me if it's true. The last time we met, you introduced me to your partner, the gentleman from *India Abroad*. As part of his agreement with you, he committed to me that he was responsible for making the signal payments, right?"

"That is correct," I said.

"He then saw that your radio is becoming more popular than his paper, right? Rohit, in confidence, I want to share something with you. I myself was going to call you in for a meeting. You see, Microsoft is looking to enter the data watch business. They are looking to send stock market data from the New York Stock Exchange floor directly to people's wristwatches."

"And the way they are looking to transmit this data is through a sideband signal. Upon researching the signals in this market, the Microsoft engineers have determined that *The New York Times* signal, the signal that we have leased to you, is the best in the market. I can now see why you were so determined to make your deal with us. But this is Microsoft, they want the best that money can buy. Maybe you can get two, three million dollars, Rohit. Who knows, even more. You can then get another signal."

I thanked him for the heads up on the interest Microsoft had in the signal, then instead of allowing our conversation to continue in that direction, I led him back to the reason I requested the meeting.

I told him that I would appreciate it very much if he could put that notice of termination of the signal agreement on hold. I told him of my plan to pitch my station to mainstream advertisers. The time was right, and should I manage to bring a few of them on board, it could take them several weeks to pay the invoices.

I needed more time.

Having realized that I showed not even an iota of interest in thinking about Microsoft, much less talking about it, he said in a lower tone, "Mainstream advertisers is the only way to do it, Rohit. Local mom-and-pop stores cannot make up any significant amount of advertising dollars in any market. I see where you are going with this. I will hold off on that notice. I cannot hold off on it forever, so keep me posted on your progress."

CHAPTER 64

The intensity of the purpose defines the attitude. It, therefore, defines us.

Following my meeting with *The New York Times* radio signal, I reached out to my friend at McCann Erickson advertising agency in Trinidad and Tobago. He made some calls to his industry contacts in New York then called me back with the name and number of an executive handling AT&T for the Indian market in New York.

Representatives from Young & Rubicam, the prestigious advertising agency handling AT&T, were now sitting on the sofa in my studio, waiting for me to demonstrate to them why they should advertise on my station. I had arranged for them to arrive shortly after seven that evening.

I could sense their curiosity growing as the clock moved toward showtime. They were trying to equate the pitch I had made to them over the phone with what would happen when I took my seat behind the microphone at 8 p.m.

In the early 1980s, the monopoly AT&T had in the telecommunications industry across America, was shaken at its core. New federal regulations would cause it to become dependent on its long-distance service. The expats were, therefore, among their target demographic.

I invited them to bring their coffee and take their places around the studio furniture. I took my seat behind the microphone. I handed them earphones. The clock moved to eight, the theme music came up, and the earphones came alive.

Without missing a beat, I emerged in my radio host persona. The listeners emerged as well. They had made it a habit to phone in their requests right from the start of the show for a chance their songs would be played. As my theme music rolled, the phone lines lit up, and so did the eyes of the ad agency executives.

The following day, Young & Rubicam issued their first AT&T order to the station and had it hand-delivered to me. It was for 455 spots spread over twelve weeks at $40 per spot, totaling $18,200.

I made a copy of the document, placed the original in my files, wrote "confidential" on the copy, faxed it to the president of *The New York Times* signal, then called to inform him that the ball had started rolling.

I pitched other agencies telling them AT&T had come onboard. General Motors and American Express soon followed.

By then, the AT&T ad spots had been produced by Young & Rubicam and delivered to the station for broadcast. The first AT&T ad appeared on air at the 8:58 a.m. station break. And as many who shared our Indian heritage were listening, so too were the powers at *India Abroad* just a few floors down from the studio.

I sat calmly on my sofa, awaiting his visit. Within minutes, Raju was in my studio. Having realized that the station secured advertising from a mainstream advertiser, which took him well over a decade to accomplish for the newspaper, Raju smiled and congratulated me.

He asked if I had time for a meeting.

He tried to show a dignified face, but his goal to snuff out the breath from the station was by now openly known. Nothing he would say had any credibility. Still, he tried.

"Rohit, you are not thinking like a businessman. We can make a lot of money. As a matter of fact, give me your fifty percent share in the radio, and I will give you twenty percent of the combined shares in *India Abroad* and the station. And I'll throw in three million dollars to sweeten the deal. Then I'll get rid of the music and make this a twenty-four hour a day news radio."

I asked Raju what the remaining time on my lease for the studio space was. He told me it was up sometime in the last quarter of the year.

Raju thought the ace card he still held in his hand, the ownership of fifty percent of the station and the ownership of my equipment, would make it impossible for me to move and continue broadcasting.

However, the newspaperman did not understand the power of music, the voice of the people, or the older Indian expat woman. Neither did he understand that people unite in the face of adversity.

I called the brokers from whom I had leased my small signal and my first studio. I explained the situation and asked if they could give me a helping hand. They immediately assured me their studio was mine to use for as long as I wanted it.

It was around 7 a.m. on September 15, 1995, as the sun was about to cast its presence across the great city, that I moved with all of my music from the *India Abroad* building to my old stomping ground, the studio that I had originally leased in 1989 when I had my small signal. I had now returned to it, this time with my big signal.

All of my equipment was left behind. When Raju arrived at *India Abroad* in the morning, the staff told him that as they were arriving to work, I was moving out.

He looked at the radio that his staff had turned on and asked, "If he has moved out, how come the radio is still playing? He has no equipment."

By the time he arrived at my old studios upstairs, he found that I had left all of the equipment behind. His final act, his last deed, had fallen short of the Bank of Karma.

I had signed on to this big signal and committed to a six million dollar operating expense over fifteen years so that the expats could have their own Indian and Indo-Caribbean radio station in New York.

At this point, I had four mainstream advertisers on hand, and my account in the Bank of Karma had grown. But I still had a way to go to balance the other bank – the Bank of Money.

CHAPTER 65

*Our thoughts and purpose
determine our karma.*

It was apparent to everyone that Gopal Raju had recognized early that by partnering with the radio station, he prevented his competitor, the other Indian expat newspaper, from making such a deal. What I didn't recognize at first was that in addition to shutting out his competitor, he wanted to stifle the growth of the radio station so that his paper could remain at the forefront of the expat media landscape.

The day I moved, I went on air and informed the expats the station was completely independent again.

A few days later, an Indian expat phoned me introducing himself as Satpal Bhinote, the owner of a small family business selling luggage.

Having secured a few mainstream advertisers, this was an opportunity for me to know if my station was a game-changer for these smaller businesses.

Mr. Bhinote sat across from me at the station, and after expressing how much he and his family and friends appreciated having a station of their heritage, he said he would like to place his ads on the station.

I told him that I would be happy to offer him a special rate that I thought would be reasonable for a small family business such as his: three spots per day over a three-month period for $4,500. He asked if he could have the same rate for a one-year period. I told him if he signed for a year, I would give him a ten percent discount. We shook hands and concluded the deal for $16,200.

I noticed he was trying to look around. I offered to show him the modest facility that temporarily housed the people's expat radio station.

"Rohit, one of my friends, is one of your biggest fans. We heard of your separation from *India Abroad*. He owns a building here in the city on 5th Avenue. When I told him that I was going to meet with you, he mentioned that should you need some space, he would be more than happy to give you a good rate. Would you like to see it?"

In exchange for a few spots of advertising time and a token amount of $1,500 a month, the boy from Black Bush Polder moved into a Midtown location on 5th Avenue.

The space was approximately 2,500 square feet. I set up the studio in the back half and my residence facing the iconic 5th Avenue. I was now waking up in the mornings and going to bed at night a block away from the Empire State Building, from where my station signal was broadcast to the expats.

Early one morning, the chairman of Habib American Bank phoned me. He welcomed me to the neighborhood and invited me to lunch at a restaurant next to my studio. As we sat over lunch, he described the station's role in the lives of the expats from the country of his birth, Pakistan.

"Mr. Jagessar, you may not know it but take it from me, you are changing the lives of Pakistanis too. We have adjusted our schedules to match yours. Your radio has taken over our lives in place of even the big American television shows. We are so appreciative of the work you are doing for all of us. And the most intriguing thing is that it took an Indo-Caribbean expat to bring us all together."

Later that day, the chairman had his secretary fax over an order for a full 52 weeks of advertising. Soon after their ads went on air, the head of their country's national airline phoned me. He introduced himself as the CEO of Pakistan International Airlines (PIA).

"Mr. Jagessar, you don't know how much we can do for you."

PIA issued an order for the station to announce their daily flight arrivals and departures.

This was followed by calls from Air India and the State Bank of India. Within six months of setting up the office on 5th Avenue, the station aired advertisements for over twenty-five brands.

Soon thereafter, it came time for me to upgrade to the next generation of radio equipment and keep improving the sound of the music. The president of *The New York Times* signal suggested I hire one of their engineers, David Antoine, as a consultant to help me achieve such technical advancement.

Like Herb Powers, the iconic engineer that had cut my album *Kuchh Gadbad Hai* to scale the charts, David had worked as sound engineer for such iconic groups as the Tramps, one of the first disco bands, as well as the engineer at well-known radio stations as KISS FM, WLIB, WBLS and WQXR.

One day, a friend told me the FDA had seized and destroyed a warehouse filled with groceries belonging to an Indian food brand. This caused the owner such a major loss that he was reduced to a tiny space and was looking to start over again.

Realizing that a mighty one was broken, I told my friend to set up a meeting with the owner of this company. My friend wondered why I would be interested in meeting a company with no apparent resources for advertising.

In preparation for going to the meeting, I took off my suit, put on a tee-shirt and jeans and slipped on a pair of casual sandals. I then ventured over to the city's suburb to have the meeting.

The owner was attired in a similar fashion. He introduced me to his wife and his assistant. No one else was there. As he was looking around his tiny space, searching for something, anything tangible to show me, he succumbed to the reality that he had nothing to show. Realization had set in.

"Mr. Rohit, as you can hear, my family and I listen to your radio not only at home but here too, at work."

He then reached over to bring the radio from his filing cabinet to his desk.

"This is a wonderful thing that has happened in our community."

He then fell silent. And as silence spoke the loudest, it told me it once was a wonderful life for him and his family.

I placed both of my hands upon the broken one, assuring him, that which is in our hands no one can take away.

I told him instead of advertising many items, we should pick one product consumers use daily and rebuild his company around that product.

His wife suggested that Indians use atta, a wheat flour, for making flatbreads. It came in twenty-pound bags and retailed for around $8.00, from which they made a profit of $2.00. At the time, they were selling 2,500 bags a year.

"I will market this product for you on a percentage basis. You will give me fifty cents for each bag that's sold."

They were relieved to have a chance to start over and expressed gratitude they did not have to immediately write a check, especially since they were tight on funds.

At the end of the first year, the broken one had risen. Sales went from 2,500 bags to over 80,000 bags.

In 2001, listeners awoke to news that an earthquake had struck the state of Gujarat back in India. By daybreak, listeners rallied together with phone calls and suggestions of what we could do as a community. I went on air and told them that we should collectively rebuild one of the villages that had been destroyed. Within days listeners contributed $129,000 to the station. Soon I arrived at the epicenter of the destruction and brought in the BAPS organization to carry out the task at hand.

The expats needed live media they could depend on at any time. There was a time, too, when they needed their music. There was a time when boundaries held them and this music behind. There was a time when they needed the shows and the concerts that belonged to them, and there was a time I held that purpose.

EPILOGUE

The Indian and the Indo-Caribbean expats depended on my radio station, the only live source available twenty-four hours a day, to inform them should something of great importance happen back home in Southeast Asia or the Caribbean.

On February 16, 1997, Dr. Cheddi Jagan, the president of Guyana, was brought to Walter Reed Army Medical Center, on the outskirts of Washington, DC.

Guyanese expats went into panic mode, and those without my subscription radios rushed to find one. They now understood what I had been telling them: a nation must have a voice.

Since the days leading up to the fight for the country's freedom, two names were embedded in the minds of the people of Guyana and the expats — Dr. Cheddi Jagan and Linden Forbes Sampson Burnham.

As days turned into nights and nights into days, many were glued to their radios. I allocated special time slots to accommodate them with the updates. A people now bonded as one. They came home to their radio station, praying together as one people, one nation, for their president, Dr. Jagan.

The man in the news that I covered on my station was no stranger to me. He was a frequent guest at our home in Black Bush Polder during his political campaigns.

Although he and other members of his political party, the People's Progressive Party (PPP), had been visiting our home since we moved there in the early 1960s, one such visit stood out.

A few months before the country's general elections in 1973, soldiers took to the streets of Guyana under specific orders of Dr. Jagan's arch-rival, L.F.S. Burnham.

On the morning of Dr. Jagan's proposed visit to our home, soldiers came.

It was around four, some thirty minutes before the rooster's clock would wake us, when the dogs started barking at a far distance down the street. Political tension hung in the atmosphere across the settlement. Within minutes, the sound of the barking dogs drew closer to our home. It was then we knew for certain it was the soldiers, and they were coming for my father.

Thoughts of the stories we heard about Mazaruni Prison came to our minds. It was a place where they took men and women into hard labor, and some never returned to be with their families ever again.

My father, by now, had emerged from our home. He was standing on our veranda, awaiting them.

Their heavy boots stomped on the wooden bridge as they marched across and into our yard.

My brother Prakash and I stood on either side of our father. We reached behind us and closed the door, ensuring our mother and sisters, Datsy and Betty, were safe inside.

Instead, they reopened the door and stood next to us.

"We have come for the guns, the weapons that you are hiding for Jagan to take over the government," shouted the soldier standing in front.

My father assured them that they had come to the right place. Having witnessed the courageous man I had seen in many such situations over the years, I remained calm.

"Please come in and take the guns, or should I bring them out to you?"

The soldiers appeared baffled. One of them even lowered his weapon, perhaps wondering about the response they were getting. My father invited them into our home to get the guns. Confused, a few of them proceeded to surround our house while a few walked up the stairs.

My father showed them the guns, pointing toward them. There they were on the wall, two guns my father had bought for my brother and me as Christmas gifts.

The lead soldier shook his head and said in disbelief, "Man, you are something."

And taking this cue from their leader, the rest of them stood there laughing.

My parents led them downstairs into our small kitchen, where my mother began making breakfast for them. No one should leave our home hungry, my grandmother would tell us.

Dr. Jagan, along with other prominent members in his inner circle, arrived at our home later that day. As they planned and discussed strategies, I started to have a semblance that life was different outside of my surroundings — outside of my oasis.

They were all attired in similar-looking shirt-jacks, but it was easy to tell who the leader was from the manner of his speech and how the others listened. He spoke about the upliftment of humanity.

This man had sat with the most powerful man in the world, President John F. Kennedy, in the Oval Office at the White House. He was now sitting with my father, a farmer, in the presence of all who came to our humble home that day.

His journey from that time in our home in Guyana to this night in 1997 at Walter Reed Army Medical Center was an eventful one.

In 1980, while on a tour of the United States, Dr. Jagan reached out to me for the first time and asked if I could help him reach the Guyanese expats in New York. I was nineteen.

By 1991, Dr. Jagan had been out of office for some twenty-seven years, and his arch-rival, Mr. Burnham, was no longer alive. The political climate was steadfastly changing, and elections were just a year away.

This time, I was on air with my small signal. Dr. Jagan phoned me from Miami to tell me he would like to come to New York to see what support he could drum up from the Guyanese expats. He expressed the doubts he knew the expats had, as his many failed attempts to regain power and rigged elections had caused them to lose hope in the country's electoral system and in him.

I told him to visit, then hung up the phone and walked the streets of Richmond Hill, the main hub of the Guyanese expats. Dr. Jagan was absolutely right. Many I spoke with described him as a man whose best days were over. Many saw him as being "in the wilderness."

There was a time many had turned to him with hope. Over time, they lost that hope believing he could never come out from the wilderness to emerge and become the country's leader again.

After a few days of walking the streets, from the tens of thousands of Guyanese expats living across the great city, I barely scraped together forty people for the first of three events in support of Dr. Jagan's intention to plant the first seed of democracy in Guyana.

This was a country that had never seen democracy. There was a time in this country when even grass didn't grow. It was broken and it was barren. Once a colony run by colonial masters until its independence in 1966, it was then overrun by fraud and deception. Although Dr. Jagan had won elections, those elections were held during colonial rule and were not under the umbrella of self-determination and democracy. Even Burnham's election to public office in 1964 was undemocratic. It was under colonial rule.

All elections held in the country after it became an independent nation were widely illegal, and therefore, they too were undemocratic. Should the upcoming 1992 election be free from fraud, the country would inhale its first whiff of democracy and emerge on equal footing with many other nations of the world.

The three events held in New York brought Dr. Jagan around $21,000. Although a modest amount, he left hopeful and happy knowing that, although small, he had received a response.

It was the last time that I would meet with him. A year later, the people's call for democracy was answered. The Carter Center joined hands with other like-minded organizations, and free and fair elections were held. On October 9, 1992, Dr. Jagan emerged to become the president of Guyana.

The seed of democracy he had planted had now blossomed into a flower. And although the country was called an independent one, it was only now it held the fragrance of true self-determination for the very first time.

As Dr. Jagan was being treated at Walter Reed Army Medical Center, the expats waited for news. It was a little past midnight on March 6, 1997, when Guyana's ambassador to the United States, Odeen Ishmael, phoned me from the hospital to inform me that the president of Guyana, Dr. Jagan, was no more.

By daybreak, I brought my staff together and made preparations to carry the broadcast from both Washington and Georgetown, Guyana. The ambassador anchored from Washington while Information Minister Moses Nagamootoo provided updates over the phone from Georgetown.

As the Guyanese president was making his final journey home, Dr. Joey Jagan, the president's son, stood next to the aircraft and read a poem in tribute to his father before a flight attendant closed the aircraft door.

I touched down in Guyana the following day to cover the events and made my way to Georgetown. The roads were empty, and businesses were closed. Many were sitting on their verandas. Guyana had fallen into a somber mood.

This told me the entire story of the life of a man born a short distance from where I grew up in Black Bush Polder. Like my grandparents, his parents, too, were brought from India to work on the sugar plantations of Guyana.

I beamed the broadcast back to New York, where expats remained glued to their radios.

As far as the communication platform I had set out to build for the expats back in 1989 was concerned, the events that unfolded were best described by them as a service to humanity. This was exactly the purpose that I had hoped to realize for the expats in place of buying that house. And upon introspection, as I sit here writing this book, I am glad that I made the right decision.

Upon the passing of President Jagan, Prime Minister Samuel Hinds was sworn in as president and later that year, general elections took place. I anchored from Freddie Sanchara's television studios in Georgetown. My reports were carried both on TV in Guyana and over my radio station in New York, where tens of thousands of expats listened in their homes. Many also gathered at various venues to listen in groups.

I made direct contact with the Election Commissioner to receive up-to-the-minute results. My broadcast became the focal point not only for the viewers and listeners but also with journalists and overseas observers on the ground. The volume of phone calls pouring into the broadcast was unprecedented. The updates were so timely that at one point, the BBC requested a dedicated phone number to call in for the updates.

The election following Dr. Jagan's death was one of the most controversial in Guyana's history. It was the first time in the country's relatively short history since independence that a foreign-born candidate would contest the election for the presidency. The candidate was Janet Jagan, and her native-born opponent was Hugh Desmond Hoyte. A little backstory here will be instructive.

* * *

In the aftermath of World War II, freedom had become a word on the lips of everyone across the world, and for their part in the war, Britain had promised the eventual freedom of her colonies, but they were delaying.

British domination was challenged like never before, and with India becoming independent in 1947, unrest was beginning to grow across the colonies.

In Guyana, the seed of freedom was firmly planted as protests over conditions on sugar plantations erupted. During these protests in 1948, five laborers were gunned down by British forces. These five became known as the Enmore Martyrs, having been shot at Enmore Estate.

On the day of the funeral, crowds gathered from the sugar belts and formed a procession that traveled more than sixteen miles to the martyrs' final resting place in Georgetown. Standing by the martyrs' resting place, the first political leader of Guyana was born. Dr. Jagan, the son of former Indian laborers, pledged to lead the fight for Guyana's freedom.

Dr. Jagan was an American-trained dentist, having studied at Northwestern and Howard University. During his time in the United States, he met and married his Chicago-born wife, Janet Jagan.

He led the country's most powerful political party, the PPP. He would become the first elected chief minister and later, premier of what was then British Guiana.

During the late 1940s and 50s, Linden Forbes Sampson Burnham, a British-trained lawyer of African ancestry, who had returned to his home of Guyana, joined forces with Jagan for a time. He would later split off to form his own party, the People's National Congress (PNC), which became the prime opposing party to the PPP.

As the two leaders of the country's major political factions split due to their ideological differences, so too did the country, with mostly those of Indo-Guyanese heritage following Dr. Jagan and those of Afro-Guyanese, supporting Mr. Burnham.

These men would both take their country's highest office at separate times. Controversy, however, would follow Mr. Burnham, who claimed the highest office more often than Dr. Jagan, even though his followers were far less numerous. Rigged elections would cast a fog over his party throughout his career and that of his successor, Hugh Desmond Hoyte.

I had met Mr. Hoyte in 1985 when I brought Kanchan to tour Guyana. At that meeting, he thanked me and told me that my music was bringing the country together.

Within three months of our short conversation President Burnham had died, and Prime Minister Hoyte, a God-fearing version of his predecessor, was sworn in as the new president of the Republic of Guyana.

The feeling of anticipation, surrounding the 1997 presidential election in Guyana, was higher than any other I had experienced. Not only was this the first time the country had a foreign-born candidate running for the highest office, but also the first election in which the long-time leaders of the two most powerful parties — Dr. Jagan and Mr. Burnham — were not running.

It was no surprise when Janet Jagan, the Chicago-born American, was declared the winner. Protests immediately followed. Mr. Hoyte wasted no time in declaring it a rigged election.

All hell broke loose. His primarily Afro-Guyanese followers took to the streets of Georgetown within minutes of the decision. Recounts were demanded. The streets filled with people shouting threats, and many would describe the scene as a riot.

From my vantage point from the Pegasus Hotel in downtown Georgetown, that's exactly what it was. Mr. Hoyte's supporters stayed in the streets, night and day, chanting their mantra, "Mo Fiya, Slo Fiya." They were saying that since they didn't feel the election was fair, they might as well burn the system to the ground and start over. *More fire. Slow fire.*

Events took a violent turn, and the country was thrown into chaos.

The New York Times described how "riot police officers fired shotguns and tear gas to disperse demonstrators who said election fraud helped an American expatriate take a strong lead. Opposition leader Desmond Hoyte said he would seek a court injunction to challenge the results."

The nights continued to pass by with no resolution in sight. During one of those nights, after my broadcast, I returned to the hotel and after some time turned off the lights and retired to bed.

I heard a touch on my door. No one I knew knocked with that rhythm, nor with such a soft touch. I listened intently, recalling memories of the dark nights in Black Bush Polder. One thing I was sure of, whoever the knock might belong to, I must work in a manner which will cause them to reveal their intent to me.

When I was a child, my father told my brother and me a man who was afraid of death was already dead. My mother would often say that in calmness and stillness, the senses are best awoken. And my grandmother told me to always be mindful of my surroundings. I would employ each of these lessons as I lay there in the still of the night.

"You have brought the newspaper faster than I had expected," I said.

"Mr. Jagessar," came a whisper from the other side of the locked door, "my leader wants you to call him."

Unaware of who he or his leader was, I answered, "Okay, but please tell your leader the dial pad on my room phone is broken and for him to please call me. I am up."

"Very well," he said.

The call, which came shortly thereafter, was short and held only two purposes for me. It confirmed the leader was Mr. Hoyte, and it served to establish he and I would meet in the morning. I stayed up for some time after the call. As I thought over what this meeting might hold, I breathed away all that stood in the way of courage.

I decided this meeting would only be used to create good. It was a chance to do just that, and my words must create the same objective. I would not meet Mr. Hoyte as a reporter of the news but as two men having a discussion. Why the former president, who was fighting for his political survival, would be interested in meeting me was not my business. My only business was to change the dialogue, so the situation could change.

The next morning was bright and sunny. My driver pulled up to the gates of the PNC headquarters, a building that had been described to me since childhood as "the belly of the beast."

So many conspiracies are said to have been hatched in that building, so many controversies fueled from within its walls. But at that moment, I remained true to my purpose. I would not allow those thoughts to be my reality. I would be brave.

Mr. Hoyte's security led me up a flight of stairs to an entrance where a door suddenly opened, revealing a tall and familiar gentleman waiting to welcome me.

"Hello Mr. Jagessar," said the former president in a soft and welcoming voice.

He was true in his role of a statesman, not revealing any connection to the riots I saw on the streets on the way to his office. He smiled warmly, and we shook hands.

His personality was so welcoming that I reminded myself of my purpose for being there.

"Chief, I hope it's safe to be here," I said with a friendly laugh, aiming to dissolve the burdens I knew the statesman was carrying from a lost election.

He matched my laughter as he said, "You are my guest. Please, come in."

Any underlying tension that there might have been was gone. The power of purpose set the tone for the meeting.

He led me back into his private office, and after taking our seats, I remember thinking how surreal the moment was. While riots were taking place in Georgetown, I was sitting and preparing to begin a conversation with the only man capable of quelling them. My goals remained clear. I would reason with Mr. Hoyte why he should end the riots and return peace to our country.

But to do that, I had to practice the lessons I had been taught from my earliest years. My grandmother had told me, "It is under the most pressure that we must breathe and make ourselves the most calm."

The image of the riots I had witnessed over days and especially on that morning had to be banished completely from my mind. I focused my mind on the proper outcome of this conversation as I began discussions with Mr. Hoyte.

Our conversation continued for a few hours, and I then understood the true intentions of the former president. This was not a man who wanted riots. This was not a man who wished to bring doubt and danger upon our country. This was a man with fear. He feared the loss of his political career, the loss of power, and the loss of control he and his party had for so long.

He feared the loss of respect from those around him. He was desperately clinging to the idea that if he could convince the people the elections had been rigged, he would regain what he feared so much to lose. But like any man with fear, he was already dead. I had only to resuscitate him.

I observed something else as our conversation continued. This man — the former president of our nation — began to mimic my breathing. He began to take slow, controlled, deep breaths and his words became slower and more measured. His body language began to speak to me that his composure was returning, and his fear was subsiding.

In a mood that expressed genuine concern for the man before me, I asked, "How are you doing, personally, Mr. President? I heard that you weren't keeping well."

He took another deep breath and exhaled, "Well," he paused, "you know, I am trying."

I managed to keep our conversation away from the elections and the riots and maintain my clarity, showing no sense of urgency in my mannerisms. That is what this man needed — clarity and peace of mind. He needed to be free from the fear of what was inevitable.

Then I observed him take in another deep breath and slowly release it. It was perfect, just how my grandmother had taught me.

And then he said, "What will you be reporting tonight? What is your take on all of this?"

I found profound purpose in that moment. I knew the purpose he had chosen me for.

This was a man fighting desperately to cling to a life that was already gone. He was now on the brink of irrelevance and perhaps even more desperate measures in the days to come.

My next words had an opportunity to change that. I wanted nothing more than for Mr. Hoyte to heal. I believed he would. As he continued to breathe, I let that moment stretch out in a long pause before responding.

"I will report that you will never be president again, Mr. President. You do not have the numbers. Your supporters have been outnumbered, and the scales are firmly weighted to the other side."

The room fell silent.

Mr. Hoyte looked at me, bewildered. He looked around the room as if trying to find something to indicate he was not dreaming or perhaps, hoping that he was. His entire political career was flashing past his eyes. There was silence. Only a small ticking clock could be heard.

He had not expected the response I had given. He had expected to hear what he would have likely heard from any other guest: exactly what he wanted to hear. But in that moment of returned clarity, I saw something change in the former president.

Acceptance. It was plain to see that he had realized the truth in my words.

He turned his chair toward mine, looked straight into my eyes, and gently took my hand. I learned much from that touch. Looking at his hands and feeling their texture, I learned though this man had lived a life of law and politics, his hands had other tales to tell, tales of a life full of struggle.

In that moment, I was reminded of the last time I saw my grandmother. As I had prepared to leave our small home in Black Bush Polder and venture out into the world, she took my hand in hers and told me to work hard. She told me I was her hope to further our family's heritage. She kissed my forehead that morning and told me to breathe.

With these thoughts my hands began to grow warmer, and so too did Mr. Hoyte's. I knew for certain, like many I had met on my travels, he was awakening to a new consciousness.

His next question lifted me out of my deep thoughts.

"Then how will history judge me, Mr. Jagessar?"

After a moment more, as I continued to look at his hands, I answered, "Chief, what the eye sees, the pen writes."

I then lifted my eyes to meet his, "It's time to go home, sir."

My response was calm, and I was mindful not to give him false hope by again referring to him as Mr. President.

As I was leaving, he requested that I drive away from Georgetown for a few hours. As I got into the car, I told my driver to take me away from Georgetown. I sat that afternoon overlooking the vast ocean, preparing the words I would say on my radio and television simulcast that evening.

By 6:00 p.m., as the driver took me back into Georgetown, there was only silence in the city. The streets, which had been in the chaos of riot earlier that day, were now empty. The driver turned to look at me, then turned back again and continued driving. And as I reported the news that night, Mr. Hoyte was watching from his home.

Soon thereafter, with the help of the CARICOM nations, both sides, the Indo Guyanese supporting PPP and the Afro Guyanese supporting PNC, reached an understanding and peace was restored in the country. Janet Jagan became the president.

After the next election cycle, the former president decided that rather than spend his last years struggling to hold on to a life that was behind him, he would spend it cherishing the ones he loved.

Changes can happen, relations can improve among the people of a country when they engage in meaningful and purposeful dialogue. Better relations can develop when we are respectful and mindful to sit and listen to the struggles of others.

That night as I was simulcasting the election coverage from Georgetown, the phones kept ringing at the studios there and in New York. I put some of the callers live on air, and the people of both countries were happy to have an opportunity to hear each other's thoughts and opinions on the elections.

On my journey back to New York, I reflected on how things were and how they turned out.

It was now 1997, a long way from the days when I made my first 45 RPM record amid the dreams of all the immigrants who had come to liberty's shores. In those early days of the 70s and 80s, the immigrants dreamed of setting up life in the new land, owning a home, and securing a life for themselves and their families.

At the time, they had little or no media and music. From then to now, I had worked to cultivate and fill their need and over time, as they rose to fill it for themselves, I moved on to their other challenges.

It was time for me to go to my next one — telling the story of the people who came by ship. I wanted to share the stories my grandmother had told my siblings and me as we sat in stillness around a small bottle lamp growing up in Black Bush Polder.

* * *

Over the next seven years, I wrote the screenplay for a film entitled *Guiana 1838*. My friend Dr. Hemant Shah, an Indian expat from Jersey City, and I produced it.

As the film was nearing production, Bharrat Jagdeo, the then president and the architect of modern-day Guyana, suggested I produce the film in Guyana because it was here the first indentured laborers landed in the Caribbean region.

In early 2004, I arrived in Guyana with my cast and crew. The president was gracious in welcoming us, and over the next several months, I completed the production.

On September 24, 2004, I returned to my old stomping ground in the Richmond Hill neighborhood of Queens.

There was a day that I had walked the streets of this neighborhood in search of work. With almost everyone at school or at work, I recall the streets had felt empty and silent, and in that silence, it felt as if I was the only one walking on this great land, and I could do anything I chose to do. And now, on this afternoon, I had returned to travel freedom's streets once more.

As I entered Richmond Hill that afternoon, I got down at our old home at 121-02, 101st Avenue. It was here, at this very address some twenty-five years before this day, that the seed for Indo-Caribbean music was planted. It soon blossomed from here and made its way onto the global stage.

By evening time, as I neared the cinema for the premiere of my film, the crowds came into my view. I lowered my window. Thousands had come from near and far to witness their story, the people's story, the people who came by ships.

That weekend, the film that told tales of a people time had once forgotten, would be remembered in the annals of American film history. It recorded the highest single screen average of all films released in the United States that weekend.

The following year, in 2005, *Guiana 1838* was adjudicated the Best Film of the Year at the Belize International Film Festival.

The people who came by ship were celebrated.

And so, my story began…

Some of the artists that I have distributed:

Abdool "Kush" Razack
Ace Cannon
Admiral Bailey
Al Campbell
Al Hert
Alice Rambali
Anand Yankarran
Andrew Tosh
Anup Jalota
Atiya
Babla
Bansraj Ramkissoon
Barrington Levy
Basdeo Jaikaran
Bashiri Johnson
Big Youth
Black Uhuru
Blueboy
Bob Marley
Budram Holass
BWIA National Indian Orchestra with Harry Mahabir
Carl & Carol Jacobs
Cecil Fonrose
Celia Samaroo
Chaka Demus
Chalice
Carlene Davis
Dean Fraser
Dennis Brown
Denroy Morgan
Devindra Pooran
Don Carlos
Dropati

Ed Watson
Fausto Papetti
Frankie Paul
Freddy McGregor
Gabby
Gem Myers
Gregory Isaacs
Grynner
Haniff Mohammed
Horace Andy
Isaac Yankarran
James Ramsawak
Jays
John Holt
John Luongo
Johnnie Osborne
Johnny P
Judy Boucher
Judy Mowatt
Kamroon Ali
Karamchand Maharaj
K.B.Singh
Ken Boothe
K.P's Sunshine Band
Krishna Ramphal
La' Riece
Lalchand Singh
Jameer Hosein
Kanchan
Ken Booth
Lakhan Karrya
Lee Perry
Leon Rampersad
Leroy Smart
Lily John

Machel Montano
Marcia Griffiths
Mark Bryan
Michael Rose
Mighty Diamonds
Maxine Miller
Max Romeo
Mohan Nandu
Moonfou
Musarrat Nazir
Narsaloo Ramaya
Nazia Hassan
New Voices of Freedom
Ninja Man
Pablo Moses
Papa San
Paula Clarke
Phil Ashley
Polly Sookraj
Poser
Prematee Bheem
Rajdai Sookraj
Rajmani Maharaj
Ramchaitar
Ramdew Chaitoe
Ras Iley
Rita Marley
Russell Patterson
Sanchez
Sarojini Budhai
Satrohan Maharaj
Slingshot
Sly & Robbie
Sukdeo Jagdeo
Sagar Sookraj

Sally Edwards
Sam Boodram
Shabba Ranks
Shelly Thunder
Sonny Mann
Sugar Minott
Sundar Popo
Tarzan Shah Mohammed
Taran Persad
The Heptones
The Jays
Tiger
The Upsetters
The Wailers
United Sisters
Wailing Soul
Yellowman
Yusuff Khan

Some of the labels that I have distributed:

Acme Records
Angel Records, India
ATA Records
Capitol Records, India
CBS Records, India
DOC Records
EMI, India
Firehouse Records
HMV, India
HMD, Canada
INRECO
Jammy's
Music India
Odeon Records, India
Paloeloe Records
Polydor, India
PolyGram, India
Pond Side Records
Rohit Records
Rohit International Records
RPG
Saregama
Scorpio
Tassa Records
Tropical Melodies
T-Series, India
WIRL Barbados
Windsor Records

Made in United States
Orlando, FL
12 January 2025